Romantic vision and the novel

ROMANTIC VISION
AND
THE NOVEL

JAY CLAYTON

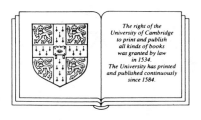

The right of the
University of Cambridge
to print and publish
all kinds of books
was granted by law
in 1534.
The University has printed
and published continuously
since 1584.

CAMBRIDGE UNIVERSITY PRESS

CAMBRIDGE

LONDON   NEW YORK   NEW ROCHELLE

MELBOURNE   SYDNEY

Published by the Press Syndicate of the University of Cambridge
The Pitt Building, Trumpington Street, Cambridge CB2 1RP
32 East 57th Street, New York, NY 10022, USA
10 Stamford Road, Oakleigh, Melbourne 3166, Australia

First Published 1987

Printed in the United States of America

Library of Congress Cataloging-in-Publication data
Clayton, Jay.
Romantic vision and the novel.
Includes index.
1. English fiction – History and criticism.
2. Romanticism – England.   I. Title.
PR830.R73C55   1987   823'.009   86–12918

British Library Cataloguing in Publication Data
Clayton, Jay
Romantic vision and the novel.
1. English fiction – 18th century –
History and criticism   2. English Fiction
– 19th century – History and criticism
I. Title
823'.009   PR851

ISBN 0 521 32776 8

For Ellen

CONTENTS

ACKNOWLEDGMENTS

I am grateful to the friends, colleagues, and institutions that supported and advised me while I was writing this book. My greatest debt is to Cecil Y. Lang, whose wit, learning, and charm have endeared him to all who know him. His support has been invaluable to me, as it has been to so many other members of our profession. I have also profited from my close association with Anthony Winner, a reader whose great intelligence is matched only by his integrity. Two scholars of the sublime inspired me by their examples and supported me with their friendship – Thomas Weiskel and Samuel Holt Monk. They are greatly missed. William Andrews, Harold Bloom, Janice Carlisle, Paul Fry, Phillip Herring, Margaret Homans, Robert Kellogg, Alan Liu, Janet McNew, Julie Rivkin, Eric Rothstein, Ronald Wallace, and Joseph Wiesenfarth read parts of this study at different stages in its composition and offered helpful comments. Over the years, in countless conversations, George Bradley, John Casey, David Field, Diderik Finne, Kim Rogal, Peter Taylor, and Craig Smyser have given me many valuable ideas.

The English Department of the University of Wisconsin–Madison has provided an excellent atmosphere in which to work. For this, and for the friends I have made there, many thanks. I also want to thank the Graduate Division of the University of Wisconsin for two summer research fellowships and the American Council of Learned Societies for a grant, given with the assistance of the National Endowment for the Humanities, that enabled me to spend a much needed year in Boston working on this book. The Houghton Library at Harvard generously allowed me access to its collections of eighteenth- and nineteenth-century literature. I am also grateful to the editors of *ELH* for permission to reprint the material in Chapter 7, which appeared in an earlier form in their pages.

The debts that it gives me greatest pleasure to acknowledge are to my parents, for all their years of support, and to Ellen Wright Clayton, to whom this book is dedicated. She listened with patience to every idea and read every chapter with a discriminating eye. No words can thank her enough for all she has given me.

Madison, Wisconsin

INTRODUCTION: TRANSCENDENCE AND THE NOVEL

Transcendence, simply defined, is the act of surpassing a limit, of "going beyond." To transcend something – an idea, a state of being, or an entire world – is to rise above it. The ability to exceed the bounds of ordinary experience has traditionally been reserved to a select group. Plato named the principal members: madmen, lovers, poets, and prophets.[1] In the Renaissance neo-Platonists found ample precedent in Christianity for praising the same figures; and Shakespeare was only following conventional wisdom when he wrote in *A Midsummer Night's Dream*, "The lunatic, the lover, and the poet / Are of imagination all compact" (5.1.7–8). By the Romantic age, however, writers began to claim the power for more people: for artists and opium eaters; for heroes, dreamers, and children; for scientists, social theorists, and revolutionaries. All who shaped the circumstances of life to the pattern of their own desire might possess what Shakespeare called the "fine frenzy." As a young man, Wordsworth saw glimpses of paradise in the world around him, and he looked forward to the time when these visions would be for everyone "A simple produce of the common day" (*Poetical Works* 5:5). Yet, even in Wordsworth's time, transcendence involved a measure of violence. One cannot question the limits of one's own world without paying a distinctive price. Wordsworth tells of transcendent experiences so disorienting that he had to grasp at a wall or tree to recall himself to reality. No matter what value one places on transcendence, the capacity to exceed the bounds of common existence is disruptive. Both the mystic's truth and the madman's delusion unsettle ordinary conceptions of reality.

In the world of a novel, such disruptions can be particularly unsettling. As a genre, the novel takes as its special province the recording of the ordinary and the everyday. Its length, prose style, and discursive conventions make possible the detailed observation of people and places, historical events and social institutions. More than any other form, the

1

classical novel has recounted the adventures of recognizable men and women in society. Hence the disruptiveness of transcendence is especially visible in this genre.[2] It stands out in relief, as it were, against the prevailing social fabric. More important, it tends to conflict with those aspects of the work that create the illusion of a coherent fictional world. To represent a visionary experience, some element in the novel must transgress the very limits of the world that the rest of the novel has established.[3]

There can be little doubt that, in a novel, a visionary character or event is more out of its element, more a "sport," than in most Romantic poetry.[4] As a result, novels that include visionary experience tend to pose certain questions about transcendence in their starkest form: How can the Ideal exist in the real world? What is the fate of an eternal Absolute in a fallen universe? The answers that most novels propose are disturbing. One remembers the fate of outcasts, like Ahab in *Moby-Dick* or Heathcliff in *Wuthering Heights*, whose monomaniacal desires drive them to their end; of saints, like Prince Myshkin in *The Idiot* or Milly Theale in *The Wings of the Dove*, whose purity isolates them; and of lovers, like Werther in *The Sorrows of Young Werther* or Jay Gatsby in *The Great Gatsby*, whose passion destroys them. Whether the Absolute is incarnated as love, goodness, or power, the result is equally severe.

The novel bears testimony to the violence of transcendence in more than just the fate of its protagonists. Structurally, as well, it records the shock that a visionary experience gives to everything around it. In effect, the visionary power is antithetical to realistic representation. Shelley writes that "poetry defeats the curse which binds us to be subjected to the accident of surrounding impressions" (505).[5] But, to most realistic novelists, the bond between characters and "surrounding impressions" is anything but a curse: It is the epistemological basis of their art. A power that distorts our ability to see the world must necessarily conflict with a form in which the accurate representation of the external scene is paramount. Since the Absolute can never be rendered in concrete, descriptive language, an authentic moment of transcendence can call into question the very premises upon which a realistic novel depends. In a fictional world, visionary experiences create unique disorders, unnatural disturbances, which cannot easily be disguised. They are "scandals," to borrow a term from Claude Lévi-Strauss, events that combine the "conflicting features of two mutually exclusive orders" (8). As scandals, perhaps they should not be disguised. Perhaps the attempt to represent an experience that claims by its very nature to be beyond representation should dictate important alterations in novelistic structure.

In addition to representation, other aspects of the novel are changed by transcendence. Most fiction tells a story, and stories move forward from a beginning, through a middle, to an end. Narrated events follow a sequence, even if the chronology of that sequence is scrambled. Transcendence, on the other hand, inevitably breaks the line of a story. A visionary experience disrupts not only the "probable" order of events, in Aristotle's terms, but the "possible" as well, for the visionary is by definition that which seems impossible. A transcendent episode should record a rupture with the very events that lead up to it and presumably cause it. If a moment of vision truly goes beyond the limits of experience, then it cannot follow seamlessly from experience. To occur in a novel, transcendence must burst the seams of the narrative.

Finally, transcendence radically alters the concept of character. When Saul was called by God on the road to Damascus, he was permanently transformed. Stopped in his tracks, blinded, dazzled with the glory of revelation, he was turned around and sent off in a totally new direction. In a novel, visionary experiences exert a similar pressure on people. A character almost becomes a different person, and perhaps should be given a new name, just as Saul became Paul.[6] In Romantic poetry this transformation is figured directly. After a moment of transcendence the poet becomes a new person, discovers a higher self, or perceives another being within his or her own being. The conventions of the novel, however, rarely allow for such absolute changes in its characters.[7] Generally, the transformation is naturalized as "growth" or "development." But, if we credit visionary poets from biblical times to the present, the new Being found in transcendence is not a natural growth at all. One never "develops" the visionary. It comes into the self with a shock.

Visionary experience, then, alters a novel in at least three of its aspects: representation, sequence, and character. Shelley, in a striking passage from his "Defence of Poetry," identifies all three as ways in which a story inevitably differs from his conception of a poem:

> There is this difference between a story and a poem, that a story is a catalogue of detached facts, which have no other bond of connexion than time, place, circumstance, cause and effect; the other is the creation of actions according to the unchangeable forms of human nature, as existing in the mind of the creator, which is itself the image of all other minds. The one is partial, and applies only to a definite period of time, and a certain combination of events which can never again recur; the other is universal, and contains within itself the germ of a relation to whatever motives or actions have place in the possible varieties of human nature. (485)

According to Shelley, poetry conflicts with narrative sequence, because a story has "no other bond of connexion" than those Aristotle mentioned – time, place, setting, cause and effect. True poetry, in

Shelley's highly Platonic formulation, employs a higher form of connection, an ideal unity. Further, in poetry character is not finite, not limited by the dress and habits of a single historical moment. Rather, it is "unchangeable," "universal"; it contains within itself the "germ" of a new kind of action, the beginning of a "relation" that is not narrative at all. This new form of relation evokes all the possible varieties of human nature without being restricted to any. Finally, poetry is not a catalogue of "detached facts." It constitutes a mode of representation that does not depend upon "circumstance" or particularity. As he says a few lines later, "The story of particular facts is as a mirror which obscures and distorts that which should be beautiful: Poetry is a mirror which makes beautiful that which is distorted" (485).

VISIONARY EXPERIENCE

In order to understand transcendence in the novel we need to define more precisely what constitutes a genuine visionary experience.[8] The Romantic visionary moment is related, on one side, to the ancient tradition of mysticism and, on the other side, to the modern epiphany. It has, however, important differences from both. Like the mystic, a visionary is in touch with some intangible reality, beyond or above this sphere of things. Yet, unlike the mystic, he does not merge with this higher realm; he remains separate and distinct, part of his own world even as he perceives another.[9] Like the modern epiphany, the visionary moment involves an intense burst of insight and a heightened sense of consciousness. Yet, unlike the epiphany, which produces a closer awareness of reality, the visionary power shuts out the senses, cutting one off from the external world.

While we are locating Romantic visionary experience in relation to other literary phenomena, we should note that it is not exactly the same kind of thing as romance. Romance builds airy castles by means of improbable plots. Shipwrecks, disguises, lost twins, secret caskets, and heroic deeds all work in succession to lead the reader to fantastic ends. Events – ceaseless, improbable events – lie at the heart of the form. As Northrop Frye has said, romance is "a sequential and processional form" (*Anatomy of Criticism* 186). The magic is in the action, not in the mind's power to halt all action. Of course, one famous definition of Romanticism speaks of the "internalization of quest romance."[10] But we should always be aware of how great a difference "internalization" makes. Keeping the events of romance within the boundaries of the mind converts their restless, onward momentum into static, lyrical moments. The pause in action that accompanies transcendence frequently prolongs itself for the length of entire poems, so that the "plots" of many internalized quest romances seem to have been cast into an enchanted paralysis.

By concentrating on visionary experience we may seem to be slighting what has often been taken as the central concept of Romanticism, the creative imagination. The two concepts, however, are closely connected. As Wordsworth says, "Imagination almost always transcends reality" (*Middle Years* 2:170). Hazlitt, too, writes that "the province of the imagination is principally visionary, the unknown and undefined" (5:9). The visionary power, in truth, forms an aspect or a stage in the larger movement of the Romantic imagination. Coleridge defines the imagination as a power that blends or unifies discordant qualities. This "synthetic and magical power," as he calls it (*Biographia Literaria* 2:16), may seem different from the violent dislocations of transcendence. But we should remember that the imagination not only reconciles opposites but also transforms the world it perceives. As Coleridge puts it, the imagination "dissolves, diffuses, dissipates, in order to re-create" (*Biographia Literaria* 1:304). Wordsworth, in his "Preface to the Edition of 1815," speaks of "the abstracting, and the modifying powers of the Imagination" that must come into play before the poet can succeed in making "two objects unite and coalesce" (*Prose* 3:33).

In its disruptive phase the Romantic imagination can usurp all the other elements of the poet's world, but such moments are necessarily brief. The "light of sense / Goes out," Wordsworth writes in his most important comment on the visionary power of the imagination; "but with a flash that has revealed / The invisible world" (P.6.600–2).[11] To some readers (particularly those raised on voluminous novels), such "flashes" of vision seem incomplete. These readers want to exclaim, "Yes, but what do you *see*? What does the 'invisible world' look like?" Questions like these, reasonable enough to deserve an answer, nevertheless proceed from a misunderstanding. Visionary moments often have no specific content. According to Kant, even if the imagination can find nothing beyond the external world, it still qualifies as a visionary power:

> For though the imagination, no doubt, finds nothing beyond the sensible world to which it can lay hold, still this thrusting aside of the sensible barriers gives it a feeling of being unbounded; and that removal is thus a presentation of the infinite. As such it can never be anything more than a negative presentation – but still it expands the soul." (Kant 127)

The inexplicitness of Romantic transcendence accounts for our emphasis on visionary *experience*, rather than on achieved visions.[12] Moreover, it is the Romantics' very silence on what if anything lies beyond the limits of this world that makes their form of transcendence attractive to many novelists. Only a "negative presentation" of the infinite can be carried over into the determinate, social world of the novel.

We have attempted in a brief space to distinguish visionary experience from a variety of related phenomena, but such generalizations naturally have their limits. Categories tend to overlap, and what one writer calls "visionary" another will find utterly mundane. In spite of these difficulties, most visionary moments have certain characteristics in common. Let us turn to some specific examples of Romantic transcendence in order to explore these characteristics. In Wordsworth's "Intimations Ode" and in the visionary passages of his *Prelude* (the well-known "spots of time"), we can identify at least six elements that are found in almost all transcendent experiences.

To begin with, the poet experiences a loss of sight. The "Intimations Ode" speaks of "those obstinate questionings / Of sense and outward things" (*Poetical Works* 4:283, lines 142–3), and the Simplon Pass episode in *The Prelude* tells of "the light of sense" going out. In essence, the flash of vision blinds the poet to all but the light from another world. Occasionally, this loss of outward perception can be gradual:

> Oft in these moments such a holy calm
> Would overspread my soul, that *bodily eyes*
> *Were utterly forgotten*, and what I saw
> Appeared like something in myself, a dream,
> A prospect in the mind. (*P*.2.348–52, italics added)

Second, a visionary often claims access to a realm beyond language. Discussing the visionary power of youth, Wordsworth writes: "in the main / It lies far hidden from the reach of words" (*P*.3.186–7). The incommunicability of visionary experience is sometimes figured by the use of a private language. This trope has a venerable history. In the "Phaedrus" Plato relates that the words of the Delphic oracle and of the Sybil were prophetic only when they seemed most incoherent. From the Bible come numerous instances of this phenomenon, the most famous of which is the pentecostal experience in Acts of the Apostles:

> And suddenly there came a sound from heaven as of a rushing mighty wind, and it filled all the house where they were sitting. And there appeared unto them cloven tongues like as of fire, and it sat upon each of them. And they were all filled with the Holy Ghost, and began to speak with other tongues, as the Spirit gave them utterance. (Acts 2:2–4)

Erasmus, like many later Romantic theorists of visionary experience, combines Plato and the Bible in his description of divine ecstasy: "Those who have the privilege of experiencing this (and it happens to very few) undergo something very like madness: they talk incoherently, not in a human fashion, making sounds without sense" (Erasmus 137).[13]

Third, visionary experience is usually static. The poet who is lost in a visionary trance is not given to moving about. "I was lost," Wordsworth writes, "Halted without an effort to break through" (P.6.597). This slowing or arrest of action is often associated with a sense of permanence, immutability, producing what is sometimes called a "still moment." The epiphanies of Virginia Woolf, which owe so much to the Wordsworthian spot of time, capture the element of stasis beautifully.[14] In *To the Lighthouse* the novel's heroine, Mrs. Ramsay, achieves a moment of perfect poise:

> Nothing need be said; nothing could be said. There it was all round them. It partook, she felt . . . of eternity; . . . there is a coherence in things, a stability; something, she meant, is immune from change, and shines out . . . in the face of the flowing, the fleeting, the spectral, like a ruby; so that again tonight she had the feeling she had had once today, already, of peace, of rest. Of such moments, she thought, the thing is made that endures. (158)

The word "eternity," in Mrs. Ramsay's meditation, introduces another aspect of transcendence, the disappearance of ordinary time. From the study of myth and religion we are familiar with the change from *chronos* to *kairos*, from clock time to sacred or ritual time. In Wordsworth's "Intimations Ode" the obstinate questionings of sense and outward things have the power to make "Our noisy years seem moments in the being / Of the eternal Silence" (lines 155–6), and in the Simplon Pass vision, nature becomes "The types and symbols of Eternity, / Of first, and last, and midst, and without end" (P.6.639–40). Another Romantic, Jean-Jacques Rousseau, found that in reveries "time counts for nothing" and "the present lasts forever, without marking its duration in any way, and without any trace of succession" (113). Dostoyevsky, exploring this same idea, has a character in *The Possessed* explain that "there are moments – you can reach moments – when time suddenly stops and becomes eternal" (223).

A fifth characteristic of visionary experience is the transformation of character, the renovation of what Wordsworth calls our "mortal Nature." Transcendence expands the self, giving the poet access to a new being. In the Simplon Pass episode Wordsworth recognizes for the first time his "conscious soul" (P.6.598). On Mount Snowden, in another visionary moment, he says that this new being is like "a mind / That feeds upon infinity," a "mind sustained / By recognitions of transcendent power" (P.14.70–5). The idea that a transformation of the entire person is a consequence of all visionary experiences comes down to us from the Old Testament. Samuel warns Saul that when the Spirit of the Lord enters him he "shall be turned into another man" (1 Sam 10:6). Dostoyevsky picks up this point directly: "Man, as he is constituted on earth, can't endure [eternity]. He must be either physically transformed or die" (609).

A final attribute of transcendence grows out of the previous one. In a visionary moment, the poet encounters the numinous directly.[15] This contact can be indicated by religious vocabulary, the invocation of a deity, or the incarnation of some spiritual power or absolute. The "obstinate questioning" passage from the "Intimations Ode" is pervaded by a tone of religious awe. In the Mount Snowden vision Wordsworth writes, "Such minds are truly from the Deity, / For they are Powers" (P.14.112–13). Earlier in *The Prelude* he connects godhood with the power of vision that lies within him:

> Of genius, power,
> Creation and divinity itself
> I have been speaking, for my theme has been
> What passed within me. (P.3.173–6)

These characteristics, common to most visionary experiences, all relate to some aspect of the novel as a genre. The first two, blindness and the inadequacy of language, have a bearing on the problem of representation. The next two, stasis and timelessness, necessarily affect sequentiality. The final two, expanded consciousness and the influx of divinity, have consequences for the conception of character. Nevertheless, the model of transcendence we have so far presented is too static.

Visionary experience can best be viewed not as a fixed set of characteristics but as a movement between two orders or structures. Considered this way, the visionary becomes a liminal experience, and the movement between structures can be charted as a series of discrete crossings of a threshold.[16] The loss of sight becomes not simply blindness but a shift from one sense to another – generally from sight to sound. In visionary moments Wordsworth feels "whate'er there is of power in *sound* / To breathe an elevated mood, by *form* / Or *image unprofaned*" (P.2.304–6, italics added). In the case of the realm beyond language, the poet figures its power as a shift from one form of discourse to another – from human words to the "ghostly language of the ancient earth" (P.2.309).

Further, the arrest in Wordsworth's visionary moment is not a true halting. To stop completely would end the action of the poem. Rather, there is a shift from one kind of motion to another – from physical action to spiritual motion. In the "Intimations Ode" all external action halts, but the poet finds himself "moving about in worlds not realized" (line 146). The shift from one form of motion to another also signals a larger movement – from one state of consciousness to another. Transformations in identity underlie the entire structure of *The Prelude*, as well as the middle section of "Tintern Abbey." In both, the poet moves from his youthful, too-exclusive love of nature to a more broadly inclusive love of nature and mankind.

Finally, since timelessness and the numinous are the most difficult aspects of transcendence to capture in the time-bound structures of language, they profit the most from a liminal structuring. Wordsworth never attempts to present more than natural scenes directly. It is their possibility rather than their presence that his poetry evokes. The only way to represent the unrepresentable turns out to be as a gap between two achieved systems of order. In the leap from one recognizable order to another, Wordsworth intimates the leap beyond all sensible orders. The gap or lacuna left in his text reflects the hole transcendence makes in ordinary life. It is a permanent reminder that the visionary power comes as a shock. The "light of sense / Goes out," not only in the realm of perception but in that of discourse as well. The ability to make oneself intelligible vanishes along with sight. The invisible realm appears not as a world in its own right but as an absence of other worlds, perceptual and textual.[17]

Before concluding this discussion, we should note the connection between the "cost" of transcendence and its liminal structure. Considered as a threshold, the visionary moment has an economic character. The gains of transcendence are offset by the costs. For a visionary experience to appear authentic, each side of the threshold must be acknowledged. The gain of a spiritual realm compensates for the loss of the real world; the sound of a new music balances the loss of sight; a higher self replaces our original identity. As Wordsworth puts it in "Tintern Abbey," "for such loss, I would believe, / Abundant recompense" (*Poetical Works* 2:261, lines 87–8). But is any recompense ever truly abundant? The novelists and poets we examine approach this question in different and often conflicting ways. As we shall see, their answers have important psychological, ethical, and literary consequences that may not immediately be apparent.

NARRATIVE FORM

We have seen that transcendence alters a novel in at least three of its aspects – sequence, representation, and character – and that in each case the alteration possesses a liminal structure. Before we can look at how the visionary power works in specific novels, we need to examine in more detail these three aspects of narrative form.

Narrative itself is a simple matter – simple in the sense of elemental, basic, an irreducible part of all other forms of discourse. The impulse to tell a story is one of the most primitive constituents of literature. It lies at the root not just of literature but of language itself, for every sentence tells a story. Each has a subject that performs an action, often on some object, usually with subsidiary characters who modify the main action.[18] To tell stories seems to be a universal human characteristic. As Roland Barthes says, "Narrative is present in every age, in every place, in every society; it begins with the very history of mankind and there nowhere is nor has been a people without narrative. . . . Narrative is international, transhistorical, transcultural: it is simply there, like life itself" ("Structural Analysis of Narrative" 79). From another perspective, Barbara Hardy makes a similar point: "Narrative . . . is a primary act of mind transferred to art from life" ("An Approach through Narrative" 31).[19]

These considerations are important, for they give substance to what is sometimes thought to be a naive belief about literature. We often imagine that stories have a life of their own. A series of events, merely by becoming part of a narrative, seems to acquire an independent life, an existence undetermined by an author. This sense of autonomous life is what allows even young children to know when a storyteller is "cheating," and it is what leads even mature readers to believe that a good story has the power to enchant. Both are merely responding to their sense that there is something in the story with its own integrity, something that demands from an author fidelity and care. We say a good story has its own "necessity" – it is the way it had to be.

Our sense that narrative has a life of its own comes from a very real source. Stories *do* possess properties that are beyond the control of the author. These properties are simple ones, the elemental qualities that narrative brings to all discourse: A story must begin, things must happen in a sequence, and the story must end. The most rudimentary narratives – "I lived," "He loved her" – possess a stubborn autonomy. It is not merely that life ends, or love dies (if only in the consummation of all life and love at the end of time), but also that those stories, in their few words, run an inevitable course, lead their lives from a beginning to an end. Frank Kermode has described this well: "Something begins that must have a consonant end. . . . There will be order" (*Sense of an Ending* 146). At the other end of the spectrum, the most complex and comprehensive narratives – *War and Peace, The Golden Bowl,* or *Remembrance of Things Past* – are, to the same limited extent, beyond the control of their authors. Again, this is not simply because "relations stop nowhere," as James said in the "Preface to *Roderick Hudson*" (*Literary Criticism* 2:1041), but because the stories begin and end in their own places. Naturally, an author chooses those places – a house in Combray, for instance, and a room in Paris – but the choice, once made, inscribes itself within the permanent conditions of narrative. Even attempts to give a novel alternative endings, as in Cortazar's *Hopscotch* or Fowles's *French Lieutenant's Woman,* merely play with the idea of multiple endings, within a field constituted by the inevitability of an ending, and ultimately succumb to the linearity of our reading.

To speak of the "life" of a narrative is, of course, to use a metaphor. The word "life" merely names those conditions of narrative that are beyond authorial determination.[20] A narrative has a life only in the way that a thesis in mathematics possesses one: As formal structures, they create certain limits and entailments on the one hand and hold out certain promises of undiscerned fruitfulness on the other. By giving a name to these conditions we separate them from their context, enabling us to notice things about them that have hitherto gone unperceived. Further, we provide a theoretical underpinning for a phenomenon that novelists have long discussed. How often have we read, in writers' journals and letters, of the immense joy an artist feels when the story suddenly takes an unforeseen turn, when the work begins to write itself? Although this process is often treated as inexplicable, it actually has clear roots in the nature of storytelling. The joy seems to arise at those moments when the artist is aware of being true to something larger than the self, of following the dictates of his or her own story. It arises, that is, when the artist perceives a special congruence between the individual requirements of his or her imagination and the universal conditions of narrative.

The fact that stories can often possess a life of their own makes narrative seem the most independent of literature's elements. It is something given, an intractable material, that a writer must accept or fight against as best he or she can. Like the world into which we are born, narrative is there to be dealt with. For a visionary artist, it is the everyday ground from which transcendence springs, the limit above which vision must rise. To put it another way, narrative is the "ordinary life" that visionary experience inevitably disrupts. Consequently, we must look closely at how the life of narrative manifests itself in each of the three areas – sequence, representation, and character – that we have been discussing.

Narrative's sequentiality is the aspect of literature that has proved most congenial to structuralist analysis. Barthes, Todorov, and others have attempted to break down complex narrative orders into their smallest component parts, which are short sequences or actions.[21] In Barthes's terminology, adapted from Aristotle, sequence forms the "*proairetic*" code, which dictates that a cause always leads to an effect (*S/Z* 18). Barthes clearly regards this aspect of narrative as its most reactionary, an element that can be subverted, "but not without scandal, since it is the *nature* of the discourse which then appears to have been betrayed" (*S/Z* 52).[22] Anglo-American criticism generally concurs in finding sequence to be the core of narrative and in seeing that core as somewhat inflexible, less malleable than the other constituents of literary discourse. The source text for this position is E. M. Forster's chapter on "The Story" in *Aspects of the Novel*. There he writes, "The story is primitive, it reaches back to the origins of literature, before reading was discovered, and it appeals to what is primitive in us" (40). But, he adds with a sigh, "Intolerance is the atmosphere stories generate. The story is neither moral nor is it favourable to the understanding of the novel in its other aspects. If we want to do that we must come out of the cave" (40–1).

For the Romantic poets, the sequence of a story often seems hostile to the freedom of the visionary imagination. It pins one down, restricts the imagination's flight, and directs the poetic attention to the details of this life. Coleridge outlines this position in a letter expressing concern about the strong narrative interest of Robert Southey's poetry: "I am fearful that he will begin to rely too much on *story* and *event* in his poems, to the neglect of those *lofty imaginings*, that are peculiar to, and definitive of, the poet" (*Letters* 1:320). Wordsworth, too, thinks that "incidents are among the lowest allurements of poetry" (in Coleridge, *Letters* 1:565–6). The momentum of action, he claims, tends to overwhelm the mind's finer discriminations. Therefore, he attempts to create a narrative that has little visible action, "a story," as he says in "Michael," "ungarnish'd with events" (*Lyrical Ballads* [*1800*], lines 18–19).

The life of narrative is also a source of the novel's representational dimension. Hayden White presents this idea with a certain polemical vigor: "Far from being one code among many that a culture may utilize for endowing experience with meaning, narrative is a metacode, a human universal on the basis of which transcultural messages about the nature of a shared reality can be transmitted" (6). Many other writers have noted the same power in a more positive register. Roman Jakobson writes, "It is the predominance of metonymy which underlies and actually predetermines the so-called 'realistic' trend" (91). Malcolm Bradbury relates the novel's enhanced referential capacity to the genre's use of prose, a word, we remember, which etymologically means sequence. "Prose, as compared with poetry, has an accentuated referential dimension: it is our normal instrument of discursive communication, is associated with our ways of verifying factuality, and is subject to complex social uses not imposed on poetry" (Bradbury 7).

Instinctively, we believe that the world of a narrative is "real" to the extent that we cannot detect an author's hand. Evidence of tampering, an "artificial" story, tends to undermine the mimetic illusion. Self-conscious novelists often exploit this principle by overtly manipulating events. The realist, on the other hand, fosters the illusion that the story has its own head, that the action follows its own lead. The fact that narrative does have its own limited "will," does follow certain inevitable patterns, aids the realistic novelist immeasurably. If the author succeeds in identifying his or her story with this larger force, then the narrative begins to seem a "given," something "out there," a reality beyond the control of any mere individual. When this happens, the narrative seems not simply independent but alien, a genuine "other." The world of the novel comes to possess all the alien majesty, all the otherness, that we attribute to reality. And this, in fact, is how we remember many of the great novels, as things that really happened.

The otherness of narrative has another influence on representation, one more subtle than those so far mentioned. The sense of otherness enhances our tendency to *visualize* the world of a novel. We desire to "see" the events of a story in a way that we customarily do not demand of lyric poetry. We can only see what lies outside the self, and the province of lyric is preeminently the world within the poet. The other is by definition exterior to the self. It lies beyond the boundary of the eye and thus is uniquely visible. When a narrative becomes "other," it grows vivid, concrete. In return, vividly realistic details can aid in making the narrative seem even more independent and other. In extreme cases, the connection between visibility and otherness can make the world of a novel seem not merely visible but opaque. Alain Robbe-Grillet explores this extreme capacity in his search for an "objective novel," a fictional world constructed solely out of descriptions of the surfaces of things. Robbe-Grillet attempts to write a narrative that is wholly other, a story that moves in a realm totally exterior to the intelligence and desires of the individual.[23] The alien worlds of his novels, however, merely uncover a propensity in narrative form that has been there from the beginning.

Finally, character has a complex but determinate relation to the life of narrative. We often think of characters leading independent lives. Becky Sharp, Emma Bovary, Huckleberry Finn – the great figures seem to live on after we have finished the books. This intangible aspect of literature has always been one of the hardest things to relate to other elements of narrative. How does a work of literature produce this marvelous appearance of life in its characters? The obvious answer, in the current context, is that the life of a character is borrowed from and determined by the life of the story.[24] An examination of primitive stories seems at first to confirm this theory. In his study of the fairy tale, Vladimir Propp discovered that characters are incidental to their functions within the narrative. One character can easily be replaced by another without altering the narrative sequence (Propp 21, 66). Todorov comes to much the same conclusion about characters in the slightly more elaborate narrative of *The Arabian Nights*. He calls the agents of this work "narrative-men," because their characters cannot be separated from the action (66–79). Every personality trait leads directly to an action. A king's jealousy, for example, immediately produces the order to cut off the queen's head. The movement from character to action is unmediated by concerns that are extraneous to that movement – concerns such as manners, morals, economic background, or social position.

These "extraneous" concerns, of course, are just the ones that we associate with the complex, multidimensional characters of the realistic novel. When we come to highly sophisticated narratives such as those in the novel, the relation between characters and action becomes more complex. Henry James posits a subtle relation between the two in a famous passage from "The Art of Fiction": "What is character but the determination of incident? What is incident but the illustration of character?" (*Literary Criticism* 1:55). Action does not simply create character, nor does character create action. Rather, each participates in the life of the other, forming a complex, reciprocal relationship. Todorov can take us a step closer to understanding this relationship: "X kills his wife because he is cruel: but he is cruel because he kills his wife. . . . Hence, it would be more accurate to say that psychological causality duplicates the causality of events (actions) rather than that it takes its place" (68–9). The life of a character reproduces, on a different level, the life of a narrative. It is as if the former is a displaced version of the latter. Yet the displacement of narrative energy into character does not diminish the life of the story; rather, just the opposite occurs. Narrative acquires a new, even greater appearance of life from the lives of its characters. But is this new appearance of life the same implacable force that we have been discussing? Not precisely. Each time the energy of narrative is displaced – from story into character, from character into "higher" being – the otherness of that energy is reduced. Character receives its first impetus from the impersonal force of narrative; at this stage (the stage of primitive narratives) both character and story seem abstract, alien existences; but, in a more complex work, character gives back to the story the appearance of a fully humanized, psychological life.

We have discovered that the otherness of narrative is a source of much that we think of as "living" in a novel – the sense we have, when we read, of being in a real world, inhabited by actual people who are swept up in events beyond their control. Now we must attempt to relate this discovery to the issue of transcendence. The visionary power, we remember, disrupts ordinary life. In a work of literature, the life that is disrupted is that of narrative. To put it more precisely, the visionary power violates those conditions of narrative that are beyond the determination of the artist. When we speak of a visionary interruption in the story, we are not talking about an intentional intrusion by the author or narrator such as is found in an authorial aside. Rather, we are examining a dislocation at a primary level of discourse, an alteration in narrative form that can neither be augmented nor suppressed without doing gross damage to the work's integrity. Once the first step is taken, once an author attempts to include a visionary experience in a work of literature, all is changed. The grounds of representation suddenly seem unstable, and the lives of characters appear volatile, given to strange shifts and transformations. More important, these changes occur in specific ways. Because the life of narrative is a distinctive phenomenon, the ways in which transcendence affects a literary work can be clearly delineated.

DISRUPTION: THE WORDSWORTHIAN MODEL

Let us begin by outlining the two major ways transcendence affects narrative. On the one hand, visionary experience can interrupt a narrative, rising like Wordsworth's "Imagination" in Book 6 of *The Prelude* to block the progress of events. We might call this moment a visionary disruption, for it severs the connection between events, disrupts the bond between cause and effect.[25] On the other hand, visionary experience can call into question all linear order, positing in its place a timeless unity. Instead of halting or interrupting the narrative sequence, it challenges the very concept of order, questioning the necessity not only of a narrative sequence but also of a finite beginning or end. This second, more radical procedure occurs in a number of apocalyptic writers – Shelley serves as our paradigm – who attempt to merge all the disparate pieces of this world into an infinite union.[26]

In the sixth book of *The Prelude* Wordsworth's Imagination comes like an "awful Power" to interrupt the very story the poet is telling. This moment in the composition of *The Prelude* has become a primary text for students of Romanticism.[27] It is important to us here because it shows, quite explicitly, how an aspect of the poet's own mind can turn against the narrative that he or she is composing. In the passage Wordsworth relates the tale of his crossing Simplon Pass in 1790. While climbing, he and a friend lose their way and are forced to backtrack. When they regain their bearings, they discover that without knowing it they have already crossed the Alps. This little incident possesses a clear narrative structure. In fact, it seems to emphasize certain traditional elements of plot. The two travelers follow the line of events in a single direction until a sudden "discovery" (*anagnorisis*) leads to a "turn" or reversal of their prior course (*peripeteia*). Just as this tale reaches its climax, however, it is interrupted. The poet's "Imagination" rises "from the mind's abyss" to halt the poet's own telling of the story. Something about the narrative he was writing forces him to interrupt it. But, paradoxically, he sees this interruption as a sign of his power as a visionary poet.

> Imagination – here the Power so called
> Through sad incompetence of human speech,
> That awful Power rose from the mind's abyss
> Like an unfathered vapour that enwraps,
> At once, some lonely traveller. I was lost;
> Halted without an effort to break through;

But to my conscious soul I now can say –
"I recognise thy glory:" in such strength
Of usurpation, when the light of sense
Goes out, but with a flash that has revealed
The invisible world, doth greatness make abode. (*P*.6.592–602)

This moment can serve as a paradigm for visionary disruption.[28] To begin with, the transcendent experience alters some element in each of the three dimensions of narrative that we have been discussing. The sequence of events is interrupted; visible representation is undone by the poet's blindness; and Wordsworth recognizes an entirely new aspect of his character, what he calls his "conscious soul." Second, each of these transformations follows a liminal pattern: Each can be charted as a shift between two levels. The poet's first sequence – the historical account of his experiences while crossing the Alps – is interrupted by another kind of event, hardly sequential at all, a discussion of the author's experiences during the composition of the poem. The object of representation shifts from the external scene, the Alps, to an internal vista, the world of the poet's own poetic processes. And the central character changes from "protagonist" (of the historical action) to "author" (of the account of that action).

At this point we can identify an aspect of visionary experience that we have hitherto been forced to neglect: Transcendence is the self's defense against otherness. In literature as in life, the visionary power represents an assertion of the individual will over the indifference of events. Just as Wordsworth had rebelled against his actual experiences in 1790, an aspect of the poet rises against the narrated event in 1804. He calls this aspect his "*conscious* soul" because it is the part of himself that defends the realm of consciousness against the infringements of the other. The poet's Imagination sets itself in opposition to any force that would deny the self's autonomy, even if such forces include his own story. In a visionary moment, the Imagination extends the self's dominion, recovers for consciousness that mastery which narrative had seemed to deny it. One question, however, needs to be asked. Is transcendence a spiritual triumph or a defensive gesture? Much depends upon how we answer, for the question itself identifies two major poles of contemporary thought. One pole sees the self as integral, an entity in its own right, and the other views the self as a product of forces beyond its control. The two positions may be roughly identified with traditional humanism and with newer, post-structuralist thought. Ultimately, such a question must be decided in moral as much as psychological terms, so before we can answer, we must make an inquiry into the value of both narrative and vision. For now, we can at least admit the uncanny accuracy of Wordsworth's claim that greatness resides in "usurpation." Whether triumph or defense, the greatness of visionary writing lies in its strength to usurp the dominion of narrative.

In similar fashion, the break in representation is a response to the otherness of narrative. The tyranny of the visible world is a common theme in Wordsworth's poetry. He tells in *The Prelude* of times "When the bodily eye" gained "absolute dominion" over his mind (*P*.12.128–31). The imagery of dominion is the same as before, only the roles have been reversed. The mind, Wordsworth cautions, must guard against "thraldom of that sense" (*P*.12.150), against becoming "a mere pensioner / On outward forms" (*P*.6.737–8), because "a soulless image" can "usurp . . . upon a living thought" (*P*.6.526–7). Wordsworth defends against this threat from the external senses by disrupting them with the visionary power. His characteristic practice of mingling the perceiving self with the object of perception is an attempt to lessen the otherness of the visible world. He aims at "A balance, an ennobling interchange / Of action from without and from within" (*P*. 13.375–6). Thus to represent an object is to represent the self, and the otherness of the image is reduced.[29] The poet, in effect, "humanizes" representation.

The transformation in Wordsworth's character responds to a similar pressure. In the Simplon Pass episode Wordsworth's ordinary self is lost, but in its place the poet recognizes a new, "higher" aspect of himself. The Wordsworthian "I," in the very midst of the poem, becomes a new character. This change is a form of sublimation: The poet exchanges a "lower" for a "higher" being. Wordsworth justifies this exchange by recourse to traditional humanistic arguments for the value of sublimation. The spiritually "higher" self is "abundant recompense" for the loss of a more primary being. What his new character is "higher" than, we should note, is narrative. Wordsworth discovers his "conscious soul" not within the story he is telling but within himself. We can recognize this sublimation as a specific instance of the larger phenomenon known as Romantic internalization. The "higher" being is not really a dramatic character at all. The external or dramatic manifestations of character – agency, visibility, otherness – have disappeared, only to be replaced by a more intimate, internal, reflective presence. This new presence initially seems "beyond narrative," a purely visionary entity; but as soon as the poet commits it to writing, it reenters narrative discourse, becoming a new character in a new story.

Wordsworth's method of writing about visionary experience, then, inevitably results in a dialectic of narrative and vision. A first order (of events, of external images) comes to seem alien or other; it is interrupted, during a visionary moment, by an assertion of the poet's self; after this interruption, a new, "higher" narrative is begun, one which represents a synthesis of self and other, the first story and the power that disrupted it.

As a textual event, this process appears as a threshold, for only the first and the last stages make their way into words. The middle term, the actual moment of transcendence, is unrepresentable. It appears as the liminal barrier itself, the gap between the two narrative orders, and its existence is discovered only in the crossing. Psychologically, this movement may be viewed as a form of sublimation; philosophically, as a version of humanism.[30] Clearly, the dialectical relationship does not end here. The synthesis is only slightly less subject to alienation than the original story, so the "higher" narrative often becomes the first term in a new dialectic. In this first form of visionary experience the upward movement can have no natural end.

UNION: SHELLEY'S CRITIQUE OF TRANSCENDENCE

Some visionaries hope to avoid the kind of disruption that occurs in Wordsworth's visionary moments. Shelley tries to circumvent the entire problem by denying that there is any necessary conflict between visionary experience and ordinary life. To believe that transcendence shuts one off from reality, isolating the visionary within the bounds of one's own self, is to Shelley a pernicious error. If we could only see the world aright, we would realize that there is no division between humanity and the universe, that all things are one. This vision of unity, Shelley says, can still be attained in childhood and in the condition called reverie. But most often, unity comes to us through the power of love. For Shelley, love is an almost mystical attraction that every soul feels toward something beyond the self, and it represents the highest state of awareness that a visionary spirit can achieve. At the end of "Epipsychidion" the poet composes a hymn to love that can serve as a paradigm for visionary union:

> We shall become the same, we shall be one
> Spirit within two frames, oh! wherefore two?
> One passion in twin-hearts, which grows and grew,
> 'Till like two meteors of expanding flame,
> Those spheres instinct with it become the same,
> Touch, mingle, are transfigured. . . .
> One hope within two wills, one will beneath
> Two overshadowing minds, one life, one death,
> One Heaven, one Hell, one immortality,
> And one annihilation. (lines 573–87)

We should note the many differences between the ways in which Shelley and Wordsworth portray their visions. Shelley's imagery shares with Wordsworth's all six of the characteristics of transcendence, but it presents them differently: (1) Instead of a movement between the senses – primarily from sight to sound – we find all mortal senses consumed in the flame of passion. (2) In place of a shift between two selves or states of consciousness, we find the loss of the individual self in oneness. (3) Whereas Wordsworth's spots of time are retrospective, recording isolated moments of transcendence from the past, Shelley's union is prophetic, looking forward to a time when all life will be lived on a transcendent plane. (4) In Wordsworth's visionary experiences, there is only a momentary break in the action; after the interruption, the narrative is resumed on a "higher" level. In Shelley's prophecy, action disappears forever; after the union, there is no need for further acts, because the lovers are always united. (5) Further, Shelley alters the Wordsworthian project of locating divinity within the self. Heaven and Hell, immortality and annihilation, will appear not within the bounds of the poet's mind, but in the union of two distinct wills, the merging of "two overshadowing minds." (6) Finally, Shelley's lovers will have no need of a new language when they are one spirit within two frames: "our lips / With other eloquence than words, eclipse / The soul that burns between them" (lines 566–8).

Although both poets seek visions, Shelley's apocalyptic ambition appears to be more radical than Wordsworth's. Everywhere we find imagery of *dissolving, fusing, mixing, merging, commingling, becoming the same, becoming one, bonding, joining,* and *uniting.* Visionary experience might be a form of human alchemy, a "philosopher's stone" that can break down our individual natures and reconstitute them as a new compound. Shelley does not envision a perfect balance between self and other so much as a loss of both, a destruction of the very concepts in a vast, apocalyptic whole. Given such aims, how does one compose a narrative at all? The task of dramatizing an experience that dissolves not only the self but also the surrounding universe approaches the impossible. To the extent that Shelley's ambition is more radical than Wordsworth's, the difficulty of his project is greater. Consequently, Shelley chooses a different strategy from Wordsworth's for recording his vision, a radical procedure more appropriate to his apocalyptic designs. Before we identify this second procedure, let us turn to some other visionary authors in order to establish that Shelley's approach is not unique.

Emily Brontë's *Wuthering Heights* contains a vision of Romantic union as apocalyptic as any in Shelley. The first Cathy loves Heathcliff with an all-consuming passion. In the famous passage where she confesses her love, the only words she can find are apocalyptic. Cathy and Heathcliff are one, the same being within two frames. She tells Nelly that she loves him, "not because he's handsome, Nelly, but because he's more myself than I am. Whatever our souls are made of, his and mine are the same" (100). Throughout the passage, Cathy exclaims of Heaven and Hell, immortality and annihilation, all in terms of her bond to Heathcliff. Without their union, creation itself would have no meaning. Their love is not a transitory passion – it is hardly an emotion at all – but something necessary, a presence:

> I cannot express it; but surely you and every body have a notion that there is, or should be, an existence of yours beyond you. What were the use of my creation if I were entirely contained here? . . . If all else perished, and *he* remained, I should still continue to be; and, if all else remained, and he were annihilated, the Universe would turn to a mighty stranger. I should not seem a part of it. . . . [M]y love for Heathcliff resembles the eternal rocks beneath – a source of little visible delight, but necessary. Nelly, I *am* Heathcliff – he's always, always in my mind – not as a pleasure, any more than I am always a pleasure to myself – but, as my own being. (101–2)

Untutored as she is, Cathy makes an eloquent advocate for Romantic union. A character in Thomas Hardy's last novel, *Jude the Obscure*, also stands as a conscious expositor of the Shelleyan position. Sue Bridehead tries to teach Jude the right words for their passion by making him recite lines from Shelley: "Say those pretty lines, then, from Shelley's 'Epipsychidion' as if they meant me!" (195). Jude knows little poetry, but even without Shelley's aid he can identify the visionary quality of his lover: "It is more than this earthly wretch called Me deserves – you spirit, you disembodied creature, you dear, sweet, tantalizing phantom – hardly flesh at all; so that when I put my arms round you I almost expect them to pass through you as through air!" (195). Even Jude's rival Phillotson can perceive the unusual nature of Sue's bond with Jude. There is an "extraordinary sympathy, or similarity, between the pair," he says. "They seem to be one person split in two!" (183). His companion calls this union "Platonic!" but Phillotson knows better. He chooses just the right term for Sue's love for Jude: "Well no. Shelleyan would be nearer to it. They remind me of – what are their names – Laon and Cythna" (185).

One of Hardy's great admirers, D. H. Lawrence, commits a pair of lovers in his novel *Women in Love* to a union more radical than any we have examined. In its final consummation, Birkin's love for Ursula leads him beyond identity. He enters a visionary state, a new oneness, where self and other are dissolved, where lovers are conscious of no distinctions. In the current context Lawrence's description of this union cannot help but remind us of Shelley:

> In the new, superfine bliss, a peace superseding knowledge, there was no I and you, there was only the third, unrealized wonder, the wonder of existing not as oneself, but in a consummation of my being and of her being in a new one, a new paradisal unit regained from duality.

How can I say "I love you" when I have ceased to be, and you have ceased to be: we are both caught up and transcended into a new oneness where everything is silent, because there is nothing to answer, all is perfect and one. Speech travels between separate parts. But in the perfect One there is perfect silence of bliss. (361–2)

Here we can see exactly how apocalyptic such a love must be. For this union to occur, the world as we know it must cease to exist. The lovers form a "perfect One," without division or difference, a unity where language itself cannot enter, because words only travel between separate beings. In this "new paradisal unit" the very concept of identity, of *I* and of *you*, has no meaning. Selfhood is subsumed in the "unrealized wonder" of a love that is simultaneously consummation and annihilation. Each individual lover ceases to be. Both are "caught up and transcended into a new oneness where everything is silent."

The passages from Shelley, Brontë, Hardy, and Lawrence all record truly radical unity. Their vision of oneness exists at the conceivable limit of desire, creates an identity past any possible expression. If they are to do justice to such union within the bounds of literature, they must stretch those boundaries to the conceivable limit of literary form. They must look for some structure equal to the intensity and magnitude of nearly infinite desires. Yet the visionary artist cannot simply indulge in grandiose rhetoric or sublime posturing, not if the artist wants to convince anyone of the authenticity of his or her vision. The artist must somehow "earn" the right to apocalyptic gestures. Numerous critics of Romanticism, including Northrop Frye, M. H. Abrams, and Harold Bloom, have shown how poets go about this task; the major Romantics create a virtually new genre, what has been variously called "Romantic mythmaking," the "poetry of apocalypse," or simply "mythopoesis." Within the tradition of the novel, however, there is no apocalyptic genre per se, only various and difficult accommodations of existing structures. Yet both poet and novelist confront the same problem – the problem of encompassing infinite desire within finite form. To understand how any apocalyptic work of literature can be written, we need a precise account of how a vision of unity affects narrative form.

Shelley's most ambitious work, the poetic drama *Prometheus Unbound*, provides an excellent place to begin our account. Northrop Frye has remarked, "It is almost literally true to say that nothing happens in *Prometheus Unbound*" (*English Romanticism* 110). It is Shelley's most important poem "because it has attained the plotless or actionless narrative which seems to be characteristic of the mythopoeic genre" (110). Instead of formulating an extensive plot, Shelley attempts to construct a narrative that is entirely apocalyptic. In order to do so, he must transform all our ideas about narrative, beginning with the concept of character. In his apocalypse, all the principal figures are seen to be but different aspects of a single being. Jupiter, Prometheus, and Asia are not so much characters as illusory "states" – illusory because, in the final transformation, the qualities that seemed to differentiate them are revealed to be false distinctions. Next, Shelley attempts to change our ideas about narrative sequence. He does this not simply by interrupting a single chain of events but by making us doubt whether sequentiality really exists at all. Is not the notion that events possess a linear order, moving forward from a beginning, through a middle, to an end, as illusory as the distinctions we call character? In the perfect oneness of eternity, all things happen simultaneously. Finally, Shelley tries to alter our understanding of literary representation. He does this not by postulating a "ghostly language" beyond ordinary words but by questioning the very distinctions with which language creates meaning. He asks if the differences between words are not simply artificial constructions, another set of illusory distinctions. In the true apocalypse all such distinctions will vanish. We shall hear not words but the Word, not language but Logos.

To say that a work of literature becomes pure Logos sounds almost as visionary as the phenomenon we are describing. Yet the places where such transformations are attempted can be precisely located in a number of texts. We cannot fail to recognize these places, because they all begin with a moment of visionary disruption. The second procedure for recording visionary experience begins where the first leaves off. We remember that Wordsworth captures the disruptive effect of transcendence by interrupting his own narrative. This disruption, however, is not radical enough for Shelley. The transformations in narrative wrought by visionary disruptions are too limited to accommodate a wholesale apocalypse. Yet Shelley does not simply strive for greater, more cataclysmic disruptions of narrative form. There is a limit to how utterly one can fragment a work of literature before the result is incoherence. Rather, Shelley's procedure both follows from and undoes the first method of recording transcendence. If Wordsworth's visionary power comes as a disruption of narrative, then perhaps the more radical breakthrough Shelley seeks can come as a disruption of the visionary power. In short, Shelley deconstructs a Wordsworthian moment of vision. He first interrupts his own narrative, then calls into question the structure of this interruption.

In *Prometheus Unbound* the crucial moment comes at the very beginning of the play. The apocalyptic events start when Prometheus calls into question a prior action: He repents his curse of Jupiter. As a result of this change of heart – a shift in his valuation of an action – total transformation occurs. The remainder of the play consists of the mythic changes made possible – "earned," if you will – by Prometheus's moment of self–questioning. Asia goes down to the lair of Demogorgon; this awful Being declares the hour of Jupiter's overthrow at hand; Prometheus is set free to marry Asia; and their union signals the greater union of all nature and humanity in one apocalyptic marriage.

Why should a simple act of repentance enable all this to come to pass? To begin with, the curse commemorates a visionary disruption. Prometheus's rebellion caused a rupture in the order of the universe. By bearing the gift of fire to humanity, he changed everything. Human beings, for the first time, were able to transcend their environment, to rise above the primitive conditions of nature. Traditionally, this change has been identified with the advent of consciousness (Hassan xiv, 190). The Promethean fire is the fire of knowledge. We recognize Prometheus's revolt as an assertion of the conscious self in defiance of an implacable other. It is an "obstinate questioning" of the order of things, a disruption in the continuity of existence, brought about by an aspect of the self that had not been apparent until the very moment of defiance. The result of this rebellion is a fall from unity into a solitude that is nevertheless triumphant. Prometheus is condemned to suffer alone for three thousand years, yet his suffering is his glory. In return for his loss, the world receives the "abundant" recompense of thought. The "higher" state of human consciousness makes up for the loss of an original unitary being.

Beyond noticing the act's status as a visionary disruption, we need to ask why Prometheus felt compelled to change his mind about it. The answer lies in the structure of rebellion itself. The act of defiance locks Prometheus into a relation of opposition, a pattern of conflict from which escape is almost impossible. This oppositional structure is the same dialectical relationship that underlies the first form of transcendence. Wordsworth resolves the conflict between self and other by increasing the dominion of human consciousness, just as did Prometheus. But, according to Shelley, it is the conflict itself, the dialectical structure, that is wrong. For Shelley, transcendence of our mortal condition can never be achieved by augmenting the existing self.

Prometheus's curse is a magnificent gesture of defiance, a fitting accompaniment to his rebellious gift of fire. In this curse the sufferer bids his tormentor to do his worst, to rain down plagues, fear, frost, fire, lightning, hail, and legions of furies. Not unexpectedly, Jupiter obliges. The king of the Titans becomes the merciless tyrant that Prometheus urges him to be. The glory of Prometheus's defiance, however, cannot disguise the strain of perversity that runs through it:

> Let thy malignant spirit move
> Its darkness over those I love:
> On me and mine I imprecate
> The utmost torture of thy hate
> And thus devote to sleepless agony
> This undeclining head while thou must reign on high.
>
> (*Prometheus Unbound* 1.276–81)

For Shelley, the perversity in Prometheus's reasoning lies in the way it commits both parties – victim and tyrant – to fixed roles. Jupiter "*must* reign on high" just as Prometheus must suffer. Each character needs the other. Without omnipotence, there would be nothing to defy; without defiance, no purpose in absolute power. The victim gives the tyrant his strength of oppression, by the very act which distinguishes the two:

> Aye, do thy worst. Thou art Omnipotent.
> O'er all things but thyself I gave thee power,
> And my own will. (*Prometheus Unbound* 1.272–4)

Since rebellion establishes the self in opposition to an other, one's very identity depends upon the structure of conflict. Wordsworth admits a similar dependence by recognizing his "conscious soul" only in a moment of "usurpation," but he justifies this conflict because of what it produces. Shelley will not accept this kind of justification. It does not matter that the "conscious soul" is "higher," Shelley would argue, because the "higher" self is nonetheless implicated in the conflict that created it. As long as one conceives of one's self in opposition to an other, the conflict must continue. The very act that constitutes Prometheus and Jupiter as separate beings condemns them to eternal enmity. Shelley takes the Wordsworthian model of the self – the dialectical model we have identified as an integral part of any visionary experience – as the root of all our problems.

We can expand Shelley's objections to the dialectical self into a critique of the liminal structure of transcendence. As long as the visionary accepts transcendence as a balancing of one thing against another, a compensatory relationship, he or she is trapped in an unending process. It is not simply that transcendence has a cost; it is that the cost of transcendence itself vitiates the act, prevents the visionary from ever seeing the world aright. Locked into his or her "higher" self, the visionary cannot perceive that transcendence creates the split it would heal. If we could only step back from our frame of reference entirely, we would see that there does not have to be any conflict between victim and tyrant, good and evil, self and other. The distinctions we would transcend are but products of the fallen structure of transcendence.

Not even Shelley can step back entirely, of course. One cannot escape. Insofar as Shelley's design is influenced by the structure of his *own* self, his writing is locked into the opposition it would overturn. The poet cannot simply do away with dialectical relations as such. The best Shelley can accomplish is to put in question the *value* of that structure. When Prometheus repents his curse, he uncovers an error that had lain at the heart not only of his own character but of our entire civilization. Mythically, the gift of fire gave birth to three thousand years of human history. It stood as the inaugural act of Western civilization. Shelley devotes most of Act 1 of his play to an indictment of that history, a critique of our chief religious, social, and political institutions. They were all erected, the poet implies, upon the same false base. By rejecting the entire course of our civilization, Shelley eliminates the traditional justification for the sacrifices required by transcendence. The essential claim of humanism, that the advances of the "higher" or intellectual self make up for the ravages of our more primitive natures, holds little weight for Shelley. The poet offers one answer to the questions we left unanswered in the preceding section. He suggests that Wordsworth's "humanism" is neither the defensive gesture of an embattled self nor the triumphant act of a civilizing intellect, but rather the cause of mankind's fall into conflict in the first place.

In poetic terms Shelley's questioning of the structure of transcendence justifies the profound alterations in our ideas about narrative that we have outlined. It must be emphasized that narrative itself does not change in the play. Its "life" goes on in much the same inexorable fashion as it did before Prometheus repented his curse. The mythic actions in Shelley's play never escape the inevitable constraints of narrative form. Only our ideas about the value of narrative are changed, just as are our ideas about the value of transcendence. Shelley's critique of visionary experience extends to both terms of the dialectic: He questions the value of both vision and narrative.

Let us conclude by looking again at one of the novels that contain an experience of visionary union. In *Wuthering Heights* Cathy claims a complete identity with another being, and this identity is expressed as love. Strangely enough, there is not a single moment in the novel when Emily Brontë attempts to dramatize this union. Their oneness remains undepicted, discussed and inferred but never actually seen. The sequential structures of narrative are not merely inadequate to the intensity of their love; they contradict it. Moreover, the closeness of their bond constitutes a profound rejection of character itself. The notion that there is "an existence of yours beyond you" challenges any unified conception of selfhood, making it impossible for the artist to record transcendence as a shift between discrete states of consciousness within a single being. Finally, Romantic representation proves an inadequate vehicle for Emily Brontë's vision. A desire for oneness subsumes all structures, including the structure of language itself. Ultimately, Emily Brontë's strategy must be a subversive one. Like Shelley, the novelist depends upon her power to call into question prior visionary structures, rather than to create her own. For both writers, visionary union can be achieved only in an apocalyptic future. As long as we remain in literature, the time of consummation will always be to come. When we read of a visionary union, we read prophecy.

1

CLARISSA

One of the ironies of literary history is that the Marquis de Sade confessed to owing a great debt to the works of Samuel Richardson. The example of Richardson, wrote Sade, teaches that one must explore the heart, not virtue, "because virtue, however beautiful and necessary it may be, is still only one of the modes of this amazing heart, the profound study of which is so necessary to the novelist and which the novel, faithful mirror of this heart, must necessarily map out in all its windings."[1] In addition to Sade, the testimony of Diderot and the practice of Rousseau and Laclos seem to indicate that the value of Richardson for the Romantic movement, at least in France, lay in his ability to provide a faithful mirror of the heart. In England, Richardson's legacy did not exclude the study of virtue, for moral delicacy remained an essential part of a man of feeling in the novels of Sterne and Mackenzie.[2] Nevertheless, when we discuss Richardson's influence on Romanticism, we usually speak only of his knowledge of the heart.

Important as Richardson was in the development of the late eighteenth-century cult of feeling, he anticipated other Romantic concerns as well, concerns that surface in the novels of Jane Austen, George Eliot, and Henry James more than in *Justine, La nouvelle Héloïse,* or *Les liaisons dangereuses.*[3] Richardson's fiction foreshadowed the interest of Romantic poets in all aspects of the interior life, not just in feeling. Clarissa Harlowe is a woman of immense intellectual and spiritual strength. Her inner world possesses all the richness, mystery, and power that the Romantics claimed to discover in the twilight realms of consciousness. If we remember that Wordsworth and Coleridge were concerned with anything that related to "modes of inmost being," we can see that Richardson was a precursor not only of those figures of "Romantic agony" who exposed the course of passion but also of those writers who explored the fate of imagination and consciousness.

In particular, *Clarissa* anticipates the Romantic problem of how to accommodate a transcendent dimension of character within the formal conditions of narrative. Before we can even approach this problem, however, we must first recover Richardson's understanding of virtue from the limbo to which the Marquis de Sade attempted to banish it. Today, we tend to associate the concept of virtue with moral conformity, self-righteousness, didacticism, and prudery. But for Richardson it stood not merely for correct conduct, but for the power to encompass within the self a consciousness of one's position within a variety of complex, often contradictory systems: natural, familial, social, and divine. The burden of such a faculty was greater than we might imagine. The difficulty of living a virtuous life consisted of more than inhibiting desires or repressing instincts. It involved confronting many of the same burdens that accompanied Romantic self-consciousness, most notably the burden of losing contact with a viable world within which to exercise one's power. Raymond Williams has remarked on the separation of Clarissa's virtue from the economic and social systems in which she lived, and he has connected this separation with the emergence of Romanticism (R. Williams 65). The novel's inability to represent transcendence within the terms established by the rest of the narrative can be seen as the formal equivalent of the isolation that Williams locates in the social and economic sphere.

Lovelace, "the arch-fiend" as he calls himself, deliberately invoking Milton's Satan, also foreshadows elements of Romanticism, although of a different strain entirely. Lovelace is the avatar of action, not consciousness, and hence he has often been seen as a proto-Byronic figure in frustrated, misdirected, and finally doomed rebellion. He prides himself above all on plots, schemes, witty language, and colorful dress. A fine freedom of invention marks his clear superiority over every other representative of his class. Yet, when measured against Clarissa's full consciousness, Lovelace's flowery language and clever pranks smack of what Coleridge calls Fancy.[4] A willful and conscious control governs his imagination, shaping his plots, tainting his manners, and directing his musings.

Lovelace's Fancy clashes violently with Clarissa's reflective vision.[5] Richardson's novel chronicles the struggle for existence between two modes of imagination – strong, personal, yet mutually destructive ways of seeing the world which can only partially be characterized by reference to social or sexual attitudes. To the loser comes nothing less than a knowledge of absolute personal inferiority; to the winner, a tragic realization of the most extreme consequences of her own world view.

VIRTUE AND CONSCIOUSNESS

Early in the novel, when Clarissa tries to examine her difficulties with her family, she begins by contrasting her present isolation with her former community: "I found Jealousies and Uneasiness rising in every breast, where all before was Unity and Love" (1:134). She glances briefly at the inheritance from her grandfather – the main external cause of her family's jealousy – but within a sentence, she has shifted her attention away from what threatens her and onto herself. The inward movement is highly characteristic. She loves to indulge in reflection, rehearsing for her friend Anna (and thus uncovering for herself) all that was wise or mistaken in her motives: "All young creatures, thought I, more or less, covet independency; but those who wish most for it, are seldom the fittest to be trusted either with the government of themselves, or with power over others. . . . We should not aim at *all* we have power to do" (1:134).

Clarissa can rarely gaze at any situation, however pressing, without creating new questions, new difficulties. What she sees at the moment is not the harsh restrictions surrounding her; still less, the personal necessity for rebellion. She sees her own desire and power, together with her own responsibility for the use to which she puts that power.[6] Although Clarissa's sense of power is ungrounded in political reality, she believes that the choices that she makes will determine both the extent and the limitations of her identity. Thus Clarissa permits herself the independence to resist her father's demand that she marry Soames, yet she renounces her lawful right to take control of her grandfather's estate. Clarissa's belief in the autonomy of her decisions may be naive, but there is a kind of glory in the naïveté that would liberate an individual from dependence on the judgments of others. Without the grandeur of defiance, Clarissa lays claim to a very wide dominion for the self; so wide, indeed, that she sometimes accuses herself of "spiritual pride." But her effort to establish the terms of her own identity, to create and control what we would call her self, lies at the heart of a quality that she usually denominates "virtue." It is this sense of the word that we must recover in order to understand the effusions of a Romantic writer such as Anna Barbauld over the "sublimity" of Clarissa's virtue.[7]

Clarissa dwells in the unrelenting light of self-scrutiny. She lives, as she will later say, so long as she is excusable to herself: "For that is the test, after all. The world's opinion ought to be but a secondary consideration" (1:295). She runs just the risk, however, of becoming too aloof from the world, too distant from others, which is one thing she has always feared. Her desire for self-knowledge can isolate her as surely as any active attempt to assert her independence, for the very scrupulousness of her self-examinations makes it hard for her to engage in many activities that the rest of her world consider a matter of course. In the letter quoted above, Clarissa mingles her fear of solitude with exactly the sort of reflection that prevents her from behaving as others might. She considers taking the inheritance in order to fund her charitable schemes, but then she stops again: "Ought I not to suspect my own heart? If I set up for myself, puffed up with every one's good opinion, may I not be *left* to myself?" (1:134–5).

Clarissa believes that a woman of sensibility should have more than the fine powers of discrimination that are both her highest joy and her special curse; she should have a feeling heart as well.[8] Ideally, a deep sensibility would enrich her relationships with other people – heightening her capacity for feeling along with her understanding – but in the actual event, it has a more mixed effect. "*Delicacy* (may I presume to call it?) *Thinking, Weighing, Reflection,* are not blessings (I have not found them such) in the degree I have them" (3:278). Lovelace, of course, repeatedly calls her unfeeling, and his friend, John Belford, praises her with the dubious compliment, "She is in my eye all mind" (4:9). But it is her very sensibility that makes her seem cold, and Clarissa is not above wishing that she might feel less if she must know so much: "I wish I had been able, in some very nice cases, to have known what *Indifference* was; yet not to have my *Ignorance* imputable to me as a fault. Oh! my dear! the finer Sensibilities, if I may suppose mine to be such, make not happy!" (3:278).

In view of these difficulties, friendship with Anna becomes a matter of social survival. Clarissa's feelings for her friend testify to her rich potential for emotion and link her to a world of normal domestic activities, a world made increasingly foreign first by her imprisonment in her room, then by her flight from home, and finally by her captivity in London. Throughout most of the novel, Clarissa's affection for Anna engages all the powers of her mind and heart.[9] (The withdrawal of her emotional investment from this relationship on her deathbed will be important evidence of the transformation that occurs in Clarissa's status as a character.) Clarissa's letters to Anna do more than establish their friendship and advance Richardson's plot; they create a crucial space in which Clarissa can exercise her gifts to their fullest without being wholly cut off from others. Like a diary, these letters create inward, subjective occasions for Clarissa, hours charged with the prospect of self-examination, soothed with a welcome seclusion.[10] Yet, unlike a diary, they provide her with a way to make contact with another person. They are, above all else, a form of communication.[11] Thus the privileged space of Clarissa's letters to Anna allows the novel to explore the solitude that engulfs so fine a sensibility, as well as the hunger for communion that such a sensibility inspires.

Clarissa's understanding of the burdens of marriage permits the novel to explore a similar dilemma. As a child, Clarissa saw what marriage, even for love, could mean to a woman of superior talents. To her mother, it meant sacrifice, first of herself, then of her children. "Would any-body," Clarissa protests, "wish to marry, who sees a Wife of such a temper, and blessed with such an understanding as my Mother is noted for, not only deprived of all power; but obliged to be even *active* in bringing to bear points of high importance, which she thinks ought not to be insisted upon?" (1:108). Mrs. Harlowe suspends her powers of judgment, of independent action, and ultimately of selfhood, acquiescing in the decisions of her husband. She has found a method of existing in the world, but that method requires great sacrifices. She suffers inward turmoil, as she tells us, for outward peace. This sacrifice, in effect, is what Anna recommends to Clarissa when Anna urges her friend to marry Lovelace despite her reservations. Anna presses all the more urgently because of Clarissa's situation in London, where the need for compromise increases with the growing number and poor reputation of those who surround her. Clarissa's ability to see the full nature of such a compromise gives her the strength to resist it. The sensibility that makes "indifference" impossible enables her to recognize the full consequences of marriage, among so many partial views of the institution. Clarissa frequently vows to remain single, but this does not mean she fears physical intimacy; rather, it is spiritual inequality, rising again and again as the only alternative to solitude, which she adamantly will not accept. Hence she clings to her family and the single state, where she has managed a fragile balance with other people without an unacceptable sacrifice of self. Her crisis comes when she must choose not between freedom and duty, as many readers have thought, but between a desolate isolation and a destructive community.

Clarissa's extreme sensibility forever teeters on the verge of solipsism. No other person in her world – not her sympathetic mother, not Anna with all her vivacity, not even Lovelace, however energetic his mind – can equal Clarissa's intelligence or understand the discriminations upon which she bases her identity. One early letter suggests the many dangers that beset such a sensibility. Clarissa is writing to Anna on the day when Clarissa first decided to meet with Lovelace in the garden:

> Your partial Love will be ready to acquit me of *Capital* and *intentional* faults: – But oh, my dear! my calamities have humbled me enough to make me turn my gaudy eye inward; to make me look into myself. – And what have I discovered there? – Why, my dear friend, more *secret* pride and vanity than I could have thought had lain in my unexamined heart.
>
> If I am to be singled out to be the *punisher* of myself and family, who so lately was the *pride* of it, pray for me, my dear, that I may not be left wholly to myself. . . .

> But I will not oppress you, my dearest friend, with further reflections of this sort. I will take them all into myself. Surely I have a mind that has room for them. My afflictions are too sharp to last long. The crisis is at hand. (2:264–5)

Here Clarissa tenders her first tentative resignation from the external world, turning in toward her capacious heart. Her pain leads her to give up even communicating her reflections: "I will take them all into myself. Surely I have a mind that has room for them." This is a terrible yet sublime moment, not just in Clarissa's own history, but in the development of what was to become Romantic self-consciousness. The reflections which she bears into herself are nothing less than the responsibility for all that has happened, and by extension, for much that is to come. By internalizing her afflictions, she both expands herself to encompass what injures her and feeds on her injuries in a somewhat morbid manner. If she is to be her own "punisher," then she will indeed be left to herself, for nothing will ever touch her so keenly as her own sense of virtue or fault. Instead of relying on her innocence of the overt crimes her family accuses her of – her innocence in relation to the external world – she dwells on what her "gaudy eye" can glean within her heart. The mind has expanded its dominion – this is both the glory and the sorrow of English Romanticism. Clarissa's heart is "unexamined" not only because of its "secret pride," but also because of its still only partially discerned tyranny. Unchecked, the heart's capacity to usurp the domain of external action and event would make it difficult for Clarissa to act at all.

Clarissa's "transcendent virtue," as Richardson calls it in the index he added to the third edition (4:408), must not be thought to lie in acting in accordance with a set of moral principles. She is, after all, only partially successful in living up to her own standards of conduct. Rather, her virtue lies in the power that makes it so difficult for her to act at all, her heightened sense of consciousness. The merely nominal signs of virtue – Clarissa's chastity, her kindness, and her often-applauded charity – signify little for a woman of such strength; in truth, they testify only to the difficulty of inventing actual achievements for an imaginative woman within the structure of a realistic novel and a male-dominated society. Clarissa often warns Anna of the mere appearance of virtue in actions, and she commands those who are capable of understanding the elusive quality to teach it. Yet this understanding cannot be a merely passive engagement with the self, a skirmish with the crucial but inevitably self-involved problems of intention; rather, it must move beyond assessing one's own motives to engage the external world, confronting the meaning of an action for other people as well as for oneself. Thus Clarissa marshals the total activity of her mind to establish the significance of an act in its inception. A truly virtuous deed implicitly carries with it the comprehension of that deed, in all its ramifications, so that, for example, Clarissa's reluctance to marry reflects her struggle to know the meaning of marriage for herself, her family, her society as a whole, and her God above. In Romantic terms, virtue embodies a fusion of vision and the object of vision in daily life, a fusion Wordsworth sought only in retrospect, when an act could be understood in the full resonance of recollection. For Clarissa, it entails this pitch of consciousness on a daily basis, a self-accountability in the present, "to the moment."

Clarissa's conception of virtue, then, should enrich her relationship with the world at large. But, like the sensibility with which it is so closely allied, Clarissa's virtue threatens to isolate her in a world of her own. Until now we have discussed the danger of this isolation primarily in terms of Clarissa's character. It might be interesting to look at her dilemma in terms of its relation to genre questions, in order to reflect on the larger issue of transcendence in the novel. As Ian Watt has shown, Richardson did much to develop a genre of realistic narrative that was especially suited to the representation of middle-class values and Protestant individualism (*Rise of the Novel*, Chaps. 3 & 6). Yet these values are the very forms of life that Clarissa's idea of virtue calls into question. Richardson's recognition that Clarissa's virtue could not survive in the bourgeois, Protestant society in which she lived had the practical consequence of making her highest aspirations incompatible with the conventions of the very form of fiction he helped to invent.[12] In the last part of this chapter we shall argue that Richardson's experiments with non-realistic and non-narrative genres at the end of his novel were attempts to accommodate Clarissa's transcendent aspirations within the bounds of his text. For now let us conclude by offering two observations. The first is that Clarissa's isolation from the other characters in the novel (which intensifies following her rape) encouraged Romantic readers in their desire to abstract a few episodes in her life as sublime or poetic moments, whose interest for those readers lay outside the moral or thematic concerns Richardson hoped to convey in his narrative. The second point is that a proper understanding of genre can shed light not only upon the formal dimension of a work, but also upon its political, social, and historical significance. By understanding the generic impasse Richardson reaches, we can better comprehend the full value of his work.

LOVELACE AND ACTION

Lovelace, with his many plots and contrivances, embodies the very spirit of action. His dexterous command of daily life, his intrusive assurance, his physical mastery of men and women, servants and society, contrast vividly with the internalized mode of existence to which Clarissa is increasingly forced to resort. His arrival among the Harlowe family sets the plot in motion, and his actions, in the first half of the novel, almost always determine the course of events. Up until the rape, Clarissa's attempts to act for herself, to escape the toils in which she has been snared, are frustrated by Lovelace's far greater capacity to conceive and execute a plot. Deeds which Clarissa believes to reflect her own intentions are often encircled, as it were, by Lovelace's larger designs and prompted by specific stratagems of his devising. The events at the garden gate are an interesting example. Clarissa meets Lovelace on that occasion determined not to leave her father's house. Despite Lovelace's every argument, she remains true to her intention. She twice raises the key to the gate in order to return to the house, but both times Lovelace prevents her by feigning to hear a sound from the other side of the wall. The second time, moreover, his plot is carried forward by an agent whom he has hired to give alarm from within. In her confusion and fear, Clarissa finds herself doing the very thing that she had resolved to prevent: She agrees to rush off into the night with Lovelace. On other occasions, such as the fire scene at Mrs. Sinclair's, she is able to turn Lovelace's best laid schemes against him. Yet her prowess lies in neither the conception nor the execution of a counterplot. It is something beyond mere design that triumphs over her antagonist. It is Lovelace's momentary – one is tempted to say "epiphanic" – vision of Clarissa's perfection that stops him in the midst of his attack. "By my Soul," thought Lovelace as he gave in, "thou art, upon full proof, an angel and no woman!" (4:394). She escapes his plot for now, as she will ultimately move beyond the reach of all mundane plots, by being beyond the touch of such earthly arts. In Lovelace's words, "*Imagination* cannot form; much less can the Pencil paint; nor can the Soul of painting, *Poetry*, describe an angel so exquisitely, so elegantly lovely!" (4:387–8).

Lovelace's active spirit, in which deeds correspond to discernible motivations, is perfectly suited to serve as the protagonist of a dramatic narrative. His letters, throughout the story, quicken the pace of the novel, frequently relieving our suspense about that most elementary of all narrative questions: What happens next? Most of the second part of the novel – from Clarissa's abduction to her rape – must be told from Lovelace's point of view, not only because of Clarissa's ignorance of the plots against her, but also, paradoxically, because she does less. She initiates few actions, and the story of her reactions would necessarily have been the story of her inner life, a minute, nuanced, constantly shifting discourse. All the shortcuts that Lovelace takes – the summaries, conceits, imaginary dialogues, and staged debates – would not have been possible for Clarissa. Nothing would have done but the exact word, the precise tenor of her self-doubts, the extensive elaboration of what she was thinking and feeling. If Richardson had not adopted Lovelace's more direct version of the action, his novel might easily have stretched to half again its present length. Richardson saw that to make his story live, the representation of Clarissa's inner life must at some point be sacrificed to a more active mode of representation – sacrificed, that is, to a mode of narrative that is analogous, on the formal level, to the very kind of action that destroys Clarissa's virtue.

The opposition between Lovelace and Clarissa, then, can be seen as emblematic of another, formal opposition, that between narrative and vision. Tony Tanner has called Lovelace "the novelist within the novel." "Without him there would be no novel. . . . He is the source of disruption and molestation, of dark, plotting energy, that makes the book, while marring the characters within it" (*Adultery in the Novel* 105).[13] This kind of narrative energy frequently does violence to the more extreme claims of the inner life – the claim of the Romantic self to possess a transcendent power or the claim of Clarissa's virtue to an expanded and inviolable dominion. By contrast, an emphasis on a mode of vision such as Clarissa's tends to devalue the realm of action, and hence to prompt Richardson to experiment with several non-narrative genres near the end of the novel. One of Richardson's letters to Lady Bradshaigh suggests his altered relation to narrative, and it looks forward to the comments of Henry James about finding more "story" in the perceptions of his young heroine Isabel Archer than in the most dramatic adventures. "Ye World is not enough used to this way of writing, to the moment," Richardson complained. "It knows not that in the minutiae lie often the unfoldings of the Story, as well as of the heart" (*Selected Letters* 289). If the most important unfoldings of the story lie in the minutiae, then how is one to value the expansive gestures of a Lovelace?

Many readers have answered this question in a way that runs counter to the intentions of the author. Even before the novel was published, Richardson's correspondents often evinced a decided preference for Lovelace's mode of action. Clarissa, some readers thought, was too cold and cautious, an unfeeling type, who raised far too many obstacles to the consummation of a plot whose natural denouement these correspondents hoped would be marriage. Lovelace, on the other hand, appeared to be a dashing character, a man of spirit, whose manner of dealing with difficulties and objections more nearly suited the taste of the novel-reading public. From this position, it was but a short step to see Lovelace as a misunderstood hero, a figure of grand passion whose flamboyant nature could find no adequate field for its expression.[14] This attitude toward Lovelace partakes of Romantic Titanism, the tendency to value energy for its own sake, and it has had a profound effect on the development of Romantic fiction. Such satanic figures as Falkland in

Caleb Williams and Ambrosia in *The Monk* owe much to the demonic energy of Lovelace.[15] Jane Austen, who as one would expect deplored this view of Lovelace, burlesqued its effect on a fashionable young man in a scene from her unfinished novel *Sanditon*. Austen's Sir Edward, who has just been discoursing on his love of the Romantic poetry of Scott, Burns, Campbell, and Wordsworth, characterizes his taste in fiction as follows:

> The Novels which I approve are such as display Human Nature with Grandeur – such as shew her in the Sublimities of intense Feeling – such as exhibit the progress of strong Passion from the first Germ of incipient Susceptibility to the utmost Energies of Reason half-dethroned. . . . [A]nd even when the Event is mainly anti-prosperous to the high-toned Machinations of the prime Character, the potent, pervading Hero of the Story, it leaves us full of Generous Emotions for him; – our Hearts are paralized – . T'were Pseudo-Philosophy to assert that we do not feel more enwraped by the brilliancy of his Career, than by the tranquil & morbid Virtues of any opposing Character. (*Works of Jane Austen* 6:403–4)

About which, Jane Austen simply observes, "His fancy had been early caught by all the impassioned, & most exceptionable parts of Richardsons; & such Authors as have since appeared to tread in Richardson's steps" (6:404).

Sir Edward's confusion of sexual depredation with sublime power is meant to be as amusing as it is ineffectual. Like Lovelace, Austen's hero was given to fantasizing about rape; but he lacked the means, not to say the will, to carry it out.[16] Lovelace, who possessed both, has been much admired for the ingenuity of his rape fantasies. More than one critic has said that a lover of "art" must appreciate Lovelace's comic vision of the subject, whatever the moralist within the reader is constrained to think. This interpretation of Lovelace is a descendant of the Romantic view held by Sir Edward, because it values Lovelace for his mode of imagination, although it is not his power but his self-consciousness, his ironic acceptance of masks or roles, that this modern reading endorses. Such an exemplary modern figure is only to be blamed, if he is blamed at all, for a sin against modernism, the error (mortal, it turns out) of confusing art with life.[17] By extension, Lovelace's rape of Clarissa becomes a slip by a comic performer on the high wire; the pathos comes to lie as much in the fact that his act is ruined as that her life is destroyed. Thus it is still important to state what should be obvious, that rape is not an aesthetic mistake, but a crime which injures its victim more cruelly than its perpetrator. Yet we can go beyond this point as well. When we turn to Lovelace's celebrated comic fantasies, his displays of sheer dramatic virtuosity, we discover that even there his imaginative power takes its origin not from a disinterested love of artistic free play, but from the aggressive instincts of a frustrated and vengeful spirit.

It is seldom noticed that Lovelace fantasizes about raping other women besides Clarissa. In particular, he dreams of raping Anna and her mother. These fantasies, which have been cited as examples of the genius of his dramatic vision, are worth looking at more closely. He first conceives his scheme while copying for Belford a long series of extracts from Anna Howe's letters to Clarissa, which one of Lovelace's agents (Dorcas this time) has stolen from the captive's room. The plan evolves slowly, over the course of two long missives, so it provides an extended glimpse of Lovelace's imagination-in-process. And the plot he conceives would make an elaborate, if unpleasant, drama. Lovelace dreams of tricking Anna, her mother, their maidservant, and Mr. Hickman into taking passage on a ship which he has purchased. He will be on board in disguise, along with his four confederates. In the midst of a storm (a storm *will* blow up, he tells us; even nature must do his bidding), the conspirators will strike. Mr. Hickman they will throw overboard. Lovelace pauses a moment, savoring in anticipation the sight of Anna's suitor "popping up and down, his wig and hat floating by him; and paddling, pawing, and dashing, like a frighted mongrel" (4:272). But he catches himself up with a rhetorical question: "But thou wilt not drown the poor fellow; wilt thou?" and then generously answers that, no, he hates supererogatory mischief. Mr. Hickman will be set ashore, with only his dignity destroyed. The fruits of this little project, as Lovelace calls it, will be three or four days spent beating about the coast, taking turns raping Anna, her mother, and the maidservant. He reserves Anna for himself – the pleasure of "overcoming" the others will be decided by lots – but, as there are to be five men and only three women, some sharing of the spoils must be allowed.

The few critics who have considered this plan in any detail seem quite taken with the wit and vitality of Lovelace's imagination, one going so far as to call it a "grand comic charade."[18] As long as such inventions remain in the mind – or in the aesthetic realm – they are, we must suppose, entirely satisfactory. Even as a fantasy, however, this plot hardly represents an innocent diversion, nor is its function comic. It is a form of violence, directed at Anna, ostensibly for daring to meddle in his plots, but more importantly for being the kind of woman who believes herself entitled to exercise the freedom of judgment and action reserved for a man. "I am too much disturbed in my mind, to think of anything but Revenge" (4:184), Lovelace begins his letter; and his plot will only be the proper "punishment" for such a "little fury," a "virulent devil," a "virago," and a "vixen" (4:185–9). "Had she been a man," Lovelace grudgingly admits, "and one of us, she'd have outdone us all in

Enterprize and Spirit" (4:189). But in a woman, such independence must be crushed. When Anna writes of coming up to London to help Clarissa, Lovelace thinks with relish of "teach[ing] her submission without reserve. What pleasure should I have in breaking such a spirit!" (4:195). This form of desire, we should note, is not sexual but aggressive, and it is the instinct of aggression that drives Lovelace to his highest flights of creativity.[19] He imagines his joy in having the two women, Anna and Clarissa, both humbled before him, and again it is the pleasure of seeing them injured and brought low that moves him: "How sweetly pretty to see the two lovely friends, when humbled and tame, both sitting in the darkest corner of a room, arm in arm, weeping and sobbing for each other!" (4:195). Lovelace's fantasy displays not so much the power of sexual desire as the energy of violence that is the motive force in the novels of Sade or in the Victorian work *A Man with a Maid*, in which gaining revenge on a woman who dares to resist him is the great aim of the hero's elaborate plots.[20]

If Lovelace's mode of imagination is the polar opposite of Clarissa's, it is not because it embodies the appeal of physical sexuality rather than the attractions of the spirit, as has been maintained (Wendt 485). Rather, it is because the aggression behind Lovelace's imagination gives rise to a kind of action that is violent and dehumanizing, whereas Clarissa's mode of consciousness results in a tendency to abandon action altogether, in favor of an internal and (from the perspective of this world) static form of existence. For novelists who were concerned with the formal opposition sketched above, Lovelace often came to represent a wayward and dangerous potential in action itself. From a certain perspective, there was something threatening to the values of individuality, freedom, and spiritual integrity in the very power that enabled men and women to create large, compelling plots. So destructive is Lovelace's mode of action, and the narrative it propels, that only Richardson's belief in a Providential redemption allows him to claim a final triumph for Clarissa's values.

In many nineteenth-century novelists, a recognition of the dangerous potential in action lay behind a shift away from the kind of narrative that would reflect the heroic aspirations of a Lovelace. In Jane Austen, such a shift led to her preference for the static virtues of a Fanny Price rather than the active, vital powers of a Mary Crawford. In George Eliot, it led to an interest in plots that followed the course of sublimation, in which the claims of the spirit were allowed to triumph, despite the absence of a Providential pattern, over the physical and social restraints that worked against them. In Dickens, who was more attracted to the forces of action, even when violent, and who was more concerned with devising a dramatic plot, it led to his ambivalent portraits of figures with powerful

or domineering characters.[21] The villains who provoke the central action
in his novels are usually grotesque beings, often physically deformed;
but they often possess a vitality and strength that may be missing from
the other characters, and their downfall is viewed with a degree of
pathos. Frequently these characters seem to incarnate something
impersonal – the forces in an industrial, bureaucratic, or litigious society
that have made them what they are and that share with them the blame
for the remorseless direction taken by the plot. In *The Old Curiosity Shop*,
a novel whose heroine superficially resembles Clarissa both in being a
paragon of innocence and in experiencing a long-protracted death, the
twisted dwarf Quilp, who pursues her to the grave, might be thought of
as a parodic version of a man of action such as Lovelace.

CLARISSA: *NOVEL OR SPECIES OF POETRY?*

It might surprise some readers to learn that Romantic poets and critics
seriously considered the question of whether *Clarissa*, one of the longest
and most minutely referential novels ever written, should be regarded as
a work of poetry. Such a question would not be inconsistent with some
Romantic definitions of "poetry." Wordsworth, Coleridge, Shelley, and
Hazlitt all maintained that poetry could exist in works of prose, and they
cited as examples works by Plato, Herodotus, Plutarch, Livy, and Lord
Bacon; the novels of Bunyan and Defoe; and prose translations of
Homer, the Bible, and Dante.[22] Furthermore, these same Romantic
writers held that brief, intense passages of a longer work could be poetic,
even if the rest of the piece were not. Shelley wrote, "The parts of a
composition may be poetical, without the composition as a whole being
a poem" (485). Coleridge thought that no work, even a short lyric, could
be all poetry: "A poem of any length neither can be, or ought to be, all
poetry" (*Biographia Literaria* 2:15). According to Hazlitt, anything that is
sufficiently visionary in nature has the potential to be poetry: "That
which lifts the spirit above the earth, which draws the soul out of itself
with indescribable longings, is poetry in kind, and generally fit to
become so in name, by being 'married to immortal verse'" (5:13–14).

The parts of *Clarissa* that, for Romantic readers, might have qualified
Richardson for a place on the slopes of Parnassus are the very scenes that
modern readers often find most tedious: the heroine's suffering and
transfiguration in the last third of the novel. Scott, for example, praises
those passages near the end of the novel that show Clarissa's fortitude in
distress as "among the most affecting and sublime in the English school
of romance"; her conduct after the rape "raises her, in her calamitous
condition, so far above all around her, that her character beams on the
reader with something like superhuman splendour" (*Miscellaneous Prose*
3:48–9). The combination of sublimity and pathos in those scenes makes

her seem almost a visionary being. As a result, in the passages where Clarissa "display[s] a noble elevation of soul, rising above earthly considerations and earthly oppression, the reader is perhaps as much elevated towards a pure sympathy with virtue and religion, as uninspired composition can raise him" (*Miscellaneous Prose* 3:86).

Anna Barbauld had set the tone for Romantic readers in her long "Life of Samuel Richardson," where she singled out what she called the "distressful scenes" in the second half of the novel as the chief glory and perfection of Richardson's art. Her list of scenes (xciii–xcv), which included the depiction of Clarissa's madness following the rape, the pen-knife episode, Belford's description of Clarissa in prison, and Clarissa's final interview with her uncle, Colonel Morden, was repeated again and again by early nineteenth-century critics.[23] It was the polemicist William Bowles, however, who put the case for a "poetical" reading of *Clarissa* in the strongest terms. In the course of making his argument "that *passions* are *more poetical* than *manners*" (xiii), he turns to the example of Richardson. He rejects the notion that Lovelace – or anything connected with him and his plots – resembles poetry in the least. Only the "most affecting" parts of the novel deserve that name:

> Though Lovelace be a character in ARTIFICIAL LIFE, the interest we take in the history of Clarissa is derived from PASSIONS. Its great characteristic is PATHOS; and this I have distinguished as a far more essential property of poetry than flowers and leaves! The passions excited make RICHARDSON so far, and no farther, poetical. There is nothing poetical in the feathered hat or the sword-knot of Lovelace; nor in the gallant but *artificial* manners of this accomplished villain. (7–8)

Bowles's contention that only those parts of Richardson's novel that excite the passions are poetry raises the question of how the poetical passages of his work relate to the rest of the novel.

To the European Romantics, the new genre of the novel was potentially the most poetical of all forms, precisely because it was capable of mixing numerous genres within its boundaries. Schlegel wrote, "I detest the novel as far as it wants to be a separate genre. . . . Indeed, I can scarcely visualize a novel but as a mixture of storytelling, song, and other forms" (*Dialogue on Poetry* 101–2). Logically, then, *Clarissa* might be thought of as one of the most poetical of all compositions, because it mixes the transcendent scenes that Scott, Barbauld, and Bowles admired with the close observation of ordinary manners and dramatic events. But Schlegel, in his discussion of *Clarissa,* excluded it from poetry, and he cited the genre of the work as his reason. Schlegel wrote that Richardson almost succeeded "in elevating to poetry the realities of modern life," but that he failed because of "the species of writing which he adopted" rather than any "deficiency of genius" (*Lectures* 2:212–13).

Hazlitt treated the question at more length, and he was even more emphatic in his opinion that Clarissa should be excluded from the halls of poetry:

> It has been made a question whether Richardson's romances are poetry; and the answer perhaps is, that they are not poetry, because they are not romance. The interest is worked up to an inconceivable height; but it is by an infinite number of little things, by incessant labour and calls upon the attention, by a repetition of blows that have no rebound in them. . . . Clarissa, the divine Clarissa, is too interesting by half. She is interesting in her ruffles, in her gloves, her samplers, her aunts and uncles – she is interesting in all that is uninteresting. Such things, however intensely they may be brought home to us, are not conductors to the imagination. There is infinite truth and feeling in Richardson; but it is extracted from a *caput mortuum* of circumstances: it does not evaporate of itself. His poetical genius is like Ariel confined in a pine-tree, and requires an artificial process to let it out. (5:14–15)

Elsewhere he added, "They have the romantic air of a pure fiction, with the literal minuteness of a common diary. The author had the strongest matter-of-fact imagination that ever existed, and wrote the oddest mixture of poetry and prose" (6:117–18).

Clearly, Hazlitt detected something in *Clarissa* that tempted him to elevate it to the status of poetry. It approaches the condition of "pure fiction" and has the power to present objects with great intensity. Yet its "matter-of-fact imagination" results only in an odd mixture of poetry and prose. The novel has access to "infinite truth and feeling," but it cannot make that quality separate out, as an essence, from the dross of everyday life. Hazlitt's curious word, "evaporate," is drawn from a chemical – or alchemical – vocabulary, along the lines of our term for what Longinus called simply *hupsous*. Pure poetry should "sublime" itself, not be extracted from recalcitrant material. No matter how intensely things are brought home to us by the novel, they never become "conductors to the imagination," by which Hazlitt means the visionary imagination. If Richardson's "poetical genius" is confined, Hazlitt thought, it is because the conditions of the novel make it impossible for the form to become an appropriate genre for vision.

In certain respects, Hazlitt's reading of *Clarissa* is not unwarranted. His sense that the scenes that deal with Clarissa's movement toward a higher world are different in kind from the earlier realistic episodes, which dramatize her struggle to survive in this world, has largely been endorsed by twentieth-century criticism. It is commonplace today to say that the last part of *Clarissa* represents a serious departure from what has come before. Sometimes this change is presented simply in terms of a falling off, a literary failure, an authorial confusion about how the story should proceed.[24] Occasionally, it is presented as an intentional shift in thematic emphasis or subject matter.[25] Most often, however, the problem is recognized as one of genre. An impressive array of critics have argued the question of whether the novel is, as Richardson maintained in a letter, a member "of the Tragic Kind" (*Selected Letters* 99), or whether, despite appearances, it is actually comic.[26] From the perspective of this world, Clarissa's death is a profound tragedy; from the perspective of the next, it becomes the climax of a divine comedy. Richardson, of course, meant both perspectives to obtain. But the first two parts of the novel so vividly realize the psychological, social, and economic concerns of the finite world that it has become difficult for many modern readers to credit the Christian vision of eternal life expounded in the devotional material at the end.

One recent discussion of genre in Richardson deserves more extended treatment here because it tacitly accepts the Romantics' preference for a transcendent rather than a realistic perspective. Margaret Doody argues that in the first half of *Clarissa* Richardson makes use of conventional features found in two genres of early eighteenth-century popular fiction, the bourgeois novel of courtship and the more fantastic and sexually charged novel of rape and seduction (Doody 149). In the second half of the novel, however, Richardson employs the conventions of seventeenth-century devotional literature, including an emblematic rather than realistic use of detail and a highly stylized treatment of the death scenes in the manner of religious *exempla* (Doody 157–87). If the conventions of the former were well adapted to the presentation of physical passion, social intrigue, and tragic conflict, those of the latter seemed the best available means to represent the soul's preparation for death. Doody's sensitivity to the complex strands of genre woven into the fabric of Richardson's text illustrates the importance of a historical approach to genre study. Yet her insistence that these diverse generic patterns form a seamless whole runs counter to most readers' experience of the novel. Richardson's scenes of "holy and unholy dying," his use of emblematic objects such as Clarissa's coffin, and his arrangement of characters and settings into instructive tableaux stand out from the dramatic narrative of the rest of the novel. For the Romantics, this disjunction of genres was not a flaw. Rather, it was seen as evidence of the intensity, the power, even the spiritual integrity of Clarissa's religious impulse. The very fact that Richardson had to resort to conventions that violated the standards of realistic narrative seemed to testify to the thoroughness of Clarissa's turn away from the things of this world. The shift from one set of conventions to another was Richardson's way of reproducing, in the finite structure of a novel, a change that lies beyond the compass of all mundane structures – the journey from this world to another infinitely beyond it.

We should note that the novel shifts from the conventions of narrative genres – the bourgeois courtship novel, the rape and seduction novel, the Restoration tragedy – to those more characteristic of lyric, poetic forms. Louis Martz has described the extensive use that "metaphysical" poets such as Donne and Herbert made of traditional devotional material to create what he calls "the poetry of meditation" (Martz 118–52). And Margaret Doody wonders why readers of *Clarissa* do not respond to the same techniques in Richardson's novel that they "are so willing to admire in the 'Metaphysical' poets" (Doody 186). The answer, of course, has to do with the complex set of assumptions created by Richardson's decision to write a novel rather than a poem. But Doody's position brings us full circle, back to the attitude of Romantic readers that the "elevated scenes" which deal with Clarissa's preparation for death are "poetic" and demand the kind of reading we would give a poem. The Romantics' sense that such "poetical" elements could be separated from the rest of the work may be as theoretically sophisticated as the modern need to find some principle that will unify all the elements in the work. As we shall demonstrate in the next chapter, an acknowledgment of disjunction has the advantage of highlighting not only the difference between lyric and narrative structures but also the contrasting social functions, public occasions, and ethical roles of the genres.

In his Postscript, Richardson says that his "Story" is to be "principally looked upon as the Vehicle to the Instruction" (8:328). Clarissa, too, says that she hopes her "Story" will be a "warning to all" (7:365), and Mrs. Norton writes that Clarissa must get well because the world needs her "Example" (7:383). At the end of the novel, however, Clarissa's character loses much of its exemplary status.[27] The problem is not merely that she is too ideal to be imitated (as some critics in the early nineteenth century complained), but that her experience of religious exaltation lies, by its very nature, beyond the reach of forms of discourse that seek to instruct by example. Transcendent states of being cannot be taught by example. Unlike other virtuous kinds of behavior – temperance, say, or charity – divine rapture cannot and should not be learned through the imitation of others. Exaltation must be achieved anew by every individual, as if for the first time. Imitative raptures are perforce invalid. We regard such states either as fraudulent or as a form of hysteria, a pathological or delusional condition. In the next chapter we shall elaborate a theory of the differing social functions of genres in order to explain why visionary experience conflicts with the ethical impulse of certain kinds of fiction. For now, we need only add that Clarissa's transcendence at the end of the novel works against the author's own ethical intentions.

Perhaps the best way to conclude our discussion of this problem is to look at the change that occurs in Clarissa's status as a character. At the end of the novel Clarissa retreats from involvement with this world. The illness that comes upon her during her unresisting days in prison takes the form of a "mistiness" before her eyes, a blindness that separates her from her surroundings. She is blessed, as she tells us, with a "gradual sensible death" (7:401), by which she does not mean that her end is reasonable but that it involves a steadily increasing insensibility, a withdrawal from the external world. She is slowly separating herself from her "vile body" (7:403), widening a gap that may always have existed between her soul, aspiring toward heaven, and her *"rags of mortality"* (7:410), the only part of her touched by and implicated in Lovelace's plots. So complete is her withdrawal from this world that she no longer even desires contact with the two friends she had most valued. "Neither do I want to see even *you*" (7:404), she writes to Mrs. Norton, and of Anna she confesses, "The truly friendly Love that has so long subsisted between my Miss Howe and her Clarissa, altho' to my last gasp it will be the dearest to me of all that is dear in this life, has already abated of its fervor; has already given place to supremer fervors" (7:412).

As has been suggested, this retreat from other people can be viewed in two ways. From a Christian perspective, Clarissa's turn from the external world is a turn toward God. She becomes the bride of Christ in an explicit rendering of the traditional metaphor (7:406). But, from a secular perspective, Clarissa's withdrawal appears to be nothing more than a lapse into the solipsism that had always threatened her. "The impulse of the soul toward God is inseparable from a retreat into the Self," René Girard has remarked, and he was attempting to characterize the overwhelmingly secular perspective of the novel as a genre (Girard 58). With this opposition, we find ourselves confronting a question that we first posed in the Introduction. Are the transcendent experiences of characters in literature signs of spiritual triumph or are they the defensive gestures of embattled selves? Most recent critics have preferred the latter option, just as most Romantic readers would have argued for the former. Where Sir Walter Scott saw the "noble elevation of soul, rising above earthly considerations and earthly oppression," an intelligent modern reader such as Leo Braudy sees Clarissa's orchestration of her own death as a last attempt to make her inner self "impenetrable," even if her body was not ("Penetration and Impenetrability," esp. 191–7).

We are still not ready to decide the issue between these two positions, but certain consequences of each position are now coming into better focus. Surprisingly, the recent skeptical approach to this question evinces a concern with the ethical issues that surround Clarissa's behavior (as is apparent from the atmosphere of disapproval that pervades most modern discussions of Clarissa's death). The Romantic or the religious reading of her character, on the other hand, seems less concerned with the moral complications raised by her death than with celebrating the sublimity of her transfiguration. Clarissa's effort to make herself invulnerable worries critics such as Braudy; it seems to betray a psychological hardening, an effort to insulate oneself from the incursions of reality that will become symptomatic of the modern, alienated temper. To the Romantics, however, this same element of invulnerability seems to testify to the spirit's capacity to emerge victorious from the trials of this world. Scott praises Clarissa for possessing a "chastity of the soul" that cannot be corrupted by an earthly event (*Miscellaneous Prose* 3:49); and Anna Barbauld ringingly declares, "Virtue has a kind of self-sufficiency; it stands upon its own basis, and cannot be injured by any violence" (*Works* 2:224).

Even more surprising are the conceptions of literature implied by the different answers to our question. We have seen how a transcendent reading of Clarissa's character implies a willingness to acknowledge a radical shift in the genre of the work. What ratifies Clarissa's experience as triumphant rather than defensive is her character's violation of the work's formal integrity. The "poetry" in her transfiguration comes solely from her independence of the conventions of the original narrative. To use a contemporary vocabulary, the transcendent reading of her character implies a "multivalent" or "equivocal" conception of the text. We have not paid sufficient attention, however, to the way in which a modern, skeptical reading of Clarissa's character depends upon a theory of the text as a unified, organic whole, what is sometimes referred to as a "monological" view of literature. To interpret Clarissa's preparations for death as defensive, one must see them as part of a continuous development in her identity, an intensification of traits that have always been latent in her consciousness. The skeptical interpretation, that is, requires that one believe in "character" as a centered, determinate structure, an organization of elements that is more or less accessible to psychological and ethical investigation. The possibility of radical transformation, of decentered modes of existence, is ruled out a priori.

It may seem ironic that critics who would take Richardson to task for his ignorance of the divisive politics of the self must adopt a monological view both of literature and of identity. Equally, it may seem ironic that readers who want to defend Richardson's vision of the transcendent spirit find themselves uncovering fissures in the literary text, seismic shifts in the work's genre, and profound alterations in the way the author defines "character." If these conclusions do seem ironic, they are ironies we must nonetheless explore more fully if we are to understand the ways in which transcendence may be represented in literature.

2

PURE POETRY/
IMPURE FICTION

English poetry and the novel underwent astonishing changes in the second half of the eighteenth century, the period sometimes called the "age of sensibility."[1] Yet, surprisingly, the developments in the two fields are rarely considered in conjunction. Poetry and the novel usually form separate topics in our literary histories, just as they do in our curricula. On the rare occasion when a critic considers the two subjects together, he or she is usually more interested in intellectual history – in topics such as "nature," the "city," "childhood," or "sensibility" – than in the study of literary forms.[2] Despite a long tradition of poetics and a more recent interest in the theory of the novel, we know very little about where and how the genres intersect.

The subject of visionary experience, however, should prompt us to think about this intersection. Transcendence, by its very definition, involves switching categories, crossing from one "kind" of thing to another. It is a boundary phenomenon, an effect constituted by the transgression of a line. When reading visionary works of fiction, critics have felt ill at ease with the standard definitions of the novel. As a result, there have been several attempts to define a mixed genre, variously named the lyrical novel, the poetic novel, or the novel as poem.[3] These studies almost always center on the fiction of the early twentieth century – in English, the works of Joyce and Virginia Woolf. Not surprisingly, they rely on a New Critical conception of poetry that stresses the successful reconciliation of discordant elements through unifying patterns of imagery or spatial form, rather than the crises or disjunctive moments characteristic of Romantic lyricism.[4] To appreciate the radically *mixed* nature of a novel that attempts to accommodate Romantic vision, we need to confront the theory of the novel with a Romantic conception of poetry that recognizes the disruptive character of the lyric moment.

In the preceding chapter we saw that Romantic readers, who viewed

Clarissa as an attempt to mix transcendent scenes with other, more realistic material, still did not interpret this work as a lyrical or poetic novel, even when as in Schlegel's case they believed that precisely such a mixture was what would make the novel the most "poetic" of all genres. This example suggests that we should investigate a thesis that, if true, would contradict much Romantic genre theory and would challenge twentieth-century notions about the seamless structure of a "lyrical novel." It may be that certain effects seem appropriate if achieved in lyric poetry (or, perhaps, in certain nonfiction genres such as the religious meditation, philosophical treatise, or spiritual autobiography) but that the same effects seem inappropriate if deployed within the generic field of the novel. To explore this possibility, it seems best to look at the genre of fiction that attempted to admit visionary experience most directly and pervasively – the Gothic novel.

It has become common in recent years to parallel the impulse that led to Gothicism in fiction with the development of a visionary poetics in the second half of the eighteenth century (Kiely 6–26). This juxtaposition makes a neat historical pattern, and it has the value of dramatizing a major preoccupation of the period. Like the visionary lyrics of Joseph Warton, Collins, and Gray, the Gothic novel strove to disrupt categories and transgress boundaries. Experiments with fragmented narratives, multiply embedded stories, surprising digressions, improbable points of view, and grotesque inversions of decorum disrupted narrative conventions as radically as any of the "sudden and bold transitions"[5] that were thought characteristic of the sublime ode. In terms of subject matter, too, the Gothic novel sought to explore extreme states of consciousness, just as did the visionary lyric. Despite these similarities, there are differences between the fictional and the poetical projects that uncover fundamental aspects of the forms involved. Modern critics have tended to overlook these differences, primarily in an effort to recover the Gothic novel as a serious genre.[6] If the supernatural horrors of Gothic novels can be shown to parallel the visionary explorations of contemporary poets and their Romantic heirs, then perhaps the sensationalism of the novels can be read as something more than cheap thrills. But historical criticism needs to be informed by a sensitivity to genres, just as genre criticism needs to be aware of historical developments. It is interesting that the authors of Gothic novels did not look to theories of lyric poetry for their justification, nor did their initial critics.[7] In the nineteenth and early twentieth centuries, this genre was certainly not identified by readers, writers, or critics with an essentially poetic aim. Even today, most people turn to a tale of terror for a thrilling plot; the chills of the genre are almost universally regarded as a narrative rather than a lyric resource.

One of the best ways to uncover the differences between the Gothic novel and visionary poetry is to explore the theory of "pure poetry" that came into prominence at approximately the same period. It will become apparent that the concept of "purity" in literature seriously complicates any comparison of narrative and lyric genres. The term appears to have been given currency by the first volume of Joseph Warton's *Essay on the Genius and Writings of Pope* (1756), where Warton advanced the argument that Pope (and other writers including Donne, Dryden, and Swift) was an author of wit and sense but that he left no traces of "PURE POETRY" (iv). Declaring that the sublime and the pathetic are the marks of "all genuine poetry" and that Spenser, Shakespeare, and Milton were the only English poets who had possessed those qualities in sufficient degree, Warton asked, "What is there transcendently Sublime or Pathetic in POPE?" (x). Pope's defenders, in turn, found it useful to mock the growing vogue for visionary poetics. Percival Stockdale scored some of his best points at the expense of those "Gothick souls" who are "only stimulated with the *transcendently* sublime," which comes from "the unnatural, the gigantick, and the incoherent" (128).

By the beginning of the next century, when Anna Barbauld was preparing her edition of Collins's poetry, it was acceptable to oppose the class of "pure poetry" to all other genres of poetry: narrative, dramatic, didactic, and other. Barbauld's definition of pure poetry, in effect, restricts the literary representation of visionary experience to the realm of lyric poetry:

> The other class consists of what may be called pure Poetry, or Poetry in the abstract. It is conversant with an imaginary world, peopled with beings of its own creation. . . . It is necessarily obscure to a certain degree; because, having to do chiefly with ideas generated within the mind, it cannot be at all comprehended by any whose intellect has not been exercised in similar contemplations; . . . All that is properly *Lyric Poetry* is of this kind. ("On the Poetical Works of Mr. Collins" iv–v)

From the writings of Warton, Stockdale, and Barbauld, it is apparent that the concept of purity in poetry was closely related to the choice of a visionary subject. As we shall see in a moment, however, the concept of purity is utterly foreign to the theoretical discussions surrounding the Gothic novel, even though these latter works treated subjects fully as visionary as any that appeared in the poetry of the time. But first we must investigate the theoretical basis for associating pure poetry with visionary experience.[8] Why was it important to Joseph Warton, the author of a volume of sublime odes, to distinguish pure poetry from other kinds? The most often quoted passage in his essay on Pope, the passage that declares "a creative and glowing IMAGINATION" to be the only thing that can turn a mere author into a poet, begins with a slightly overwrought plea for the distinction between true poetry and all other forms of writing: "All I plead for, is, to have their several provinces kept distinct from each other" (v). How is this intense concern for purity related to an interest in the visionary?

The ground purity shares with vision lies primarily in the realm of religious experience. Anna Barbauld's talk of "pure poetry" belongs to the rhetoric of religion, as does her sense of poetry's obscurity, its aura of incomprehensible mysteries. The division of literature into pure and impure forms resembles the religious impulse to categorize experience as sacred or profane, holy or unholy. In the Bible, holiness means "to be set apart," and much of the power of visionary poetry derives from the sublime lyric's claim to be holy in this literal sense, a form set apart from all other types of writing. Joseph Warton's odes draw on this religious source explicitly. His most famous poem, the ode "To Fancy," invokes a power that "breathes an energy divine" and "gives a soul to every line." Significantly, this power must be approached with caution. It is sacred, pure, holy; it is "set apart," and it will set the song it inspires apart from all profane types of poetry:

> Ne'er may I strive with lips profane
> To utter an unhallow'd strain,
> Nor dare to touch the sacred string,
> Save when with smiles thou bid'st me sing. (*Odes* 9–10)

Warton's caution about touching the sacred string, the care he takes to propitiate the power he invokes, points to another way in which the category of "pure poetry" participates in religious forms of thought. The holy is always an object of awe or even terror. Mary Douglas has demonstrated the deep connection that exists between this religious feeling of awe and the concept of purity. She argues that modern as well as primitive notions of the pure are inextricably involved with a sense of danger. In the eighteenth century writers were equally interested in the connection between exaltation and danger. Burke defined the sublime in precisely such terms: "Whatever is fitted in any sort to excite the ideas of pain, and danger, that is to say, whatever is in any sort terrible, or is conversant about terrible objects, or operates in a manner analogous to terror, is a source of the *sublime*" (39). The poets of the period also saw terror as a source of vision. Perhaps the most striking example is Collins, whose "Ode to Fear" called on the power of "frantic *Fear*" to grant him "the Visions old" seen by Greek poet-prophets and by Shakespeare. In the decades to come, the terror of ghosts, the awful in nature, and the horror within man would all become standard resources for evoking the awe that was regarded as an essential part of visionary experience (Spacks 67–102). The lyrics that contained these subjects, as well as the "redis-covered" poems of Ossian, were invariably the modern exemplars of "pure poetry" chosen to stand beside the Gothic superstitions of Spenser, the witches of Shakespeare, and above all the prophetic visions of Milton (see, e.g., Drake, "On Lyric Poetry").

Critical treatments of the Gothic novel during this period followed a very different line. Far from seeing the Gothic novel as a form of "pure fiction," proponents of the new genre actually reveled in its "impurity." The first authors of this type of fiction explicitly characterized the form as a mixture of antithetical elements. The most famous comments to this effect can be found in the prefaces to the first two editions of Horace Walpole's *Castle of Otranto*. In the first preface he admitted that "some apology" was necessary for including supernatural events in a work of fiction. "Miracles, visions, necromancy, dreams, and other preternatural events, are exploded now even from romances" (264). The considerable success of his work may have lent Walpole confidence, for in the "Preface to the Second Edition" he was ready to claim that these preternatural events were necessary to correct a deficiency of imagination in the modern novel. Explaining the odd combination of elements, he wrote:

> It was an attempt to blend the two kinds of romance, the ancient and the modern. In the former all was imagination and improbability: in the latter, nature is always intended to be, and sometimes has been, copied with success. Invention has not been wanting; but the great resources of fancy have been dammed up, by a strict adherence to common life. (266)

Unlike Warton, who was concerned to identify the "pure" in poetry, Walpole's primary ambition for his novel was to blend discordant elements and hence to "reconcile the two kinds" (266). Clara Reeve, who in her *Progress of Romance* made one of the earliest and clearest attempts to define the two kinds, followed Walpole in claiming that she had mixed the two genres in her Gothic romance *The Old English Baron* ("Preface" 298–9). So pronounced was this interest in mixing "kinds" that we might speculate that the frequent violation of natural limits in the later works of Lewis and Maturin – not only the use of supernatural incidents but also the fascination with incest, patricide, and cannibalism – reproduced, on the level of subject matter, the genre's theoretical preoccupation with impurity.[9]

Impurity, of course, is closely related to purity; each term implies the other, if only by exclusion. In a secular age (or form), when the sacred no longer seems directly available, impurity may be the only way one has of approaching the divine.[10] Foucault has maintained as much in a discussion of "profanation" or "transgression" that seems applicable to the Gothic novel. "In a world which no longer recognizes any positive meaning in the sacred," he writes, "transgression prescribes not only the sole manner of discovering the sacred in its unmediated substance, but also a way of recomposing its empty form, its absence, through which it becomes all the more scintillating" (30). If Foucault is right, then transgression is a way of investing the impure with the power of the sacred. Anthropologists have sometimes been puzzled that impurity seems to possess the same religious power as purity; both are set apart and both are dangerous. Mary Douglas explains this seeming paradox by reference to the interdependence of form and formlessness. The power of form depends upon the threat of formlessness, just as the need for disorder arises from the potential rigidity of order (Douglas 94–113). Speculations such as these might help us to understand the seemingly contradictory charges often leveled against the Gothic novel – of being formless, on the one hand, and of being obsessed with forms, with multiple points of view and embedded structures, on the other hand. Whichever way one views the genre, its attitude toward form would thus testify to an effort to recompose the empty zone of the sacred. This conclusion, however, leaves unexplored the issue with which we began. If we grant that the transgressions of the Gothic seek the same (essentially religious) power as visionary poetry, then why is the structure of one form always regarded as impure, and the structure of the other as pure? It is not enough to say that the two terms are inextricably related. We still must confront the question of how a genre lays exclusive claim to one side of the relation rather than the other.

To answer this question, we must touch upon a variety of cultural and social presuppositions. To begin with, there is the matter of conventional expectations. Sublime poetry has traditionally been associated with great religious or civic occasions. Rhetorically, it is a high form, and decorum dictates that it deal with matters of import, whether to the conduct of the state or to the life of those individuals whose spiritual condition is of general concern – heroes, rulers, religious leaders, even poets. The power that sets such high subjects apart, and makes them dangerous, must be regarded as purifying rather than polluting if the social order is to preserve its authority. Even when the poet assumes the mantle of the prophet, his or her criticism aims at a renovation of the state or of the human spirit, and thus its corrosiveness serves the ends of purification. The sanctity of poetry's high mission, then, is insured by the needs of society, perhaps most when a prophetic furor appears to trespass upon dangerous ground.

By contrast, the novel, as it developed in the eighteenth century, was tied by convention to the issues and concerns of ordinary people. These concerns were typically social rather than metaphysical, and they found their expression in stories about marriage, family, profession, and class or in adventures that moved through a wide range of natural settings and alien cultures (Watt 35–59, 80–5). When the issue *was* metaphysical, the drama turned on the crisis of a private individual more often than of a public figure. As Samuel Johnson described the form in 1750, it attempted to "exhibit life in its true state, diversified only by accidents that daily happen in the world, and influenced by passions and qualities which are really to be found in conversing with mankind" (67).

Because of the genre's close ties to the "passions and qualities" of daily life, transgression inevitably assumes a different role in the form. An event that violates the ordinary conditions of the novel seems to upset a world that is very close to our own. If a sublime ode depicts an act of transgression, it reflects the poet's desire to trespass upon divine, not human, prerogatives.[11] To gain the power of vision, the poet must sometimes rise to forbidden heights, soar in regions not meant for mortal eyes. The Gothic novel, on the other hand, trespasses on laws that are fundamentally social in character. Acts of incest and patricide may seek to inspire a holy terror, a fear that can be described in the vocabulary of the sublime, but one's reaction to that terror is governed by a sense that the violence is anything but "set apart" from one's own life.[12] Far from purifying the social order, the events of the Gothic novel seem to strike at the bonds that constitute society. It appears to harbor an asocial desire, a lawless urge to undermine the relationships that make a human community possible. Despite this appearance, however, the genre has a more conservative thrust. After titillating its readers with all manner of "unnatural" acts, it frequently restores the status quo by rationalizing everything that had appeared to transcend natural limits (as Ann Radcliffe does) or by punishing the satanic hero (as does Maturin in *Melmoth, the Wanderer*). Tony Tanner has recently suggested that adultery is an apt model for transgression in any novel, even one that does not seem concerned with the sexual, because adultery violates a social contract that is analogous to the one that institutes the novel (*Adultery in the Novel* 3–24). Gothic works, to be sure, follow the pattern that Tanner has outlined, for their violence infringes precisely on the social dimension of our lives. For this reason alone, it may have been important to think of the Gothic novel as an impure form.

Another reason for the divergent responses to visionary poetry and the Gothic novel is their comparative difficulty. The high style of the sublime ode consisted of a densely packed, figurative, and allusive language that required learning and concentration for its proper appreciation. The prestige of this difficulty should not be underestimated when considering the tendency to view poetry as a pure form. Mastery of arcane knowledge and difficult techniques has always been a sign of initiation into mysteries of a religious nature. In the eighteenth century, difficult ideas and techniques were themselves frequently taken to be sources of the sublime. Burke praised Milton's description of Death for being "dark, uncertain, confused, terrible, and sublime to the last degree" (59), and he concluded that a "clear idea is therefore another name for a little idea" (63). Even today, when the connection between obscurity and divine mysteries is less assured, we still associate difficulty with a special kind of seriousness, a seriousness that demands the dedication, even the asceticism, of a saint.[13]

The novel, on the other hand, is among the most accessible of all forms. Rhetorically, the genre relies on a middle or a low style, and its prose resembles the language with which men and women go about the business of their daily lives. It is a popular form, serving a general rather than a specialized readership. Anna Barbauld singled out the novel's simplicity and ease of reading as the characteristics that most distinguished it from poetry: "Poetry requires in the reader a certain elevation of mind and a practised ear. It is seldom relished unless a taste be formed for it pretty early. But the humble novel is always ready to enliven the gloom of solitude" (*Works* 3:138–9).[14] Walpole clearly understood both the importance of this accessibility to the effect of the novel and the incongruity of using such an accessible style to write of sublime subjects. In the first preface to *The Castle of Otranto*, in which he pretended that his fiction had been translated from the Italian, he lamented that he had been unable to copy the elegant language of his original. Significantly, he blamed this flaw on the problem an English writer has trying to maintain a "pure" style in narrative forms of writing: "It is difficult in English *to relate* without falling too low or rising too high; a fault obviously occasioned by the little care taken to speak pure language in common conversation" (Walpole 265).

What is perhaps most revealing is that the dangers associated with poetry and the novel differ fundamentally. The dangers of reading and writing poetry befall only those who dare to challenge the gods. Such temerity brings down punishments of a sort not encountered by ordinary mortals. The most common are madness, loss of sight, or early death, each of which is symbolized by the fate of some preeminent figure (or figures) from the annals of poetry.[15] Perhaps Gray's ode "The Progress of Poesy" best captures the link between visionary experience and this heroic risk taking. At the climax of the poem, the poet Milton is portrayed as rising on "the seraph-wings of Extasy" to spy "the secrets of th' Abyss" (lines 96–7); but he pays for his vision of forbidden realms with the loss of ordinary sight:

> He pass'd the flaming bounds of Place and Time:
> The living Throne, the saphire-blaze,
> Where Angels tremble, while they gaze,
> He saw; but blasted with excess of light,
> Closed his eyes in endless night. (lines 98–102)

The dangers associated with novels are far more plebeian. Fiction threatens one's conduct, not one's mind, and it tends to lead apprentices astray and women to ruin. In part, this difference can be attributed to sociological factors. Since the pitfalls of novel reading were thought to imperil an audience composed primarily of young people, women, and the lower classes, its dangers were regarded as less heroic. Critics were concerned about the proper development, morality, and productivity of such groups, not the condition of their inner lives. As Ioan Williams comments, critics in the essay-periodicals "were seriously worried about the effects of novel-reading on the female mind and on the reproduction of the race" (13). But there are other reasons for this difference, reasons that are intrinsically related to the nature and effects of the different literary genres. With its minute attention to familiar details, its characters drawn from recognizable spheres of life, and its demotic style, the novel provided powerful models for people to emulate in their actual lives. As Samuel Johnson put it, "These books are written chiefly to the young, the ignorant, and the idle, to whom they serve as lectures of conduct, and introductions into life" (68). The ease with which people identified with the story of a novel made it apparent that the power of the form resided in its potential to influence one's character and conduct. The danger of the novel, that is, lay primarily in its effect on the ethical dimension of life.[16]

This last point opens a perspective on the subject that makes it necessary to broaden our field of inquiry. We can no longer ignore the fact that the topics both of purity and of the danger of certain kinds of literature had a rich classical background, a body of arguments so familiar to most educated readers of the eighteenth and nineteenth centuries that it was usually unnecessary to restate them. The topic gained its centrality from the concerns of Plato, who in *The Republic* maintained that the representations of poets posed a danger to the ideal state; and most arguments about the morality of fiction since that time have been colored by his position. Aristotle, in response, introduced the other idea whose history we have been tracing, the notion that "purification" is an essential aspect of certain kinds of literature; and this idea, Aristotle's famous concept of *catharsis*, lies concealed within many eighteenth-century accounts of the function of pure poetry.

Plato saw the fictions of poets as a danger to his republic, because such stories – in imitating the fallible condition of men and women and, still worse, in portraying the gods as jealous, wrathful, immoral, or deceiving – offered potentially corrupting examples to their audiences. (This argument survives, in modified form, in Johnson's concern about the novel's capacity to imitate the vices as well as the virtues of mankind.) Significantly, lyric was the one form of poetry that Plato was willing to permit, although only on the condition that the lyric poet imitated the good exclusively. Plato thought the lyricist who praised heroes and gods in his or her own voice was less likely to deceive listeners with false representations (*Republic* 3.397, 10.607). By contrast, narrative and dramatic forms posed an immediate and present danger to the state, because they had the power to imitate the triumphs and follies of their heroes directly. Further, the poet who aspired to imitate the great deeds of life was inevitably drawn to the "rebellious principle" in men and women, because a character who is "wise and calm" does not make an interesting story. Such a character "is not easy to imitate or to appreciate when imitated" (*Republic* 10.604–5), and the reason is not hard to discover: passion and conflict are necessary for drama. Hence, from Plato onward, narrative and dramatic forms were suspected of presenting a specifically *ethical* danger that lyric did not pose.

Aristotle, who based his theory of poetry primarily on narrative and dramatic works, was concerned to show that the imitation of actions, even corrupt ones, did not necessarily lead to the corruption of the audience. He attempted to accomplish this end through two radically different strategies. First, he restricted the concept of character (*ethos*) in fictional representations to those actions that explicitly revealed a moral purpose. Much that we think of as indicative of character – bad habits, unacted desires, vicious opinions – did not exemplify *ethos* unless clearly connected to a development in the plot (*Poetics* 29 [6.17]). When a characteristic did prompt an action, the course of the plot clearly indicated whether the trait was a virtue or a vice. The influence of bad example was thus minimized by the power of what came to be called poetic justice. Nevertheless, Aristotle recognized that our reaction to the fate of characters often exceeds what is strictly due to their moral station. This element of disproportion in our aesthetic response made necessary Aristotle's second defense of fictional forms.

The term *catharsis* is generally defined as the "purgation" or "purification" of feeling through pity and fear. Aristotle regarded this process as one of the great goods that literature bestows on society. Interestingly, he sometimes implied that this benefit is conferred independently of, or in addition to, the ethical good done by characters and plot. When Aristotle discussed the kind of protagonist best suited to tragedy, he said several times that the misfortunes of certain characters would *neither* satisfy the moral sense *nor* call forth pity and fear, as if these two effects of tragedy were distinct (*Poetics* 54 [13.2]). If these qualities were separable, then catharsis would have an independent value, and literature's power to purify the feelings would be a valid end in itself. Whether Aristotle really meant the power of catharsis to be separable from the ethical content of tragedy has been the subject of much debate. Fortunately, we do not need to argue the question, because the writers we are considering almost universally regarded it as settled.

In the second half of the eighteenth century, the ability to produce pity and fear was increasingly assumed to be a major (and separate) source of literature's value. Notice how frequently the terms "sublime" and "pathetic" (fear and pity) are employed by the authors of this period to describe the qualities that raise a work, or some part of a work, to the level of pure poetry.[17] The reader's experience of these feelings was seen as a benefit of literature that had little or nothing to do with the specific ethical argument (or plot) of the piece. Thus the passage that produced these feelings could be regarded as a detachable, morally independent unit, a moment of pure poetry that could appear in any text, no matter what its thematic tendency or formal arrangement. This line of reasoning may help to explain the puzzling practice of many early nineteenth-century critics who felt free to praise an author's imaginative power despite the fact that they were condemning the immorality of his or her story.[18]

Romantic readers were perhaps aided in arriving at this view by Aristotle himself, a figure whose writings are usually taken to epitomize a view of art opposed to the "expressive" ideal.[19] In the *Politics*, however, Aristotle discussed the power of certain kinds of music in terms that could well have supported the tendency to separate emotional affect from the particular content of a piece. For Aristotle, of course, music was a mimetic art because it imitated and possessed character: A mournful strain inclined listeners to solemnity; a lively air, to gaiety. As a consequence of possessing character, music necessarily played a role in the ethical sphere of life: "It follows from all this that music has indeed the power to induce a certain character of soul" (*Politics* 466 [8.5]). So far, Aristotle's account of music parallels his defense of the ethical value of tragedy.[20] But one kind of music had a different effect: Songs played on the pipes (or poetry in the Phrygian mode) were expressly denied to have an adequate ethical dimension. What is most important about this distinction is that the Phrygian mode was the "enthusiastic" genre of the lyric that served as the model for the visionary conception of lyrical poetry that we have been examining. Aristotle wrote, "Furthermore, the pipes are not an instrument of ethical but rather of orgiastic effect, so that their use should be confined to those occasions on which the effect produced by the show is not so much instruction as a way of purifying[21] the emotions" (469 [8.6]). Here, in the domain of "enthusiastic" lyrics, catharsis is unambiguously regarded as a quality distinct from *ethos*. Because of this separation, Aristotle thinks it necessary to add a further defense of catharsis, one that amounts to a special rationale for inspired or visionary poetry.

> Any feeling which comes strongly to some souls exists in all others to a greater or less degree – pity and fear, for example, but also excitement. This is a kind of agitation by which some people are liable to be possessed; it may arise out of religious melodies, and in this case it is observable that when they have been listening to melodies that have an orgiastic effect on the soul they are restored as if they had undergone a curative and purifying treatment. (473–4 [8.7])

For their purifying power alone, Aristotle thought lyrics of the enthusiastic kind were suitable for adults, but he warned that this genre of poetry should not be used for the instruction of the young because it did not possess a sufficiently *ethical* value.

If Aristotle himself was prepared to separate the benefit of visionary experience from the other powers of art, how much more eager would be a writer such as Joseph Warton who believed that the highest virtue of poetry was to affect "our minds with such strong emotions" that "no man of a true poetical spirit, *is master of himself while he reads*" (*Essay on Pope* 2:409, Warton's emphasis)? It is this conception of literature that made the value of "pure poetry" seem unrelated to the larger, broadly ethical concerns of men and women in fiction. It is this conception that made events in a novel that appeared to transgress natural limits seem, at best, to require a special justification and, at worst, to be evidence of an "impure" design.

We can now understand more fully why Romantic readers were prepared to separate the transcendent scenes in *Clarissa* from the larger ethical design of the narrative. When readers elevated a few passages of sublimity and pathos to a position of prominence, they were only following a logic inherent in the theory of pure poetry. When Hazlitt complained that Richardson wrote "the oddest mixture of poetry and prose" (6:118), he was really testifying to his sense that a novelist who attempted to mix transcendence and ethics – "the romantic air of a pure fiction, with the literal minuteness of a common diary" (6:117) – would invariably wind up with an impure substance. In the next chapter we shall examine a novel that was written in the midst of the high Romantic era. Perhaps because of the period in which she wrote, Jane Austen regarded the issue of the ethical value of different genres as anything but an abstract literary problem. Her novel *Mansfield Park* represents something of a challenge to the Romantic theory of poetry that values a literature "purified" of ethical concerns.

3

MANSFIELD PARK

> . . . having talked of poetry, the richness of the present age, and gone
> through a brief comparison of opinion as to the first-rate poets, trying
> to ascertain whether *Marmion* or *The Lady of the Lake* were to be
> preferred, and how ranked the *Giaour* and *The Bride of Abydos*; and
> moreover, how the *Giaour* was to be pronounced, he shewed himself
> . . . intimately acquainted with all the tenderest songs of the one poet,
> and all the impassioned descriptions of hopeless agony of the other.
>
> (*Persuasion*, Vol. 3, Chap. 11)

Marmion or *The Lady of the Lake?* Today such a question is hardly
calculated to excite our warmest attention. For the reading public in Jane
Austen's day, however, it was a matter of some interest. So perhaps it is
worth hazarding an answer. Captain Benwick, the sentimental lover
whose fiancée has recently died, would surely give the laurel to *The Lady
of the Lake*: Its portrait of Ellen Douglas, a Romantic maiden harassed by
noble suitors yet steadfastly true to her lowborn first love, is too
interesting by half, whereas the horror of Lord Marmion's guilty secret
would hold few attractions to an admirer of tender songs. Anne Elliot,
on the other hand, a woman of greater sense and more sincere emotion,
might well appreciate *Marmion*'s treatment of the theme of remorse,
although she could scarcely relish a character who lets his lover be buried
alive. But perhaps we have got it all wrong. The martial fire of Marmion
might better suit a Captain's taste, whereas the renunciation by King
James of his love for Ellen might strike a responsive chord in Anne
Elliot's breast. Of course the question cannot be answered, nor was it
meant to be. We have taken Captain Benwick's earnest inquiries more
seriously than they were meant, in order to dramatize once again the
enormous difference between the world of Jane Austen's fiction and the
Romantic poetry of her day.

In the past Austen's opposition to the Romantic movement was taken
for granted. The comic undercutting of Gothicism in *Northanger Abbey* or

the reproof to excessive feelings delivered by *Sense and Sensibility* seemed clear enough at the time; and Scott himself emphasized the younger novelist's distance from his own grand and gloomy subjects, in the course of a generally favorable review of *Emma*. In the latter part of the nineteenth century, much of the discussion of this author revolved around Charlotte Brontë's charge that Austen lacked all poetry and passion.[1] So long as one associated the Romantic with dark cliffs and secluded glens, tumultuous battles and guilty passions, murderers, ghosts, and kings, then a novelist of quiet domestic comedies represented the antithesis of everything that Captain Benwick loved in the poetry of his age.

In recent years, however, critics have attempted to bring more sophisticated conceptions of Romanticism to bear on the question of Austen's place in literary history. The contributors to a special issue of *The Wordsworth Circle* looked to themes of Romantic enclosure, to shared epistemological techniques, and to a common attitude toward the acceleration of history to buttress their contention that Austen should be accorded a place in future accounts of the Romantic movement (Swingle, Kroeber, Walling, respectively); and at least two articles (Tave, Auerbach) and a full-length book (Morgan) have since responded to their suggestions. The pendulum seems to have swung so far in the other direction that one scholar of Romanticism has protested vigorously that the attempt to call Austen a Romantic not only obscures "the special historical significance of Austen's work" but also confuses "the entire subject of Romanticism" (McGann 19). It must be admitted that, despite the intelligence of much of the new work on Austen's "Romanticism," the enterprise as a whole has not succeeded in clarifying the novelist's relation to her period. Quite the contrary, Austen's position in literary history seems far more uncertain than it was in the days when Scott could compare her portraits of ordinary life to the works of "the Flemish school of painting" ("A Review of *Emma*" 67).[2]

Jerome McGann is right when he says that Austen's relation to Romanticism has a significance beyond the interpretation of her novels. Although her work clearly possesses some affinities with other works written in the period, she is not a Romantic. Whether she is subversive or not, a feminist or a conservative Christian moralist, to call her particular stance Romantic is to confuse rather than to clarify matters. The few attitudes that she shares with Romantic poets exist only in the context of a pervasive antagonism toward the movement, an antagonism made manifest by the irony that she directs toward particular ideas, conventions, and works of the Romantic poets, as well as by her characteristic plots and themes. The attempt to turn Austen into a closet

Romantic obscures the true significance of the few Romantic elements in her fiction. Both the nature of her opposition to Romanticism and the extent to which she was unable to evade some of its characteristic attitudes tell us something about the degree to which the prevailing ideology of the period was able to dominate its age.

This chapter attempts to clarify Jane Austen's position in literary history by examining the nature of her opposition to Romanticism, particularly as evidenced in her treatment of the central topic of this study, Romantic visionary experience. At the same time, the chapter is an effort to discover some of the consequences of Romantic vision by tracing the objections that were raised to this mode of experience at the time. Although the discussion will not overtly address Austen's political beliefs, its examination of the formal strategies that the novelist employed may suggest the outlines of the ideology she was attempting to counter. As we saw earlier, the genres, techniques, and structures an author finds effective (or even necessary) can shed light on issues other than formal ones. The author's "problem" novel, *Mansfield Park*, has been chosen for discussion because it engages in a more complex argument with Romantic structures of feeling than any of her other books. *Northanger Abbey* and *Sense and Sensibility* present the case against Romanticism in terms of oppositions – imagination versus reality, feeling versus sense – that, however subtly handled, are ultimately too reductive to be equal to the subject she was challenging. Austen's most recent biographer has called *Mansfield Park* "one of her most autobiographical volumes" (Halperin 223). The part of that autobiography which Fanny Price dramatizes is the author's deep concern with both the attractions and the dangers of a Romantic vision.

A VISIT TO SOTHERTON

Fanny Price, a pale, shy woman of great sensitivity but little strength, possesses many of the qualities of a fine Romantic heroine. She loves nature; her memory delights her. With the right companion, she is apt to fall into a rhapsodizing strain; alone, she tends toward melancholy. On her visit to Sotherton, the Rushworths' ancestral home, her imagination has prepared her for an experience of what one might call the historical sublime. She wants to hear anything about the family's "rise and grandeur, regal visits and loyal efforts" so that she can "warm her imagination with scenes of the past" (*Mansfield Park* 85). The tones are those of young Waverley, delighting in all that his aunt can tell him of the romance in his family's past; and the scenes with which Fanny hopes to warm her imagination are the very kind that would overheat the fancy of one of Scott's young heroes. In a novel by Jane Austen, however, an enthusiastic youth must brace herself for misfortunes less spectacular than Waverley's. Rather than plunging her into a conflict between nations, Fanny's high expectations lead only to a momentary disappointment. As the party approaches the family chapel, Fanny exercises her mind with thoughts of Scott's castles:

> Fanny's imagination had prepared her for something grander than a mere, spacious, oblong room. . . . "I am disappointed," said she. . . . "There is nothing awful here, nothing melancholy, nothing grand. Here are no aisles, no arches, no inscriptions, no banners. No banners, cousin, to be 'blown by the night wind of Heaven.' No signs that a 'Scottish monarch sleeps below.'" (85–6)

Fanny's desire for the "awful" partakes of the Romantic hunger for the sublime; her "melancholy" evokes the favorite mood of Romantic maidens; and her hope for "aisles," "arches," "inscriptions," and "banners" springs from the Romantic passion for a Gothic and chivalric past. Chivalry, further, is what makes her think of Scott, from whose *Lay of the Last Minstrel* she quotes.

Fanny, of course, has little in common with Scott's dark, passionate women. To begin with, no one would ever accuse her of a tempestuous spirit. She is far too temperate. Moreover, Fanny's veneration for the past has room for a firmly Johnsonian moral. Discussing the institution of family prayers, she says, "It was a valuable part of former times" (86). Finally, the dramatic context of the scene in the chapel puts Fanny's Romantic tendencies within a larger perspective. Edmund, Fanny, and Mary Crawford engage in an extended debate on the duties one owes to others and the freedom one owes to oneself. In fact, every allusion to Romanticism in the novel serves to develop a contrast between the pleasures of solitude and the value of community.

The benefits of community, Edmund tells us, lie in "fixing our thoughts" (87); devotions in a closet can lead to mental "wandering" (87). It is within this context that the dangers in Fanny's Romantic tendencies should be viewed. Awe, melancholy, the grandeur of the past are not bad things in themselves.[3] Only when the mind is "indulged in wanderings" (87) do they become threatening. Mary Crawford is generally thought of as the restless character in the novel. But Fanny's expectations about the chapel illustrate that she too can be tempted to wander, not physically but imaginatively, and that this form of straying can equally isolate one. On the road to Sotherton, Fanny's love of nature encourages her to do without the company of others: "She was not often invited to join in the conversation of the others, nor did she desire it. Her own thoughts and reflections were habitually her best companions" (80). Later, we shall learn that Fanny has a "rambling fancy" (209), especially when out of doors; in the midst of nature, she is apt to fall into a "sort of wondering strain" (209). To a fully Romantic spirit, which Fanny's, of course, is not, such "wondering" might lead to a visionary wandering of the mind.

The next incident at Sotherton, the walk in the "wilderness," extends, while qualifying, the opposition between wandering and fixity.[4] As the three young people stroll through the trees, following "a very serpentine course" (94), Fanny grows tired and desires to sit down. This Mary Crawford cannot abide. She must move; only resting fatigues her. The contrast between Mary's restlessness and Fanny's immobility has attracted much attention. But those readers who maintain that the novel uncritically endorses Fanny's stillness underestimate the book's complexity.[5] Fanny is never rewarded for the physical weakness that leads her to prefer rest to motion.[6] In this instance, her need to sit still brings her only solitude and neglect, for Edmund and Mary desert Fanny to measure the wilderness together. Mary has started a frivolous argument about how far they have walked, and her waywardness on the subject has become as captivating as the serpentine woods. Austen is having fun with the romance topos that equates error with errantry, especially when she has Mary remark that they "have been winding in and out ever since we came into [the woods]" (95). Fanny, who cannot care about such a trivial matter but who would like to go with them for reasons of her own, must stay behind to wait for the others. Because the novel so clearly censures Mary's restlessness, readers may mistake Fanny's immobility for a positive trait; but Austen frequently criticizes one quality without endorsing its opposite.

Mary's character brings a tremendous impetus to the story. No matter what the situation, she serves as a stimulus to the narrative. She is the perfect creature for a plot, the principle of liveliness and action incarnate in a young woman. She has a natural love for stories and is twice praised for her narrative ability (49, 87). D. A. Miller calls this talent "the same undisciplined 'novelism'" (18) possessed by Emma, and, in a disciplined form, by the author. It is only with her and her brother's arrival that the action of the novel really begins. The Crawfords bring parties, concerts, theatricals, and excursions into the quiet world of Mansfield Park, as well as jealousy, adultery, and intrigue. From the beginning Mary's goal is matrimony (42), an excellent way to set in motion a comic novel's marriage plot. She conceives of matrimony as a "manœuvring business," the one transaction "in which people expect most from others, and are least honest themselves" (46). This happy conception, uniting duplicity, self-deception, and desire, would give almost any plot ample impetus to unfold. When she conspires with her brother to make Fanny accept his necklace, Mary proves herself adept in just the sort of tricks that keep a plot in motion.

Mary's brother Henry, who owes something to Richardson's Lovelace, is also a master of plots and deceptions. Like Lovelace, he possesses the character of a true dramatic hero. He is an intuitive actor, grasping the essence of every role almost before he comes to it. More important, he can act for himself. Julia pays him high tribute as a man of spirit: "Those who see quickly, will resolve quickly and act quickly" (61). Again, D. A. Miller has emphasized the right point: "Henry prizes the narratable," by which Miller means he values situations that keep alternatives open, the outcome in suspense; Henry values, in short, the moments that keep a story going rather than those that bring it to a close (Miller 24–7). Henry's love of "narratable" situations, however, leads him into trouble. An overbold huntsman, he is accustomed to breaking a girl's heart as easily as he would a tall hedge. But this time he is too impetuous for his own good. His attempt on Fanny's heart ends by breaking his own.

The contrast between the Crawfords and Fanny is one of the distinctive features of the book, but it is not sufficient in itself to define Fanny's position in the novel. If we return to the scene in the wilderness at Sotherton, we discover that Fanny's solitary station on a bench in the park has a significance beyond that of the contrast to Mary. Fanny has been sitting in front of a locked gate for twenty minutes when she hears footsteps approaching her on the path. It is not Edmund and Mary, who seem to have forgotten her, but Maria, Mr. Rushworth, and Henry. Fanny has some company at last, but only a minute passes before the prospect of the hill beyond the gate tempts the newcomers to leave her again, and Mr. Rushworth is sent for the key. While he is gone, Maria and Henry begin a flirtation, much to Fanny's distress. Henry taunts Maria with being afraid to pass the gate without Mr. Rushworth's "authority," and he suggests that she is prohibited from doing it. "Prohibited!" – the challenge is more than enough to spur Maria to an act she had already desired to perform (99). The sexual implications in this scene are strong: The gate is a threshold, beyond which the licensed becomes illicit, an innocent stroll becomes a more dangerous straying. Such moments are rare in Jane Austen. Although illicit or adulterous affairs have a role in all her novels, they almost always take place off stage. Understandably, most critics have focused their attention on the guilty pair.[7] Yet Fanny's part in this scene should interest us as well. After failing to persuade Maria not to go, she is left alone on her bench again – still, solitary, and "sorry for almost all that she had seen and heard" (100). She sits for an entire hour while Edmund, Mary, Mr. Rushworth, Henry, Maria, and Julia move around her station, eagerly pursuing objects that only Fanny fully perceives.

Although exquisitely conscious of all the other characters' comings and goings, she can neither prevent acts that she thinks precipitous nor mitigate the unhappy consequences of the events that transpire. In this scene she is as close to a non-narrative being as a character in fiction can reasonably become.[8] But she is not the "stable, nondesiring center of judgment" that Bersani would have her (77), for she is full of unfulfilled wishes and pressing fears; it is just that her desires have no effect on the chain of events that constitute the plot of this episode. Her nonexistence as a narrative force in this scene should help us to perceive how radically her status changes in the second and third volumes, where virtually the entire direction of the narrative is determined by her act of refusing Henry's offer of marriage. Because this act is one of denial, which superficially resembles the state of not acting, readers have confused it with the passive condition that is forced upon her here. We should not need Freud to show us how decisive an act negation can be. Fanny's "no" is one of those choices between limited and final alternatives that Tave calls "heroic" (*Some Words* 33).

If Fanny's actions (or inaction) are not critical in the chain of events, she nevertheless occupies a significant structural position in the text. A still center at the heart of the action, Fanny's place might remind us of those passages of lyric that punctuate the narratives of high romance, from Spenser to Sir Walter Scott. Such a passage – the classical *locus amoenus* – often constitutes a threat to the narrative order of a poem, and hence it could be used by Spenser and his successors as a threatening as well as merely pleasant interlude.[9] The lyrical passages that interrupt the stories of Scott's *Marmion* or *The Lady of the Lake* provide clear places of rest, seductive invitations for the hero to pause, thus suggesting an alternative to the frenzied action of the rest of the poem. They possess a power to enchant, a static charm that in some ways rivals the allure of the central narrative. Ellen Douglas, Scott's Lady of the Lake, casts a spell with her song that enwraps the wandering Knight King James in peaceful but lonely sleep: "Soldier, rest! thy warfare o'er, / Sleep the sleep that knows not breaking" (canto 1, stanza 31). The danger is that the hero, and by extension the narrative, will become becalmed in a kind of lyric stasis, entranced by the beauty of his own vision. According to Angus Fletcher, the point of contact between these static places and the active narrative possesses a distinctive structure. The movement of narrative is characteristically represented by the the image of a labyrinth, particularly a serpentine or winding path in the woods. Wandering in this maze can be actual or psychic, but usually it is both. The place of lyric is symbolically a kind of temple, often one personified by the figure of a young woman. At the point where these two structures intersect lies a threshold, a gate through which it is perilous to pass (Fletcher, *The Prophetic Moment*).

All the elements of high romance are present, in ironic form, in the garden scene in *Mansfield Park*. The "wilderness" is a labyrinth, in which the wandering characters follow "a very serpentine course." Fanny is the spirit of the temple, a passive figure who waits at the center of the story. And the locked gate is literally a threshold, one which is fraught with psychic as well as sexual peril. Yet, in Jane Austen, these Romantic motifs are domesticated within the confines of a realistic novel. Heroic action is reduced to the scale of Sotherton's neatly planned "wilderness," and the dangerous allure of passivity is embodied in the pallid charms of Fanny Price.

The elaborate machinery of romance may seem far removed from the machinations of polite lovers at Sotherton, but there is a more noticeable resemblance between the scenario in one of Coleridge's Romantic crisis lyrics and the situation of Austen's heroine. In "This Lime-Tree Bower My Prison," one of several Romantic poems about the trials of being left behind while other people wander in gladness, Coleridge finds himself placed in a position that resembles Fanny's. Because of a slight injury, the poet is prevented from taking a walk with his friends. Instead, he must sit by himself, his consciousness of the others' activity his only companion. The poem opens on a note of self-pity that might remind us of Fanny's own tendencies in that direction. Coleridge laments that he has lost "beauties and feelings" – precious states of consciousness – that in future years would have served as a source of consolation for the miseries of old age. His desire to store up memories might remind us of Fanny's hoard of precious objects in the East room, each of which had "an interesting remembrance connected with it" (152), and of her habit of looking for "immediate consolation" in her musings (151). Coleridge's proleptic blindness in the first lines of his poem ("when age / Had dimm'd mine eyes to blindness" [lines 4–5]) hints at a different form of darkness, the loss of all awareness of his immediate surroundings that occurs during his visionary experience later in the poem. For Fanny, too, losing sight of what most interests her receives a repeated emphasis ("She watched them till they had turned the corner, and listened till all sound of them had ceased" [96]; "By taking a circuitous, and as it appeared to [Fanny], very unreasonable direction to the knoll, they were soon beyond her eye; and for some minutes longer she remained without sight or sound of any companion" [100]).

The most important feature of Coleridge's poem for our purposes is the opposition between the poet's stillness and his friends' wandering. Stillness condemns Coleridge to solitude, to a prison that, in his melancholy mood, seems likely to separate him from his companions forever ("Friends, whom I never more may meet again" [line 6]). Action frees the others to "wander in gladness" (line 8), participating in a joyous communion not only with one another but with all of nature. Coleridge's escape from this dilemma is to "wander" in vision along with his friends, imagining their progress even as he remains physically behind. Yet Coleridge's visionary walk threatens to isolate him more completely than his actual disability has done. The desire to be elsewhere with his friends, the desire that on a whim evaporates distance, can in more extreme circumstances do away with the external world entirely. At its most intense, Coleridge's vision dissolves not only his own immediate surroundings but also those that he imagines his friends observing. Thus the poet thinks of his friends as gazing round on the wide landscape but seeing nothing with their bodily eyes. His fervent hope changes from the desire to be with them to the wish that they may gaze "with swimming sense" until "all doth seem / Less gross than bodily" (lines 39, 40–1).

Fanny, of course, does not grow visionary during her solitary moments in the garden. The point of contact between her static form and the wandering action does not become a transformative or liminal site. There are other moments in the novel when she comes a bit closer to a visionary response to her position. But here she never even verges on a Romantic epiphany. If we knew nothing about *Mansfield Park* but the date of its publication, 1814, the year that saw the appearance of Scott's *Waverley,* Byron's *Corsair,* and Wordsworth's *Excursion,* what is the chance that we would have guessed that its young, imaginative heroine would spend an hour alone in nature worrying only about the conduct of her absent companions? Let us turn to some other aspects of Fanny's story in order to discover both what tempts her to an occasional Romantic posture and what prevents her from ever becoming a fully Romantic character.

THE MANSION OF MANY APARTMENTS

A passage from the letters of John Keats can help us to understand Fanny's slow development. Keats, who published his first book four months before Jane Austen's death, has some affinities with the earlier novelist. Although more in love with "Flora, and old Pan" ("Sleep and Poetry," line 102), Keats too expresses some doubts about the Romantic self. In a well-known letter written on May 3, 1818, he compares life to a "Mansion of Many Apartments" (*Letters* 1:280). The first room in this great house is "the infant or thoughtless Chamber" (1:280). As we move through life, we advance from one room to another, each chamber adding something to our spiritual development. This little "simile of human life," as Keats calls it (1:280), has an amusing pertinence to Fanny's story. Her youthful days are spent in an infant or thoughtless chamber, her "little white attic" at Mansfield Park. As she develops into a woman, she begins to move through the more important rooms in the mansion. More than one critic has described her entire career as a journey through the various rooms of the house. Alistair Duckworth puts it this way: "As the novel progresses, Fanny moves closer to the center of the house, her inward journey marking her rising worth" (75).

The second room in Keats's Mansion is "the Chamber of Maiden-Thought" (*Letters* 1:281). This is a room of many joys. Here "we become intoxicated with the light and the atmosphere, we see nothing but pleasant wonders, and think of delaying there for ever in delight" (1:281). But one of the consequences of living in this room is "that tremendous one of sharpening one's vision into the heart and nature of Man" (1:281). The movement from childhood to Maiden-Thought necessarily involves an increase in consciousness; we are "imperceptibly impelled by the awakening of the thinking principle – within us" (1:281). According to Keats, Wordsworth had come to this point when he wrote "Tintern Abbey," and Keats praises the older poet for seeing "into the human heart" (1:282), even if the heart he saw into was his own. Fanny has her own Chamber of Maiden-Thought: It is, quite literally, a chamber devoted to the thought of maidens, the girls' old schoolroom, fitted up with a few comforts and given a new name, the East room.[10]

This room, poor though it is, serves as Fanny's refuge from all the cares of life: "The comfort of it in her hours of leisure was extreme" (*Mansfield Park* 151). It is her one private place, her only sanctuary. Here she retreats to be alone with herself, to indulge the sensitive part of her nature in its most melancholy reflections or secret desires. We first see the East room when she flees from the pressure her cousins have put on her to act in the play. In fact, almost every time we find her in her "nest of comforts" (152), she has fled there to avoid or to recover from some unpleasant encounter with another person: "She could go there after any thing unpleasant below, and find immediate consolation in some pursuit, or some train of thought at hand" (151). The room is in effect a microcosm of her consciousness, and a retreat to her room is equivalent to a retreat into her self. The danger for Fanny in the Chamber of Maiden-Thought is, in Keats's words, to "think of delaying there for ever in delight."

As Wordsworth is the presiding spirit or genius loci of this second stage of life, it is appropriate that Fanny's East room contains a transparency of Tintern Abbey: "Its greatest elegancies and ornaments were . . . three transparencies, made in a rage for transparencies, for the three lower panes of one window, where Tintern Abbey held its station between a cave in Italy, and a moonlight lake in Cumberland" (152). Just as much to the point, Fanny has a Wordsworthian delight in the flux and reflux of the memory. "There seems something more speakingly incomprehensible in the powers, the failures, the inequalities of memory, than in any other of our intelligences," she tells Mary Crawford. "The memory is sometimes so retentive, so serviceable, so obedient – at others, so bewildered and so weak – and at others again, so tyrannic, so beyond controul!" (208–9).[11]

For Fanny, as indeed for Wordsworth, the "speakingly incomprehensible" powers of memory are essential to the achievement of one of her favorite states of mind: nostalgia. With her brother William, she takes a melancholy pleasure in dwelling on the past; she confesses that it is "perhaps the dearest indulgence" of his whole visit (234). Together, "all the evil and good of their earliest years could be gone over again, and every former united pain and pleasure retraced with the fondest recollection" (234). Fanny feels the power of this activity so keenly that Austen pauses to comment that the memories of childhood can strengthen the bond between brothers and sisters, at times even beyond that of married partners:

> An advantage this, a strengthener of love, in which even the conjugal tie is beneath the fraternal. Children of the same family, the same blood, with the same first associations and habits, have some means of enjoyment in their power, which no subsequent connections can supply; and it must be by a long and unnatural estrangement . . . if such precious remains of the earliest attachments are ever entirely outlived. (234–5)

Fanny's appreciation of these "precious remains of the earliest attachments" might remind us of Wordsworth's thankfulness for the memories he shared with Dorothy. Austen, of course, could not have known Wordsworth's tribute in *The Prelude* to "the beloved Sister" whose daily presence served as a reminder to the poet during a time of despair of what he had been in the past, and thus "Maintained for me a saving intercourse / With my true self" (*P*.11.335, 341–2; see also 14.232–66).[12] But she could have read the short poem published in *Poems in Two Volumes* (1807), "The Sparrow's Nest," where he traced many of his finest feelings to his feelings for his sister:

> The Blessing of my later years
> Was with me when a boy:
> She gave me eyes, she gave me ears;
> And humble cares, and delicate fears. (*Poetical Works* 1:227)

It is not influence that we need argue here, however, but the resemblance between two structures of feeling. George Eliot may have felt the similarity when she wrote about Maggie and Tom Tulliver's shared memories of childhood in *The Mill on the Floss*. She seems to echo both

Wordsworth and Austen in the passages where she maintains that "the thoughts and loves of these first years would always make part of their lives" (36) and that "there is no sense of ease like the ease we felt in those scenes where we were born, where objects became dear to us before we had known the labour of choice, and where the outer world seemed only an extension of our own personality" (133).

Fanny's memories of home are so piercing that occasionally they seem as much a malady as a blessing, and we should remember that "nostalgia" is etymologically connected with the malady of homesickness, a condition that in the late eighteenth century was often thought of as physical illness.[13] When Sir Thomas resolves to send Fanny back home to Portsmouth, she is overcome with the joy of her memories: "The remembrance of all her earliest pleasures, and of what she had suffered in being torn from them, came over her with renewed strength, and it seemed as if to be home again, would heal every pain that had since grown out of the separation" (370). We should note the crucial role that separation has played in Fanny's feelings. One cannot be nostalgic for something unless one is divided from it. Hence absence is built into the very structure of nostalgia. The painful pleasure she takes in her fondest memories comes from what she has suffered "in being torn from them." That is why nostalgia provokes such a mixture of joy and sorrow, what Fanny calls a "blended" mood. Equally important is the element of displacement in the feeling. Fanny's love of the ragged furniture in the East room depends on this principle of displacement, a rudimentary instance of the association of ideas: "She could scarcely see an object in that room which had not an interesting remembrance connected with it. – Every thing was a friend, or bore her thoughts to a friend" (151–2). As a structure of feeling, then, nostalgia enshrines one's distance from the original object of desire even as it supplies one with a substitute for that object.

Fanny's nostalgia can be seen as part of a larger state of consciousness, the familiar mood known as Romantic melancholy.[14] This mood forms the very atmosphere of the Chamber of Maiden-Thought; to breathe it in sharpens one's sense of the sadness of human suffering even as it makes one's "tears delightful" (*Mansfield Park* 152). The objects that Fanny adores in the East room all have painful as well as pleasant memories associated with them, yet they are more precious for that very reason. As Anne Elliot, the heroine of another Austen novel, puts it, "When pain is over, the remembrance of it often becomes a pleasure. One does not love a place the less for having suffered in it" (*Persuasion* Vol. 4, Chap. 8). In *Mansfield Park* Austen shows that she thoroughly understands the deep, compensatory joys of Romantic melancholy:

. . . though there had been sometimes much of suffering to her –
though her motives had been often misunderstood, her feelings disre-
garded, and her comprehension under-valued; though she had known
the pains of tyranny, of ridicule, and neglect, yet almost every
recurrence of either had led to something consolatory . . . and the
whole was now so blended together, so harmonized by distance, that
every former affliction had its charm (152).

The charm of melancholy is that it can console one for "every former
affliction"; the danger in the charm that can make "tears delightful" is
that it will not let one forget. One clings to past sorrows, rather than
growing beyond them. In this state, Keats says, "We see not the ballance
of good and evil. We are in a Mist" (*Letters* 1:281). Fanny's "blended"
mood includes her former sufferings, the "pains of tyranny, of ridicule,
and neglect," as an integral part of its larger, compensatory structure.
The pain of the past becomes a permanent element in her present
consciousness.

The compensatory structure of Romantic melancholy, which we
discussed briefly in the Introduction, is the identifying mark of what
Keats calls, in a different letter, "the wordsworthian or egotistical
sublime" (*Letters* 1:387). Hence it is significant that this same principle of
compensation should play such an important part in Fanny's identity. In
"Tintern Abbey," Wordsworth's memory compensates for the loss of
his past by the sad but moving compromise of including that loss as part
of his present self. The past appears only as a painful difference from the
here and now, but memory claims the pain of that difference as an
essential attribute of identity. If this claim is sublime in its willingness to
embrace great sorrow as the burden of identity, it is egotistical in its
insatiable desire to absorb all differences into the self. In Keats's
terms – almost identical with those of Wordsworth – the movement
from "the infant or thoughtless Chamber" is accompanied by an
enormous loss of joy, but one receives some return for that loss in a new
ability to see "into the human heart." A similar balancing of gain and loss
determines that "blended" mood, Fanny's melancholy, in which "every
former affliction had its charm" (*Mansfield Park* 152).

By the end of the novel Fanny will have moved into the third and final
"Chamber of Life" (Keats, *Letters* 1:282). To do so, she must learn to
forgo the melancholy pleasures of the Romantic self. This development
requires her to emerge from the Chamber of Maiden-Thought, to leave
behind the compensatory joys of the East room. Necessarily, Fanny's
"coming out" will involve greater contact with the rest of the world. She
will exchange the solitary walls of her individual consciousness for the
shared, communal boundaries of Mansfield Park. When Keats attempts

to describe the last room in his Mansion, he emphasizes two things, both of which are missing from Fanny's youthful world. Keats writes, "After all there is certainly something real in the World"; and he feels the need to repeat this point – "but I know – the truth is there is something real in the World[.] Your third Chamber of Life shall be a lucky and a gentle one – stored with the wine of love – and the Bread of Friendship" (1:282–3). The image of communion turns Keats's third room into a sacramental space, a room where the "real in the World" takes on a power to bless. Northrop Frye, in another context, calls this lucky and gentle state the "Sabbath vision" (*Secular Scripture* 187–8), and his phrase reminds us that Fanny's story ends with a kind of Sabbath peace – marriage to a minister and happiness "as secure as earthly happiness can be" (473). The important point to be made about this final chamber is that it does not belong in any Romantic mansion at all. Its stores of love and friendship do away with the need for the painful pleasures of compensation. Fanny must learn to prefer the real things of the world to her private memories, and the wine of love and bread of friendship to her "blended" mood of melancholy.

According to the Romantic paradigm outlined in the previous section, Fanny's visits to the East room should form still moments, lyric interruptions in the bustle and commotion of the rest of the action. Such, of course, is not the case. Jane Austen frustrates our lyric expectations. Rather than allowing Fanny's Wordsworthian love of memory to develop into full-blown "spots of time," where the visionary force of one's own thoughts momentarily halts the action, the novelist makes each of Fanny's four trips to the East room a major turning point in the course of the story. We scarcely ever see Fanny alone in her sanctuary. Edmund interrupts her reverie on the first occasion to tell her the distressing news that he has decided to act in the play. Both Edmund and Mary Crawford track her down the second time we see her attempting to hide in her refuge. This scene, in which the two lovers rehearse their parts before Fanny's unwilling eyes, constitutes one of the most painfully comic moments of drama in the novel. Sir Thomas finds her the third time, and he reads her a lesson in the duties owed to others. Finally, Mary Crawford disturbs Fanny's fourth trip to the East room, this time to talk of Henry and to interrogate Fanny on the state of Edmund's feelings. By making each of Fanny's attempts to hide from others into vividly dramatic occasions, Austen prevents the dangerous allure of lyric from damaging the narrative form of her novel.

The third scene in the East room, Fanny's interview with Sir Thomas, merits a bit more attention. This scene constitutes a crucial "turn" in the plot – one recognized since Aristotle as an essential part of the action of a drama. At a point near the end of a comedy, the plot often seems to darken; the trials of the hero or heroine begin to look more serious than before. As Northrop Frye puts it, "An extraordinary number of comic stories, both in drama and fiction, seem to approach a potentially tragic crisis near the end" (*Anatomy of Criticism* 179). Stuart Tave has noticed this feature in all of Jane Austen's plots, a moment when the heroine must learn to accept unhappiness (*Some Words* 17–18). This moment precedes the happy ending of Austen's novels and may be more important than their comic resolutions. In *Mansfield Park* Sir Thomas's lecture to Fanny initiates the dark phase of the plot. He accuses her of "wilfulness of temper," "self-conceit," and "ingratitude"; he tells her that she has proved herself "of a character the very reverse of what I had supposed" (318–19). This chastisement represents what we might call the mortification of the heroine, a punishment that will shortly be embodied in the action by Fanny's exile to Portsmouth. As in so many comic plots, the heroine must be misunderstood, so that she can then be "recognized" for what she is and receive the fruits of the plot's "reversal."[15]

The interruption of potentially lyric moments by the forces of drama can be seen even more clearly in the humorous episode of Fanny's star gazing. Shortly after the visit to Sotherton, the whole party assembles for an evening at Mansfield Park. Fanny and Edmund are standing at a window, looking out upon a brilliant, unclouded night, while the rest of the group are busily gathering around the piano for a glee. Fanny's Romantic pleasure in gazing at the stars is suitably contrasted to the more sociable joys of youthful flirtation:

> Fanny spoke her feelings. "Here's harmony!" said she, "Here's repose! Here's what may leave all painting and all music behind, and what poetry only can attempt to describe. Here's what may tranquillize every care, and lift the heart to rapture! When I look out on such a night as this, I feel as if there could be neither wickedness nor sorrow in the world; and there certainly would be less of both if the sublimity of Nature were more attended to, and people were carried more out of themselves by contemplating such a scene." (113)

This speech may well be a "set-piece out of eighteenth-century aesthetics," as Litz maintains ("*Persuasion*: Forms of Estrangement" 225), but it is the aspect of eighteenth-century poetics that most decisively influenced Romantic lyricism. The sublime in nature brings us feelings that "poetry only can attempt to describe." In our response to the sublime, we are carried out of ourselves in a kind of ecstasy. This transcendent mood enables us to forget that there is wickedness or sorrow in the world and helps to "tranquillize every care." Thus the experience of the sublime serves as a very direct form of compensation for the inevitable ills of this life. Fanny's heart is lifted in rapture beyond any earthly concerns, caught up in a harmony that protects her from ordinary cares. For however brief a period, she participates in an epiphanic rather than a dramatic order.

It is only fitting, therefore, that a tiny bit of drama should puncture Fanny's enthusiasm. Her pleasure in having Edmund to herself at the window has been extreme. Now she tries to entice him to go out with her onto the lawn:

> "It is a great while [Fanny said] since we have had any star-gazing."
> "Yes [Edmund answered], I do not know how it has happened." The glee began. "We will stay till this is finished Fanny," said he, turning his back on the window; and as it advanced, she had the mortification of seeing him advance too, moving forward by gentle degrees towards the instrument, and when it ceased, he was close by the singers, among the most urgent in requesting to hear the glee again.
>
> Fanny sighed alone at the window till scolded away by Mrs. Norris's threats of catching cold. (113)

Fanny's offer of an aesthetic experience is interrupted by the more social attractions of Mary's singing. Fanny's melancholy, her sighing alone at the window, surely must be intended to make us smile; but Edmund's rudeness cannot be admired. What we can be certain of is that the scene itself makes a dramatic rather than a lyric claim upon our attention.

Jane Austen's persistent undercutting of Romantic lyricism finds a parallel in Keats's attitude toward "the wordsworthian or egotistical sublime." In the letter where he coined this phrase, Keats makes a grand attempt to define the true "poetical Character" (*Letters* 1:386). Keats's ideal poet would have no self, no character of his own. He would be a "camelion Poet," delighting in everything: "It has no character – it enjoys light and shade; it lives in gusto, be it foul or fair, high or low, rich or poor, mean or elevated – It has as much delight in conceiving an Iago as an Imogen" (1:387). Keats's poet focuses all his attention on his subject, not on his own feelings. He is essentially dramatic. Because of Keats's respect for this last quality in the poet, Keats's own works have frequently been compared to Shakespeare's; and it seems more than a coincidence that Jane Austen's dramatic bent has often been called Shakespearean as well. Richard Whately, writing in 1821, is only the first of many critics to call her talent for "giving a dramatic air to the narrative" Shakespearean.[16] For Keats, the dramatic element in the poet prevents him from succumbing to the egotistical sublime. It saves him from that Wordsworthian aggrandizement of the solitary self that we have seen to be a danger in Fanny's development. Finally, Keats says, "A Poet is the most unpoetical of any thing in existence; because he has no identity – he is continually in for – and filling some other Body" (1:387). Fanny, like other more Romantic heroines, is a bit too poetical for her own good. But Jane Austen's dramatic imagination is, in Keats's special sense, "the most unpoetical of any thing in existence."

We can discover a certain affinity between Austen's dramatic procedure and Keats's own practice in one of his best lyrics. Geoffrey Hartman has brilliantly described Keats's efforts in "To Autumn" to eliminate the epiphanic dimension of the Romantic ode yet still retain a lyrical intensity (*Fate of Reading* 124–46). Keats desires a lyricism that is poised – "stationed," to borrow another of Keats's terms – on the brink of drama. Unlike Wordsworth's epiphanic "spots of time," which interrupt the course of the narrative and halt all action, Keats's lyrics always seem about to burst into narrative. The slow, descriptive time in "To Autumn" is so charged with growth and process that the poem almost (but never quite) develops a story of its own. Autumn is personified in stanza two, on the verge of becoming a character, and Spring waits in the wings at the beginning of stanza three, ready to turn an implied contrast into a full dramatic debate; yet, instead, the poem subsides into music – the hedge-crickets sing, the gathering swallows twitter in the skies – and it is descriptive once more. The possibilities of narrative have everywhere been indicated, yet the lyric moment has been preserved.[17]

In the genre of the novel Jane Austen is able to take this process farther still. She frequently excites us with the prospect of epiphany. When Fanny sits alone in the "wilderness" at Sotherton, when she removes to the East room to meditate, or when she stands at the window looking at a brilliant night sky, we half expect an experience that "poetry only can attempt to describe." Yet each of these scenes is instinct with drama; and the advantage of a novel is that the drama can be realized. The threat of lyric is drawn off in narrative, yet the narrative order has received a lyric grace.

THE CURE OF GENRES

In the last chapter of *Mansfield Park* the narrator refers ironically to "the cure of unconquerable passions" (470). The use of the word "cure," even in such a flippant phrase, is a sign of the importance of the occasion. Edmund's "illness," his misplaced passion for Mary, must be curable, or the novel could never come to a satisfactory conclusion. In Jane Austen the cure of error is the appropriate and inevitable end of narrative.[18]

The cure of Edmund's romantic feelings requires the substitution of a different sort of passion, the growth of a different kind of affection entirely. Fortunately for Edmund, he has possessed in himself a model of this alternative way of loving all along:

> Loving, guiding, protecting her, as he had been doing ever since her being ten years old, her mind in so great a degree formed by his care,

and her comfort depending on his kindness, an object to him of such
close and peculiar interest, dearer by all his own importance with her
than any one else at Mansfield, what was there now to add, but that he
should learn to prefer soft light eyes to sparkling dark ones. (470)

The feelings of a guardian, a protector, a teacher, and a coun-
selor – feelings amplified and supported by the natural pleasure one takes
in seeing one's own importance reflected in another's eyes – such feelings
are hardly glamorous, but they seem singularly appropriate to a man
who is destined shortly to move into the living at Thornton Lacey. This
new model of love is pastoral. As a clergyman, Edmund will be charged
with the care or "cure" of others, so it is fitting that the cure of his
passion should be effected by his habit of caring for another.

Even at her most ironic, Jane Austen rarely loses sight of the necessity
that curing and caring go hand in hand.[19] Her early fiction is often
regarded as parodic, but the irony of *Northanger Abbey* or *Sense and
Sensibility* is more curative than destructive. She seems less interested in
ridding the world of Gothic or sentimental novels than in curing the
genres of their excesses. The notion of caring for the forms of literature
might seem to imply an almost "religious" attitude toward genre. It
would thus seem appropriate to compare Austen's corrective irony with
the efforts of some poets to cleanse poetry of all "impurities" – a project
that, as we discovered in Chapter 2, turns poetry into a mode of sacred
experience. But Austen's concern for genre is fundamentally different
from that of the theorists of "pure poetry." Her care reflects a social (and
secular) conception of the role of the author. The cure of genres, for
Austen, is an ethical rather than a spiritual imperative. In Edmund's
defense of the clergyman, the effect of the example of his character on the
conduct of his parishioners was as important as his religious or spiritual
counsel. In like fashion, we can distinguish an ethical concern for the
example literary works offer a community of readers from a religious
desire to purify the forms of aesthetic experience for the sake of that
experience itself.

Austen frequently raises the question of the ethical value of different
genres. If we return to the passage from *Persuasion* with which we began
this chapter, we can see that Austen's reasons for opposing Captain
Benwick's taste in literature proceed from her doubts about the ethical
influence of certain kinds of poetry. After the Captain's tremulous
display of his knowledge of the poems of Scott and Byron, Anne Elliot
diffidently suggests that he try reading works in some other genres:

. . . she ventured to hope he did not always read only poetry; and to
say, that she thought it was the misfortune of poetry, to be seldom
safely enjoyed by those who enjoyed it completely; and that the strong

feelings which alone could estimate it truly, were the very feelings which ought to taste it but sparingly. (100–1)

The humor of the situation cannot be missed, and indeed, Austen reinforces the comedy in the last line of the chapter: "Like many other great moralists and preachers, [Anne] had been eloquent on a point in which her own conduct would ill bear examination" (101). Still, the humor in no way disguises the author's serious point. Richard Simpson, the nineteenth-century critic of Shakespeare, understood it perfectly: "[Austen] seems to have had an ethical dread of the poetic rapture" (244). The "strong feelings" that allow one to respond to "the tenderest songs" and "the impassioned descriptions of hopeless agony" can carry the reader into a transport of emotion. The danger of such ecstasy, for Anne herself as much as for Captain Benwick, is that it will lead one into a private world, a state beyond the reach of everyday concerns. Anne, it must be remembered, has felt the temptation of such withdrawal during her suffering for the loss of Wentworth. The "misfortune of poetry," the ethical danger it presents as a genre, is that it can encourage one to isolate oneself from the social world.

Anne allows herself to talk so long of these matters only because she hopes to do the younger man some good. Her object is education, Austen tells us with a smile, and the import of the lesson wholly ethical. Like Aristotle in the *Politics*, Anne feels that certain genres have a more ethical effect than others; and, like the philosopher, she thinks those that are "the most emotion-stirring" are the least likely "to promote virtue" (*Politics* 473, 470 [8.6–7]). Austen continues:

> . . . she ventured to recommend a larger allowance of prose in his daily study; and on being requested to particularize, mentioned such works of our best moralists, such collections of the finest letters, such memoirs of characters of worth and suffering, as occurred to her at the moment as calculated to rouse and fortify the mind by the highest precepts, and the strongest examples of moral and religious endurances. (*Persuasion* 101)

Gilbert Ryle argues that Austen's moral ideas follow an Aristotelian pattern, and he suggests that the novelist may have acquired these ideas from her reading of Shaftesbury (Ryle 114–18). Perhaps Austen's strongest affinity with Aristotle lies in her assumption that ethics and politics (in the broad sense of the word, which includes all the subjects necessary for the creation of a proper community) are integrally related and that the genres of literature have different and important roles to play in the formation of that community. The prose of moralists and the memoirs of worthy characters help one fulfill one's role in society by rousing and fortifying the mind and by teaching the need for endurance through the example of character. Certain forms of literature can "cure" because they care, more directly, about the public actions of men and women, and consequently about the shape of society. Austen herself never wrote in the genres Anne mentions, for which most of us may be thankful, but her novels aim at much the same end.

When we hear of an ethical concern about the influence of the arts, we are apt to think of a Mrs. Grundy and the objections to novel reading in the nineteenth century, or of the conservative pressure groups of our day; and Jane Austen's own conservative vision of society does little to reassure some people about the validity of this kind of question. But an awareness of the different social effects of genres is crucial to the theories of some critics at the other end of the political spectrum as well. Mikhail Bakhtin, for example, insists that genres be defined as socially conditioned and socially operative systems. Significantly, one of his central distinctions falls between the genres of poetry and the form of the novel (275–300). In terms roughly parallel to those that we have seen the Romantics using, he opposes the monologic (or pure) discourse intended by poetry to the dialogic, refracted, and hybridized (that is, impure) prose of the novel. Unlike the English Romantics, however, he privileges the impure rather than the pure because the former reflects the heterogeneous character of our language(s) and because it acknowledges the conflictual position that all utterances, all instances of discourse, occupy in society. Furthermore, he evaluates the different genres on the basis of the degree to which they hide or disclose the complicity of their language with that of the rest of society. Thus he attacks poetry and celebrates prose because the former pretends that its speech owes nothing to the discourses of the world around it.[20] Bakhtin's reversal of the Romantic hierarchy seems vulnerable to the criticism of Paul de Man, that it depends as much as the older view of literature upon an opposition that should be examined critically ("Dialogue and Dialogism" 105). But the example of Bakhtin shows that a care for form can be part of a utopian project to cure society, without participating in a conservative vision.

On the surface, many of the technical resources Austen relies upon in her fiction resemble those that Bakhtin celebrates as socially liberating in the dialogical novel. Her use of irony to "refract" the speeches of her characters so that the text at many places appears "double-voiced"; her awareness of the "stratification" of various styles of language and manners that occurs within a presumably shared code; her sensitivity to the danger that lies in privileged or "ennobled" terms, the risk that such terms may become instruments of social domination when misused through ignorance (Mrs. Norris) or vice (Mary Crawford); and, above all, her use of dialogue to express conflicting attitudes and irreconcilable perspectives – these resources demonstrate the extent to which Austen's fiction reflects the novel's socially conditioned, inherently "impure," form. All the same, Austen would reject the ideology that underlies Bakhtin's work. She does not view the acknowledgment of multiplicity as a potentially revolutionary gesture, but rather as an unavoidable recognition of the way men and women live in a complex – she might say overcomplex – social world. Her conservatism is precisely Aristotelian. It attempts to *conserve* what the author views as good not by exclusion of conflicting realities but by a faith that the life of an individual, even in the midst of so many competing forces, still is capable of possessing a *telos*, a direction and purpose.[21] This union of faith with knowledge of the world – of an Aristotelian belief that life possesses a meaningful, unified, and knowable shape with an ironic sense of the duplicitous, heterogeneous, and opaque social forms in which that shape is to be found – is perhaps why she can be called conservative by some readers (Duckworth, Butler) and subversive by others (Kirkham, Gilbert and Gubar).[22]

In the course of this chapter we have tried to show how the treatment of Fanny in *Mansfield Park* reflects Jane Austen's opposition to Romanticism. The criticism of Fanny's tendencies toward Romantic states of consciousness seemed connected with some of the larger issues of this study, particularly with the way in which the distinction between poetry and the novel has been conceptualized. This is not surprising, for Austen's fiction has traditionally been held up as the very antithesis to the Romantic conception of poetry. G. H. Lewes drew the comparison repeatedly, and he explicitly connected her "deficiencies in poetry and passion" with her excellence as a novelist qua novelist.[23] The contrast, moreover, illustrated in a striking way the social and ethical orientation of the novel as a genre. Virginia Woolf's reading of Austen brings out many of the same points. In the course of describing the "poetical" element in the fiction of Meredith, Hardy, and Emily Brontë, Woolf comments that Jane Austen "had not the impulses of a poet" and that this lack was what enabled her to compose a "perfect" novel, for the former writers "insisted upon introducing qualities, of thought and of poetry, that are perhaps incompatible with fiction at its most perfect" (*Second Common Reader* 211).[24] The example of Austen's *novelistic* talent seems to confirm the suggestion that the lyric flight of what was called "pure poetry," with its tendency to create isolated, detachable moments of feeling, cannot be included in the genre of the novel without endangering the ethical intelligence that Austen regarded as the principal strength of the narrative form.

Having presented Austen's counterstatement to the claims of Romantic lyricism, it is perhaps only fair to confront her position with a work of fiction that invests the visionary power of Romantic poetry with extraordinary prestige. In the next chapter we shall look at *Wuthering Heights*, a novel that has probably been called "poetic" more frequently than any other piece of fiction in English.[25] Emily Brontë's conception of visionary experience resembles the pattern we described as Shelleyan, rather than the Wordsworthian model that we have been discussing in this chapter. Hence *Wuthering Heights* will prompt us to examine the difficulty of reconciling a vision of union with the social and ethical concerns that a narrative genre tends to raise.

4

WUTHERING HEIGHTS

"Nelly, I *am* Heathcliff."
(Chap. 9)

This sentence may be the most famous expression of love in the whole course of the English novel. Catherine and Heathcliff call to mind the most notable romantic pairs in myth and literature: Orpheus and Euridyce, Romeo and Juliet, Tristram and Iseult. In the Introduction this passage was compared with the visionary conclusion to Shelley's "Epipsychidion," where the poet fervently declares that he will be united with his lover in one being: "We shall become the same, we shall be one / Spirit within two frames." The similarities between the two utterances are both numerous and striking,[1] but there are differences to be noticed as well. Shelley's moment of union with his lover will come sometime in the future: The poetry is prophetic; the consummation, still to be achieved. In *Wuthering Heights* Catherine and Heathcliff seem to have already achieved a complete fusion of beings. Their union exists in the present: "He's more myself than I am," Catherine says. "Whatever our souls are made of, his and mine are the same" (100).

The lovers' union seems to exist in the present; but if we look more closely, we discover that in fact it occurred in the past, and only in the past, for even as Catherine proclaims her oneness with Heathcliff she and her lover have begun to become two. She confesses her passion for Heathcliff only after the two of them have been separated by her actions.[2] Catherine's speech follows by a few scant hours her acceptance of another man's marriage proposal. When Nelly reasonably inquires how Heathcliff will bear the separation, Catherine exclaims, "He quite deserted! we separated! . . . Who is to separate us, pray? . . . Oh, that's not what I intend – that's not what I mean! I shouldn't be Mrs. Linton were such a price demanded! He'll be as much to me as he has been all his lifetime" (101). Only after this vehement protest does Catherine begin the declaration of love that has become one of the touchstones of romantic literature.

By now such a paradoxical situation should come as no surprise. The lovers' division at the very moment when their union receives its most enduring expression is a natural consequence of all that we have learned about visionary experience. The union of two souls in one ecstatic being is difficult to represent directly, for language cannot do justice to the event. Milton is the inevitable guide in the English tradition to this subject (*Paradise Lost* 8.620–30), but Shelley also explores the problem in depth. Words, which are distinct, separate units, cannot capture the state of oneness. "The words *I*, and *you* and *they* are grammatical devices invented simply for arrangement and totally devoid of the intense and exclusive sense usually attached to them. It is difficult to find terms adequately to express so subtle a conception as that to which the intellectual philosophy has conducted us" (Shelley 478). The difficulty is compounded by the fact that the completion of transcendence precludes any need to speak. Shelley believes words sad substitutes for the reality of vision: "When composition begins, inspiration is already on the decline, and the most glorious poetry that has ever been communicated to the world is probably a feeble shadow of the original conception of the poet" (504). What is true for poets equally applies to lovers. True union is self-sufficing. Catherine would have no cause to proclaim her oneness with Heathcliff if such a state still existed. As D. H. Lawrence puts it, "How can I say 'I love you' when I have ceased to be, and you have ceased to be. . . . Speech travels between separate parts. But in the perfect One there is perfect silence of bliss" (*Women in Love* 361–2).

Catherine's declaration of love attempts to recover a lost state of being even as it claims that this lost unity will endure forever. Nelly's warning about the lovers' impending separation bears fruit in an immediate and unintended fashion; Heathcliff, having overheard only the early part of this conversation, leaves Wuthering Heights that very night, not to return until after Catherine's marriage. Psychologically, Catherine's speech is a form of denial, as its conclusion makes abundantly clear: "He's always, always in my mind – not as a pleasure, any more than I am always a pleasure to myself – but, as my own being – so, don't talk of our separation again – it is impracticable; and – " (102). Further, if what Catherine says were true, then the novel itself would never have been written. Like the stories of those other famous lovers, Catherine and Heathcliff's tragic tale depends upon their being separated. This point, obvious enough on the face of it, acquires added significance when we notice how Catherine's separation from Heathcliff briefly shifts the story onto familiar novelistic ground. Catherine's reasons for accepting Linton's proposal read like a catalogue of the nineteenth-century novel's social concerns. Her feelings for Linton are prompted by considerations of class, fortune, youth, disposition, manners, and appearance, rather than by a passion that is "of little visible delight, but necessary." The former are qualities upon which a heroine can reasonably be expected to base a decision, factors that can be weighed in the kind of ethical scale employed by Jane Austen or George Eliot. The vocabulary of moral choice enters Catherine's discussion of Linton – "I accepted him, Nelly; be quick, and say whether I was wrong!" (96) – whereas questions of right and wrong play no part in her attitude toward Heathcliff.

There are other reasons why Catherine's words cannot be taken at face value, and these have a special pertinence to some of the larger themes of this study. Catherine's first visionary experience – her dream of desolation in heaven and of joy on earth – occurs now, when the pressure of the separation she is attempting to deny forces her into this powerful form of compensation. Another point concerns the language of Catherine's avowal of love. The imagery of this speech is its principal claim to fame, and it has been subjected to much critical scrutiny. But for all the attention to this paragraph, it has not sufficiently been observed that the images are themselves an important sign of the compensatory nature of Catherine's vision. "My love for Linton is like the foliage in the woods. Time will change it, I'm well aware, as winter changes the trees – my love for Heathcliff resembles the eternal rocks beneath" (101). Figurative language is itself a sign of the distance Catherine has come from a literal union with her lover. Metaphor, comparison, and hyperbole are tropes that balance one thing against another, measure similarity and difference, and exaggerate beyond all proportion, in a linguistic to-and-fro utterly removed from the undifferentiated realms of visionary union. The very words that bind the figures together – "like" and "resemble" and "as" – reveal the pressure on the terms to spring apart. In place of the perfect silence of *is*, we receive the compensatory beauty of *as*.

If this paragraph from Chapter 9 does not record a moment of Romantic union, where should one turn for an instance of this kind of visionary experience? Should one go outside the text, into speculations about Emily Brontë's own mystical experiences? Fortunately, this once-standard approach seems to have exhausted its interest. The text is the only thing we have access to, and our study is tracing the fortunes of visionary experience as it is mediated by various genres, modes, and textual constraints. If we move backward in time from Catherine's already-compromised declaration of love, looking for a place in the text that records an authentic moment of union, we can locate nothing but a gap, a hole in the narrative beyond which the topic of union becomes prominent. This gap is clearly identifiable (remarkably so for a novel, because the genre usually tries to disguise such places), and the gap is the only place where the origin of this grand passion can be located.

In Chapter 4 Nelly tells the story of Heathcliff's introduction to the family at Wuthering Heights. When Catherine first meets this disreputable-looking creature, she learns that it has been the cause of her losing a present from her father, a riding whip that he had promised to bring her from Liverpool. She shows her feelings "by grinning and spitting at the stupid little thing, earning for her pains a sound blow from her father to teach her cleaner manners" (45–6). Catherine then refuses to have the boy in her room that night, and Nelly abets her in this cruelty. As a result, Nelly is sent out of the house, depriving us of our only source of information. When she comes back "a few days afterwards," she finds that Catherine and Heathcliff "were now very thick" (46). In the gap between these two sentences lies the birth of love. There is no other place to look, because the novel makes no subsequent attempt to trace motives or find explanations. We can count on the fingers of one hand (and not have need for the thumb) the references to their bond that occur before the pressure of their separation elicits a compensatory force of response. The representational void is so great that William Wyler, making his movie of *Wuthering Heights*, felt required to fill it both with a place – Peniston Crags, where the lovers meet even after their death – and with an action, a sexual embrace.

If the place in the text where the lovers come together is no more than an absence, a significant silence, the figures for their love are all-pervasive. This substitution of trope for topos (place or site where a theme is presented) is one of the characteristic dis-placements involved in figurative language. Looking again at the sentence in Chapter 4 that marks the gap in the narrative, we discover that a figure – Heathcliff's name – receives an interesting emphasis:

> This was Heathcliff's first introduction to the family: on coming back a few days afterwards, for I did not consider my banishment perpetual, I found they had christened him "Heathcliff:" it was the name of a son who died in childhood, and it has served him ever since, both for Christian and surname. (46)

The silence of the text about one matter is covered by the voicing in the text of a name that is a figure for wildness, desolation, and silence, a name that furthermore belonged to another child, once seemingly silenced forever but now figuratively brought back to life.

What to make of this absence hidden by a figurative presence? We would be wise to consider whether the novel is asking us to assume a deconstructive stance toward its own story. Such a possibility seems more likely when we remember that we are dealing with the "texts" of several narrators, each of which is subject to severe doubts. Several critics have recently taken this approach. In his latest work on the novel, J. Hillis Miller has come to read *Wuthering Heights* as a self-deconstructing book. Passages of the sort we have been examining, he says, lead us on an endless chase, drawing us ever deeper into the text in search of a center that will never appear.[3] The will-o'-the-wisp, in particular, is the hope of discovering a "supernatural transcendent 'cause' for all events" (*Fiction and Repetition* 52), a hope that is of all things the most impossible for a text to realize. Hence the question of whether or not a visionary union ever occurs must remain "undecidable": "It is the most important question the novel raises, the one thing about which we ought to be able to make a decision, and yet a thing about which the novel forbids the reader to make a decision" (69). So far, we must agree with Miller.[4] But the conclusions he draws from this analysis are less certain. Is the discovery of an "undecidable" feature of a text necessarily an invitation to radical skepticism? May not indeterminacy play a role in literature other than that of demystification?

Miller's answers to questions like these reveal an important assumption underlying his argument. Criticism, like all reading, is up against a blank wall, because there is no final resting place for the reader in his or her restless movement from figure to figure. The search is for a "center," a "transcendental signified," to use Derrida's term, that would fix and confirm a single meaning. Here are Miller's actual words for this dilemma: "This missing center is the head referent which would still the wandering movement from emblem to emblem, from story to story, from generation to generation, from Catherine to Catherine, from Hareton to Hareton, from narrator to narrator" (67). Miller's critical vocabulary inscribes the problem of transcendence within the traditional categories of presence and absence, an inscription that Wordsworth would not have objected to but which Shelley (and, as we shall see, Emily Brontë) abhorred. Miller's analysis of these categories is very clear, and it explains why the search for a "transcendent presence" must always be vain: "If 'something' is incompatible with any sign, if it cannot be seen, signified or theorized about, it is, in our tradition, no 'thing.' It is nothing. The trace of such an absence therefore retraces nothing" (67).

Like Jacques Derrida, Miller believes that the categories of presence and absence are unavoidable. In another work, Miller writes, "The blank wall beyond which rational analysis cannot go arises from the copresence in any text in Western literature, inextricably intertwined, as host and parasite, of some version of logocentric metaphysics and its subversive counterpart" ("Critic as Host" 248). But one wonders if Derrida and Miller have not too narrowly conceived the problem. Even employing the same premises, there may be other things to think about besides the metaphysics of presence. Is the problem of logocentrism the only host that tempts deconstruction? Emily Brontë, like Shelley, suggests the possibility of turning the indeterminacy of a text to other ends. For her, the inherent difficulty of textuality becomes a lever for shifting the burden of inquiry away from the perennial issues of "rational analysis," the questions of being as presence that Derrida insists are the instituting gestures of Western philosophy (*Grammatology* 97). That this shifting of the question may be a movement away from rationality itself, or at least from "a reason thought within the lineage of the logos" (*Grammatology* 10), is no more than what a radical visionary desires.

To begin this other inquiry, to initiate questions that reach beyond the lineage of the logos, one must start to ask not what a text means, still less what a text is, but rather what a text does. In an apocalyptic perspective, literature is action before it is knowledge, experience before being. So we need to consider what a text accomplishes in sending its readers on an endless chase. As with other doomed quests, perhaps the journey itself has some rewards unconnected with the possibility of ever reaching the grail – unconnected even with the presence or reality of the grail. Even if the movement from figure to figure can have no determinate end, the action of displacement testifies to a form of power that is beyond rational analysis, precisely because it is indeterminate. It inhabits the text, in ever-changing patterns and with ever-renewing strength, for each authentic reading of a text encounters this power in a new way. The very indeterminacy of the text guarantees that its power will be radically "other," something that works outside of or in spite of human understanding. The failure of reason ever finally to decide the questions raised by such a text makes it properly apocalyptic. A conception of visionary literature's power as something other than human, something finally *unknowable*, is anything but far-fetched when dealing with an author who, in her poetry, consistently portrays the process of writing as a form of demonic possession.

For Emily Brontë, the "undecidability" of a work of literature relates neither to the presence or absence of a "transcendent cause" nor to the meaning or lack of meaning of ghostly traces; it relates to the otherness of the power that she and countless readers have felt her texts to possess. The displacements of figurative language testify to the strength of this power, a strength that should no more be described as irrational than as rational, for both categories belong to the structure of the single identity. In Emily Brontë's poems this power is described as something external to the human being, but the categories of internal and external equally distort the issue: They are a clumsy part of her inheritance from the Romantics. She often speaks of a stern visitant, an alien and uncontrollable power, toward which she is profoundly ambivalent. Margaret

Homans, in the best reading we have of Emily Brontë's poetry, correctly describes her attitude toward this power:

> The visionary visitant of later poems takes many forms, but he is always masculine, and he is threatening as well as inspiring, dangerous as well as beloved. He is threatening more because, being external, he can withdraw her poetic powers at will than because of any dangerous content in the visions he brings. (*Women Writers and Poetic Identity* 100)

The very simplicity of the categories in some of Emily Brontë's poems can help us to demonstrate the complete otherness of this power. In one poem she calls it her "God of Visions" (*Complete Poems* 176, A26). There, she prays for her "radiant angel" to be her advocate before the bar of "Stern Reason" (stanza 2). Her devotion to this alien power has led her far beyond the things of this world, "Wealth," "Power," "Glory's wreath," and "Pleasure's flower" (stanza 3). Such service, of course, can have but one end, an apocalyptic casting off of human structures that leaves her unable to speak for herself: "No, radiant angel, speak and say / Why I did cast the world away" (lines 9–10). Her own attempts to make her experiences communicable are, significantly, phrased in terms of power, not insight. Further, she, like Shelley, tries to strip power of its tyrannical structure. When one with this "other" being, she has the option of assuming three positions rather than two, thus escaping to a certain extent the rigid oppositions of bipolar categories.

> [I] gave my spirit to adore
> Thee, ever present, phantom thing –
> My slave, my comrade, and my King! (lines 23–5)

This is the most powerful moment in the poem, but it is still only partly successful in undoing the inevitable hierarchy of power. She does skirt the worst consequences of identification. By making her "God of Visions" slave, comrade, and king all at once, she preserves for herself a freedom of mobility among various versions of a self, instead of a single rigid identity as the helpless adorer of the other. But the rhetoric of externality ultimately has its revenge on this freedom. Within the crude terms of inside and outside, the poem can be resolved only through ignoring a frustrating contradiction. Through identification, the power has become her own, an internal rather than an external strength, "since," as she asserts, "my own soul can grant my prayer" (line 38). But everything else in the poem reveals that only the "God of Visions" can speak adequately of her plight. Homans puts the dilemma well: "That the speaker thus displaces her powers of speech indicates that language is alien to her" (115).

This poem, along with the others that struggle with the problem of external possession, such as "The Night-Wind" (140, A7), "Shall Earth no more inspire thee" (147, A6), and "Stars" (184, A28), cannot do justice to the complexity of the author's sense of otherness. Trapped by their own categories, they phrase the problem of the alienness of language as a question of mastering (or failing to master) a poetic voice. But the otherness that the poems both fear and seek exists in language itself, not in the source of inspiration. The difficulty is not truly one of mastery at all. In the novel she discloses a far more complex understanding of the otherness of texts.

Let us return to the gap in *Wuthering Heights* that is marked by the figure of Heathcliff's name. This sentence will provide a concrete example of how the process of displacement in a text can possess an alien or non-human power. The name "Heathcliff" represents an especially vivid case of the alienation inherent in figuration. The boy christened with this figure is dispossessed of his old identity. Not only is this name imposed from without, it belonged to someone else to begin with. Thus the boy loses his individuality and is assimilated to a position within a flexible but inescapable system, that of the family. As a single word, both Christian and surname, it seems even less related to his individual being than usual names, a label denoting his "place" within the sliding system of kinship. As a position, this place can apparently be filled by any orphan or child. At this point, however, we come upon a paradox. Although the arbitrary imposition of a name dehumanizes him, it also brings him within the fold of the family. To have a role, a place in a system, reduces one's individuality yet makes one a partner in the transpersonal endeavor of civilization. Naming, then, civilizes Heathcliff but only at the cost of alienation.

Jacques Lacan can help us some of the way toward understanding this particular paradox. One of the most intriguing aspects of his psychoanalytic theory is that he sees language as alienating, yet regards alienation as a crucial part of our humanity. For Lacan, the thing that makes us human is our acquiescence in the otherness of words, particularly in our adjustment to the symbolic dimension of names: "That a name, no matter how confused, designates a particular person – this is precisely what the passage to the human state consists in. If we must define that moment in which man becomes human, we would say that it is at that instant when, as minimally as you like, he enters into a symbolic relationship."[5] What Lacan calls the Name-of-the-Father plays a crucial role in this acquiescence to otherness, for it is this name, beyond all others, that teaches us the "Law," a concept that has complex meanings in Lacan's writing but which for our purposes can be defined as the awareness that one must submit to a place or position within a system larger than oneself. Names teach this lesson by instructing us that people possess roles or functions that are independent of their biological identities. Hence names reveal the role of roles, the otherness that can and must exist within the self to make one a member of a human community.

The imposition of a name on Heathcliff, by exaggerating the paradox involved in becoming human, reveals how ambivalent Emily Brontë feels about the entire process. Just as important, it discloses that the problem of the other cannot be contained by the thematics of external possession. Emily Brontë and Lacan, in their very different ways, both believe that otherness exists *within* texts, whether written or lived. Yet Lacan's version of psychoanalysis can only take us so far in our discussion of *Wuthering Heights*. Emily Brontë parts company with Lacan's conception of textuality at the same point where she diverges with modern theories about indeterminacy, and it is by no means certain which of the three visions of textuality is the most profound. Emily Brontë refuses to take either the realistic stance of Lacan or the skeptical posture of Miller toward the otherness of the text. For her, the "unreasonable" element within the reason that makes us human is, both for good and for ill, wholly apocalyptic.

The degree to which Lacan and Emily Brontë differ can be measured by considering how the former would analyze Heathcliff's rebellion against the values of civilization. Few novels have dramatized the revolt against society as a rejection of the Law of the Father more vividly than *Wuthering Heights*.[6] Heathcliff's hatred of Hindley represents a rebellion against a father figure who is, as a figure, twice removed from biological paternity, for Hindley is not even the kind image of a father, Mr. Earnshaw, who originally adopts the orphan. Heathcliff's violent resistance to civilization might be seen as resistance to the otherness of language when it becomes an arbitrary system or form of Law. The arbitrariness of this system is brilliantly underlined by the novel, for Heathcliff learns to turn all the forms of society – all its laws – against the "rightful," which is to say the hereditary or biological, owners of Wuthering Heights.

So far, Emily Brontë and Lacan's analyses of the situation would seem to agree. But their stances toward this kind of rebellion differ entirely. Lacan views such a rejection of civilization from the "realistic" perspective of psychoanalysis, which regards the undoing of psychic structures solely as a form of regression. In Lacan's terms, Heathcliff remains fixed in the stage of the "Imaginary," a word that seems particularly apt when applied to a character who lives in a world haunted by the ghost of his lover. The term seems even more on the mark when we note that the Imaginary stage, in Lacan, is the locus of the individual's aggressive impulses, which are expressed primarily in terms of jealousy or rivalry, and that it tends to organize the world in terms of certain simple, bipolar categories, including master-slave and ownership-dispossession. For

Emily Brontë, however, the attempt to "locate" Heathcliff's attitude toward the other within an account of individual development misses the point. Psychoanalysis's realistic approach to such phenomena domesticates the potentially apocalyptic force of otherness.[7] In a radical perspective, the other has no "place" within the human at all; it is the trace of a power that points beyond the human entirely.

Emily Brontë gives this power a name so familiar, so circumscribed by its Romantic heritage, that it is difficult for us to recover the negative or antithetical way in which she uses it. The word she chooses is "Imagination," a term whose superficial resemblance to Lacan's "Imaginary" can be made to uncover their diametrically opposed meanings. In Lacan's term we are meant to hear the root of "image" – or even the Freudian "imago." In Emily Brontë's power, on the other hand, we should recognize a distinct hostility to the image, and especially to those images (like that of the body) that reinforce the boundaries of the individual self. The word "Imagination," of course, falsifies the power, for it fixes it as something finite and assigns it an intelligible meaning, but any other term would do the same.

In her poem *To Imagination* (174, A25), Emily Brontë labors to undo these inevitable limitations of the word. There she defines "Imagination" as a power that creates images but is not itself contained by any image. "Truth may rudely trample down / The flowers of Fancy newly blown" (lines 23–4), but the value of Imagination does not lie in any single manifestation of its activity, because "thou art ever there to bring / The hovering visions back" (lines 25–6). The process of imagining is not subject to the limits of the image, even though each particular vision is.[8] Thus Imagination becomes an unfocused or unmotivated form of desiring, the urge not to represent something but to go beyond representation. For Emily Brontë, Imagination might be defined as the will-to-power over representation. Fulfillment of this desire may be impossible – just as is Romantic union – but the desire nevertheless remains, and it is the power of this desire that drives the text in its endless displacements from image to image, figure to figure. Although each image represents the coming to earth of Imagination in a new, finite representation, we can feel the energy that wills a change in the transition from figure to figure. What we still admire in Emily Brontë's poem is that it so thoroughly understands the limits of the power it invokes. She does not trust the "phantom bliss" (line 31) of her visions, because to put faith in a product of Imagination is to falsify it, to attribute a truth-value to one of its images. Imagination can only "whisper with a voice divine / Of real worlds as bright as thine" (lines 29–30). Even here, in the very lines that attempt to deny reality to one of the figures for

Imagination (the figure of visionary worlds), it fixes Imagination in another figure, that of a "voice divine." The poem knows that it can never escape from falsifications, but it also knows that it must not cease from trying.

In *Wuthering Heights* Emily Brontë is even more aware of the seductive falsifications of what Lacan would call the Imaginary but which we must recognize as the conditions that make representation possible in any text. She dramatizes this awareness by presenting representation as a process that parallels the forces that separate Catherine and Heathcliff. So let us turn to an examination of what separates the two lovers. The moment when they are divided can be located with precision, although there is nothing extraordinary about this, because division or alienation is something that language is especially capable of capturing. The scene appears in the narrative, fully described, in a way that the moment of union never does. Their division occurs in Chapter 6, at the exact moment when Catherine and Heathcliff look through the drawing room window at Thrushcross Grange. They see a splendid space of crimson and white and gold, with a silver chandelier shedding light down upon two spoiled children. Edgar and Isabella are standing at opposite ends of the chamber, crying over a puppy that they have almost pulled in two. In this brief glimpse, Catherine is forever divided from Heathcliff, because she acquires a self through an act of identification. The thin pane of the window, like the glass of a mirror, reflects the ocular character of the moment in which Catherine recognizes the other as a model for her self.[9] At her advanced age, Catherine acquires a separate self.[10]

It has long been recognized that Catherine's stay with the Lintons separates her from Heathcliff. When Catherine and Heathcliff are caught by the window, Mr. and Mrs. Linton immediately make a wide distinction between the two children. Catherine is treated as a lady, bathed, fed, and combed in the very room where Edgar and Isabella had been playing. Heathcliff, on the other hand, is driven away from the house with rude remarks about his being a frightful thing, a gypsy or a Lascar, something quite unfit for a decent house. Catherine stays five weeks at Thrushcross Grange, separated completely from Heathcliff. There she acquires all the accouterments of a social identity – fine clothes, manners, the rudiments of style and poise. Her newfound sense of self is buttressed by the internalization of all those values that go into the composition of what Freud would call an ego–ideal. Upon her return to Wuthering Heights, her every action dramatizes how far she has grown from her former friend. Catherine draws back from Heathcliff with a burst of laughter when she first sees him, and she tells him he should wash his face and brush his hair if he wants to touch her. So profoundly has her exposure to the Lintons changed her that we would be justified in speaking, in Lacan's phrase, of "a veritable capture by the other" (*The Language of the Self* 100n27).

Catherine's original union with Heathcliff had possessed no taint of identification. Their union might rather be compared to the narcissistic state in which the boundaries between self and other have not yet been established (though it should not be reduced to such a paradigm). Heathcliff is correct in saying that Catherine herself is responsible for their separation: "Because misery, and degradation, and death, and nothing that God or Satan could inflict would have parted us, *you*, of your own will, did it" (198). But he is mistaken in saying that she did it of her own will. In the spectacle of identification, the will plays no part. Catherine is so unaware of what she has done that she cannot understand why Heathcliff should be offended at her, just as later she cannot comprehend why her marriage to another man should separate her from Heathcliff.

The first of their many arguments occurs shortly thereafter, when Heathcliff draws Catherine's attention to the number of evenings she has spent with the Lintons. Catherine's reply is interesting: "What good do I get – What do you talk about? You might be dumb or a baby for anything you say to amuse me, or for anything you do, either!" (86). Words were hardly necessary for Catherine and Heathcliff before her change. "Speech travels between separate parts," as Lawrence says. Now that Catherine has become an individual, words and actions are needed to keep her amused. Arguments such as this one continue and increase in fury, until one of them concludes with Catherine's death. Vastly more representational space is given to fights between this famous pair of lovers than to their union. But the sort of actions and words that Catherine now demands from her friend are, of course, the stuff of drama, the very thing that makes narrative representation vivid and engrossing.

Catherine's increasing division from Heathcliff is matched by a new division within herself. For the first time she feels conflicting impulses and has to make choices between irreconcilable desires, and we should be reminded of Lacan's association of this stage with the origin of aggressivity. Even Nelly notices the change in her young charge. Catherine's conflicting desires to stay close to both Heathcliff and the Lintons "led her to adopt a double character without exactly intending to deceive anyone" (83). This sort of duplicity, intentional or not, is an inevitable result of Catherine's first identifications. Her desire to be like the Lintons depends upon a prior sense of her difference from them. In bringing the other within, Catherine internalizes the division (or difference) that initially allowed her to perceive the other as enviable.

Now we are ready to take up the question of representation again. By showing us the evil that results from imitating another, the novel introduces the topic of representation as one of its themes. Imitation is revealed to be an inherently dangerous activity: It produces alienation in the self as the price of bringing the self into conjunction with the other. As Emily Brontë makes clear, imitation sets up a division within the very thing it means to organize as a single unit. Thus the reader learns to trust those modes of existence that do not depend upon the process of imitation for their very being. This suspicion of representation contributes to our sense of the visionary quality of Catherine and Heathcliff's union. We continue to believe in the visionary existence of their bond, even when they have been divided from one another, precisely because the bond itself has never been represented. As something beyond the alienating touch of imitation, their union remains inviolate through every succeeding change.

Emily Brontë's critique of the self is every bit as severe as Shelley's.[11] Her ideal is a model of existence that almost precludes the concepts of individuality, of self-sufficiency, or of character. When Catherine says to Nelly, "Surely you and every body have a notion that there is, or should be, an existence of yours beyond you" (101), she implies a radically dispersed sense of individual existence.[12] We have seen that her very ability to put such an idea into words signals her withdrawal into a distinct and isolated self, into a being that can say "I" and "you" in the first place. Yet, by introducing the topic of such an unlimited being, Catherine underlines the inadequacy of any self constituted out of imitation of the finite boundaries of the other. "Whatever our souls are made of," Catherine says of Heathcliff, "his and mine are the same, and Linton's is as different as moonbeam from lightning, or frost from fire" (100). The "sameness" of their souls is one way (a figurative way) of expressing the lack of that "difference" that is the inevitable product of any act of identification.

We can observe Emily Brontë's horror of the self in a striking passage that occurs in Chapter 12, a few months before Catherine's death. During the delirium that seizes Catherine when she is ill, she has several visionary experiences, all of which are of interest for our discussion. One in particular needs to be examined in the present context, because it draws attention to the alienation that is an inevitable component of the imitative self. Significantly, a mirror and Catherine's own reflection play prominent roles in the vision. Catherine tells Nelly that she sees an old black press that stood in her bedroom at Wuthering Heights, even though she is now locked in her room at Thrushcross Grange. Reflected in the press, she sees a face. Nelly tells her that there is no press in this room, but Catherine replies:

"Don't *you* see that face?" she enquired, gazing earnestly at the mirror.

And say what I could, I was incapable of making her comprehend it to be her own; so I rose and covered it with a shawl. (150–1)

Catherine's inability to recognize herself in the mirror is a sign of how much identification has changed her. In a sense she is right: the face in the mirror is not the real Catherine. It is merely the identity she has acquired through imitation of the other.

"It was *yourself*, Mrs Linton" [Nelly says]; "you knew it a while since."

"Myself," she gasped, "and the clock striking twelve! It's true, then; that's dreadful!" (151)

As recognition of her altered self returns to her, she becomes aware of the hour, another figure of limitation.

The other visions in this chapter are equally disturbing, yet they rank among the most memorable passages in the novel, in part because they all involve regression to the period in Catherine's life before she was married to Edgar and thus treat of that time when she was, in her own words, "half savage and hardy, and free" (153). But their patently regressive nature signals their limited, merely personal reference. They are trapped within the structures that her self has established. They are filled with nostalgia, a yearning to return to prior states. In their compensatory power, they resemble the retrospective epiphanies of Wordsworth more than the skeptical visions of Shelley. These visions include her first description of Peniston Crag, with its fairy cave; an account of a lapwing nest in the middle of the moor; a memory of the first night that she was made to sleep apart from Heathcliff; and a vision of Wuthering Heights with a candle in her own window to light her way home after death.[13] The only trace that remains of a more apocalyptic form of strength is the violence of her delirium. In her madness she seems to be straining to shatter the self she has created, to break free of the bonds that limit her to a distinct identity, restrict her to a particular body, place, and time. But the process of identification cannot be reversed. Once burdened with a self, there is no escape from the self's requirements. Even visionary experience becomes not liberation into an invisible world, but regression within the closed circuit of memory. The self can see only what the self has wrought. Catherine's vision is restricted by the very limits that it seeks to escape. To put it another way, transcendence is structured by the very thing that makes it necessary. Even figures of liberation from self, time, and reality are conditioned by all they attempt to undo.

One thing in the novel, however, seems to break free of all limitations. In death, Catherine and Heathcliff appear to transcend the bounds of self,

time, and the world. The possibility that Catherine's bond with
Heathcliff survives the limits of mortality represents a profound challenge to ordinary conceptions of text as well as of life. This possibility is
raised at several points in the novel. In her delirium Catherine prophesies
that she will not rest until Heathcliff joins her in the grave; and after her
death Heathcliff calls upon her to haunt him. According to various
sources in the novel, some more reliable than others, Catherine does
haunt him. Her ghost, or something very like it, seems to visit
Lockwood in a dream; Heathcliff appears to be in touch with her spirit in
the last days before his own death; and the country folk tell tales of seeing
Catherine and Heathcliff's ghosts walking near the church and on the
moors.

The impression that Emily Brontë is offering death as a challenge to
limited conceptions of life is reinforced by a reading of her poetry, where
death is frequently presented as a release into a higher world. In a passage
from her best known poem, "The Prisoner" (or "Julian M. and A. G.
Rochelle"), a woman comes near to death, which seems a transcendent
state of ineffable bliss, only to be dragged back to a painful reality:

> "But first a hush of peace, a soundless calm descends;
> The struggle of distress and fierce impatience ends;
> Mute music soothes my breast – unuttered harmony
> That I could never dream till earth was lost to me.
>
> "Then dawns the Invisible, the Unseen its truth reveals;
> My outward sense is gone, my inward essence feels –
> Its wings are almost free, its home, its harbour found;
> Measuring the gulf it stoops and dares the final bound!
>
> "Oh, dreadful is the check – intense the agony
> When the ear begins to hear and the eye begins to see;
> When the pulse begins to throb, the brain to think again,
> The soul to feel the flesh and the flesh to feel the chain!" (lines 77–88)

This passage forms the centerpiece of every discussion of Emily Brontë's
"mysticism," and it is often cited as the heart of her entire literary
endeavor.[14] The sufferer falls into a trance in which all sense of natural
surroundings disappears and an awareness of the Invisible takes its place.
The loss of sight is replaced by a visionary music, "unuttered harmony,"
and the limits of a mortal self are exchanged for "eternal liberty."

Emily Brontë's vision of death, then, would seem to answer the need
for an actual representation of transcendent experience, including the
"unrepresentable" experience of Romantic union. This seems to be the
role of death in some of Shelley's poetry as well. In "Adonais" the poet
cries "No more let Life divide what Death can join together," a line that
could easily have been spoken by Heathcliff. But there are problems with
these suppositions. As a number of readings of *Wuthering Heights* have

demonstrated, we cannot be sure whether Heathcliff is really haunted or not. The issue of life after death is left deliberately ambiguous. In "Adonais," too, death is but one of a whole series of figures for union, none of them any more adequate than the others. Death's privileged position at the end of the series derives only from its usefulness as an image for the end of all figures:

> Life, like a dome of many-coloured glass,
> Stains the white radiance of Eternity,
> Until Death tramples it to fragments. ("Adonais," lines 462–4)

Despite its apocalyptic purport, the "Death" that tramples the dome of Life into fragments remains a figure, and a particularly obvious one – personification. Colors, we remember, are a classical term for tropes. With this in mind, we should recognize that the trope of Death forms but another hue in the many-colored glass dome, one more of Life's "stains" on the unrepresentable whiteness of Eternity.

In "The Prisoner" the visionary passage quoted above appears only as an interruption in a story that seems to contradict or render meaningless the prisoner's vision. As Homans notes in her reading of this poem, the woman lives happily ever after on earth, seemingly satisfied with a mute, tranquil, and unappealing life as the wife of the man who had been her tormentor (*Women Writers and Poetic Identity* 115–22). Moreover, a closer look at the visionary passage itself reveals that the experience is structured, like most of the Wordsworthian visions encountered in earlier chapters, as a liminal moment. The actual impression of transcendence is conveyed in the text not by the representation of life after death, but as the movement across a gap between two represented orders, life and death.

Much confusion has been caused by the error of reading Catherine and Heathcliff's deaths as a direct and literal attempt to represent their merging into a visionary union.[15] But we cannot ignore the intentional ambiguity of this afterlife: Emily Brontë was quite capable of eliminating any uncertainty on that score. (Of course, such a decision would have damaged the novel, reducing it in some respects to the level of a mere horror story.) It does not matter in the least whether or not the two characters live beyond the grave. Death is not a literal presentation of union, nor is it meant to be. Death's status in the novel always remains figurative.

Far from being reducible to a single, literal meaning, death is given numerous, conflicting interpretations. Almost everyone in the book has a different reading of its significance. In addition to Catherine's prophecy of restlessness in the grave, we have Nelly's Christianized sentimentality about death when she describes Catherine's corpse as "that untroubled image of Divine rest" (202). In opposition to the superstitious tales of the country people, there is Lockwood's famous comment at the end of the novel, "[I] wondered how any one could ever imagine unquiet slumbers for the sleepers in that quiet earth" (414). For the second Catherine, death seems merely an occasion for guilt: Both Nelly and Heathcliff play on her anxiety that her behavior will lead to the death of others. For her father, Edgar Linton, death is primarily a financial concern: Will his daughter be provided for? Will Heathcliff inherit his sister's property? Indeed, Catherine herself at times talks of death as though it would lead to a "glorious world . . . incomparably beyond and above you all" (197), rather than to a restless after-existence on this earth.

With so many competing interpretations of death to choose from, we are compelled to regard death as a trope requiring further interpretation, rather than as an attempt to locate Catherine and Heathcliff's union within the bounds of the text. As a trope, death is so open to interpretation that it might almost be a figure for interpretation, a representation of the distancing power of textuality itself. If that were the case, then one could equally say that death is a figure for the role of figures in the novel, because the salient characteristic of all figures is that they require interpretation. Like the figure of union, like Catherine and Heathcliff's visions, the figure of death holds apart the very things that it seems to unite.[16] But, in pursuing this kind of speculation, we run the risk of missing or forgetting whatever it is that is causing the multiple figures to be deployed. We must always keep in mind that some desire, itself unrepresented, is structuring the numerous evasions represented by ghosts, visions, figures of union and of death.

It is an unusual vision indeed that can bring itself to undo such powerful figures. Emily Brontë's work forces us to take all its figures as provisional, merely *possible* interpretations. According to Miller, *every* text deconstructs itself, all works call into question their own presuppo-sitions.[17] But surely there is some difference in this regard between a work such as *Wuthering Heights*, which relentlessly and openly challenges the conditions of textuality, and a work such as *Pride and Prejudice*, which takes the greatest pains to hide the places where its status as text cannot help but put in question the adequacy of its represented world. This difference is the measure of a radical or apocalyptic project.

In the strength that deploys such powerful figures of transcendence and then challenges the very structure of their deployment, we find the authentic power of a prophet, the furor that led E. M. Forster to rank Emily Brontë, along with Melville, Dostoyevsky, and Lawrence, as one of his four exemplars of the prophetic novelist (125–47). It is the violence of prophecy that drives the text through one evasion after another, and it is the power of prophecy that we share when we participate in the text's undoing of its own evasions. Only in this violence do we find traces of Emily Brontë's apocalyptic desire, her will-to-power over all structures, stages, and forms. But if this prophetic violence is a trace of *something*, of the will, say, then why is the prophetic will not simply another figure, with all the limitations that implies? As Harold Bloom, the foremost exponent today of a will-to-power within texts, puts it, "Every notion of the will that we have is itself a trope, even when it tropes against the will, by asserting that the will is a linguistic fiction" (*Poems of Our Climate* 396).

At some points in *Wuthering Heights* Emily Brontë does seem to experiment with the will as a *figure* for transcendent power. Nelly portrays Catherine's willfulness as the quality that most distinguished her as a young girl: "She was never so happy as when we were all scolding her at once, and she defying us with her bold, saucy look, and her ready words" (52). Heathcliff, too, in his desire for revenge, seems to possess a more than natural strength of purpose, an almost satanic will to achieve his ends. This use of will is the Byronic trope par excellence, and its attractions for Emily Brontë were great, as numerous passages in the poetry and the novel testify. But the prophetic will, as a power that runs through the text rather than an image within the text, never becomes a trope at all. Emily Brontë rejects the will as a figure for the visionary power far more decisively than the tropes of union or of death, and the reason is not hard to guess. The will is too bound up with the self. Catherine's high-spirited, imperious ways are too close to selfishness. Heathcliff's satanic characteristics, so named explicitly by Nelly, Isabella, old Mr. Earnshaw, and Hindley, all relate to his physical appearance or his plans for revenge, his position *within* society, within its laws and customs, not to his aspirations beyond the limits of this sphere. More important, the long, visionary sufferings Heathcliff undergoes in the days before his death seem designed to strip him of his very will, to purge from him the circumscribed goals of the self.

Heathcliff's death is worth examining at more length. The dismantling of his will becomes not simply another place where the displacements of tropes can be demonstrated, but rather a way in which the mechanism of displacement itself can be called into question. It constitutes the novel's greatest challenge to the adequacy of deconstruction by itself as an approach to textuality. Heathcliff's loss of will is first signaled by his renunciation of his plans for revenge just as they are nearing fruition. "It is a poor conclusion, is it not?" he asks Nelly; "I get levers and mattocks to demolish the two houses, and train myself to be capable of working like Hercules, and when everything is ready, and in my power, I find the will to lift a slate off either roof has vanished!" (392). Nothing prevents his revenge, except the loss of the self that desires it: "I could do it; and none could hinder me – But where is the use? I don't care for striking, I can't take the trouble to raise my hand!" (393). He no longer has any desires connected with the external world. He can scarcely see the world around him; for days he cannot eat or sleep; he has a wild, feverish aspect, an unnatural appearance of joy. In the intensity of his visionary rapture, he resembles nothing so much as the Poet in Shelley's "Alastor," who starves to death while pursuing his own ineluctable vision. Like Shelley's Poet, who can see nothing except the "two starry eyes" that seemed "to beckon him" (lines 490–2), Heathcliff stares at what Nelly calls an "unearthly vision" (404):

> Now, I perceived he was not looking at the wall, for when I regarded him alone, it seemed, exactly, that he gazed at something within two yards distance. And whatever it was, it communicated, apparently, both pleasure and pain, in exquisite extremes: at least, the anguished, yet raptured expression of his countenance suggested that idea. (405)

It should be clear by now that this vision possesses the same fallen structure of all the other visions in the novel. One cannot claim a special privilege or status for this moment. There is no way of knowing whether a supernatural experience "occurs" or not. Nelly's narration continually indicates the possibility, even probability, of its delusional nature. But having acknowledged its secondary and ambiguous status, we need to make several other points about Heathcliff's experience. First of all, we should notice that Heathcliff does not seek death. Too often, his final days are read as a yearning for death. Heathcliff makes it completely clear that death is as irrelevant as life to his experience: "I have neither a fear, nor a presentiment, nor a hope of death," he says (395). Rather, he describes his experience as an approaching change, an alteration of some sort that has nothing to do with death, just as it is unconnected with life – both are incidental to its progress: "Nelly, there is a strange change approaching – I'm in its shadow at present – " (393). When Nelly asks what he means by a change, Heathcliff says, "I shall not know that, till it comes. . . . I'm only half conscious of it now" (394).

Even more interesting is the way Heathcliff's faculty for perceiving resemblances seems to break down. Everywhere he turns, everything he sees, is an image of Catherine. It is as if the representational faculty in the self had overloaded and was now running wild: "I cannot look down to this floor, but her features are shaped on the flags! In every cloud, in every tree – filling the air at night, and caught by glimpses in every object by day, I am surrounded with her image! The most ordinary faces of men and women – my own features – mock me with a resemblance" (394). Such phantasmagoria goes beyond the attempt to undermine the logical structure of representation. To point to the workings of "displacement" in this passage would be almost a joke. The text here moves beyond the demonstration that figures are a form of desire to a critique of the finite structure of desire. Heathcliff's "change" might be described as the loss – or swallowing up – of all individual desire, all the desires of the self, in one apocalyptic desire: "I have a single wish, and my whole being and faculties are yearning to attain it. . . . I am swallowed in the anticipation of its fulfillment" (395). A desire that subsumes the desiring subject, that swallows up the "I," is apocalyptic indeed. It is like Catherine's union with Heathcliff – not a pleasure, not a source of visible delight, but something unconnected with pleasure or desire as the self understands them.

Here we approach a final perception about the apocalyptic element in Emily Brontë's writing. *Wuthering Heights* reveals desire for any object to be fallen desire. Like speech, individual desire can only travel between separate parts, between the self and a longed-for other. Hence all desire for the objects of this world is ultimately "figurative," in the sense that the union it intends is prevented by the very conception of the desire. This insight is not unique: It is shared by Old Testament prophets and Christian mystics, by a Marxist visionary such as Herbert Marcuse and a Freudian revisionist such as Norman O. Brown. From an apocalyptic perspective, desire for the things of this world is illusion, maya. The longing for money, possessions, prestige, social position, or temporal power testifies to the same kind of displacement that underlies the structure of a literary text.

This position looks forward to the criticism that René Girard has made of the novel as a genre, that all desire, even ethical desire, is mediated and that the origin of this mediation is a moment of imitation analogous to the acts of identification that we have examined in *Wuthering Heights*. Girard's critique of desire in fiction, however, only calls into question the hope of locating the original, undisplaced object of desire. To put it another way, it deconstructs every attempt to specify the ultimate "meaning" of a particular desire. Although Emily Brontë's work comes to the same conclusion about the fate of desire in our world, she would reject the notion that this deconstruction represents the final word. The apocalyptic element in her writing refuses to relinquish the possibility that beyond this frame of things there is a realm of pure or unmediated desire.

This apocalyptic aspect of *Wuthering Heights* is not vulnerable to deconstruction in the same way that the figurative elements of the text are, because the former is neither an image within the text nor a meaning of the text, but a stance that the work prompts us to take toward all the images and meanings in our world. From an apocalyptic perspective, the work is a call for a critical attitude toward representation rather than a specific act of representation. When one adopts this attitude toward desire, it becomes possible to imagine an unmediated form of desire – desire not *for* anything, not for any single vision or representation, but for the enlarging power of desire itself, and for the fulfillment that such self-sufficing desire would bring.

Northrop Frye has devoted much of his career to the task of describing the kind of desire that might lie beyond all possible representations of desire. Here is a passage from his most recent book, discussing the fate of desire in an apocalyptic world:

> Such a world cannot be perceived, or even comprehended theoretically, by what is usually called the ego: we have described it as the way reality looks after the ego has disappeared. . . . Metaphors of unity and integration take us only so far, because they are derived from the finiteness of the human mind. If we are to expand our vision into the genuinely infinite, that vision becomes decentralized. [We find] a world that may change as much as our own, but where change is no longer dominated by the single direction toward nothingness and death. (*The Great Code* 165, 168)

Frye is writing about the apocalyptic books of the Bible, not about a novel with strongly realistic elements. In the Introduction we noted that the novel as a genre has never developed a truly apocalyptic form. In *Wuthering Heights*, for example, Heathcliff may "change" in a direction that is no longer a path toward nothingness and death; identities may tend to become radically dispersed or "decentralized"; and the personal ego, the individual desiring self, may disappear. But, unlike works cast in more genuinely apocalyptic forms – unlike *Prometheus Unbound* or St. John's Apocalypse – the novel gives us no way to decide. Not only do the narrators, Nelly Dean and Lockwood, mediate the apocalyptic elements by their natural or realistic skepticism, but also, and more significantly, the novel allows no possibility of the change being extended to the rest of the universe. The second Catherine and Hareton, the worlds of Wuthering Heights and Thrushcross Grange, are not transformed and renovated. The second half of the novel does not fulfill the prophetic elements in Emily Brontë's vision.

This has often been taken as evidence that the story of the second Catherine overturns or refutes the vision of the first half of the novel. Nothing could be farther from the truth. The second generation does not cast doubt upon the prophetic side of Emily Brontë's vision. Shelley wrote that "Poets, according to the circumstances of the age and nation in which they appeared, were called in the earlier epochs of the world legislators or prophets: a poet essentially comprises and unites both these characters" (482). In *Wuthering Heights* the second part of the narrative might be the work of a poet as "legislator." The second Catherine's love for Hareton in effect reinstitutes a society, establishes the terms of a "civilization" at Wuthering Heights and Thrushcross Grange. The story of the second generation explores what Freud would call the "social side" of desire. Emily Brontë recognizes that this social side of desire is necessary to life in our world. Without the subordination of desire to such shared structures as language her novel itself could not have been written. She understands, in short, that the prophet depends upon the very limitations and values that she challenges. But *Wuthering Heights* contains a more radical knowledge as well. It reveals that the proper institution (or renewal) of the social side of desire depends upon the existence of an asocial, apocalyptic vision of desire. Just as the prophet relies on the legislator, the legislator requires a prophet. In *Wuthering Heights* the two characters are comprised and united in one.

5

WORDSWORTH AND THE CONFLICT OF MODES

Emily Brontë's apocalyptic questioning of ordinary modes of representation – whether lyric or narrative – suggests that we should look again at the claims of both modes.[1] Our reading of *Clarissa* demonstrated that from the visionary perspective of Clarissa's virtue all available forms of action in this world were potentially violent and dehumanizing. Plot, in that novel, originated in the moment when Clarissa's position became radically unstable, and it was kept in motion by Lovelace's unceasing efforts to capitalize on the heroine's vulnerability. Clarissa's heroic intransigence amounted to a refusal of all secular plots, including her family's plot of economic improvement through marriage, Lovelace's first plot of seduction and betrayal and his later plot of rape and forgiveness, and even Colonel Morden's plot of retribution and Mrs. Norton's plot of Christian fortitude. Clarissa's virtue could be vindicated only through the transcendence of the world of plot in death. As a result, Romantic readers tended to interpret that novel in accordance with the theory of "pure poetry," which dictated that sublime moments, such as the heroine's death, could be detached from the moral concerns of the rest of the novel. One consequence of this habit of reading was to devalue narrative, particularly as it was incarnated in the chief narrative genre of the period, the novel. Works of prose fiction whose authors attempted to integrate visionary experience into their narrative, such as the Gothic novels that flourished in the years following the publication of *Clarissa*, were still viewed not as "pure" fictions but as "impure" combinations of discordant elements.

Hence Jane Austen found it necessary to defend the forms of prose narrative that she valued against the prevailing critical fashion. When she addressed these critical voices (embodied in a character such as Captain Benwick, who preferred impassioned poetry to any species of prose), she attempted to turn the terms of the debate upside down, arguing that the limitation of poetry lay in its very purity. Narrative, by contrast, was an "ethical" form precisely because it was "impure"; it had the capacity to reflect, for good or for ill, the conflictual, heterogeneous, and dialogical position of an individual in the social order. Austen criticized transcendence as an escape from the ethical imperatives both of social life and of the literary forms that were principally employed to represent that life, namely narrative and drama.

If Emily Brontë's apocalyptic perspective leads us to question the validity of all earthly forms, then how does that affect the argument over the special merits of one literary mode or another? One can, of course, put Emily Brontë's objections aside, rejecting the apocalyptic perspective entirely. But even if one feels no sympathy with an apocalyptic world view, the way in which her critique of representation anticipates important aspects of the contemporary critical debate might make one hesitate to dismiss her perspective. The more fruitful course would be to reexamine the formal concepts we have been tracing, in the hope of opening the debate over those concepts to the more radical perspective that Emily Brontë's work provides.

THE PHENOMENOLOGY OF LYRIC AND NARRATIVE

Wordsworth's influential experiments with lyric and narrative set the terms of the discussion for many later poets and novelists. The poems he and his friend Coleridge called "lyrical ballads" mark a new and complex understanding of the relationship between lyric and narrative. In the "Preface" that Wordsworth added to the second edition, the poet defines this new relation in terms of action and feeling: "The feeling," he says, "gives importance to the action and situation, and not the action and situation to the feeling" (*Prose* 1:129). This is a nice formulation, crucial in the history of Romantic thinking about narrative, and it would serve to elucidate the intentions of many later novelists. But it does not shed any light on the issue of the value of forms per se. In order to rethink the question of value in and of forms, we need to probe beneath the terms in which Wordsworth and most of his critics have cast the problem.

Wordsworth's greatest influence on the topic lay in his tendency to view the difference between lyric and narrative in terms of an opposition between internal and external modes of experience.[2] To put the dichotomy in crude terms, the poet postulates a realm of feeling, consciousness, or inward being, on the one hand, and a world of action, deed, or event, on the other. These realms are dialectically related, and hence the forms that are habitually used to represent each realm are interrelated rather than distinct and are defined by their interaction rather than their separation. This method of equating formal principles with thematic terms has clear affinities with twentieth-century phenomenology. Geoffrey Hartman has called Wordsworth an "instinctive phenomenologist"

(*Criticism in the Wilderness* 29), and such a phrase seems appropriate to a poet who maintains both that the "individual Mind" is exquisitely fitted "to the external World" ("Prospectus to *Excursion*," lines 63–8) and that the shapes of consciousness have a discernible relation to literary form.

One of Wordsworth's most important statements about the relation between lyric and narrative appears in "The Ruined Cottage," the poem that he later combined with the fragment known as "The Pedlar" to form the first book of *The Excursion*.[3] The passage amounts to a warning to the unnamed narrator of the poem, and through him to the reader, that the story of Margaret's sufferings will be different from the sort of narrative one is accustomed to finding in poetry. The Pedlar says:

> 'Tis a common tale,
> By moving accidents uncharactered,
> A tale of silent suffering, hardly clothed
> In bodily form, and to the grosser sense
> But ill adapted, scarcely palpable
> To him who does not think. (lines 231–6)

Wordsworth opposes strong or violent narratives to another state, here unnamed but carefully delineated. The opposition is between external and internal modes, plainly enough, but the specific terms used to describe them are worth further attention. Narratives can possess "moving accidents" that "clothe" events in "bodily form," making them "palpable" to the "grosser sense." Strong story lines seem to have a special relation not only to vivid characterization but to external mimesis as well. Wordsworth associates powerful actions with the visible, the palpable, the gross; and such associations are habitual with him. He spurns "gross and visible action" in a letter defending "The White Doe of Rylstone" (*Middle Years* 1:198). He claims that the "mind is capable of being excited without the application of gross and violent stimulants" in the "Preface to *Lyrical Ballads*" (1800), and he goes on to blame "frantic novels, sickly and stupid German Tragedies, and deluges of idle and extravagant stories in verse" for the "degrading thirst after outrageous stimulation" among readers of his day (*Prose* 1:129–30).[4]

On the other side of this opposition, we find "silent suffering," a tale that is "common," by which the poet means simple and universal, a nearly motionless form of experience that is "ill adapted" for representation at all. Most important, we find the requirement for thought. To understand such an action, one must become more thoughtful or reflective, one must be prepared, in short, for a more internal mode of experience. Again, this attitude is characteristic. If plots are popular, Wordsworth writes in the "Essay, Supplementary to the Preface" (1815), it is because the "selection and arrangement of incidents" keeps the mind "upon the stretch of curiosity" but "without the trouble of thought."

True poetry, on the other hand, "send[s] the soul into herself, to be admonished of her weakness, or to be made conscious of her power" (*Prose* 3:83). In "Simon Lee" he "apologizes" for not telling a real tale, but then he gently chides the reader:

> O Reader! had you in your mind
> Such stores as silent thought can bring,
> O gentle Reader! you would find
> A tale in every thing. (lines 65–8)

Wordsworth's letter defending "The White Doe of Rylstone" rings changes on most of the terms we have encountered: "If the Poet is to be predominant over the Dramatist, – then let him see if there are no victories in the world of spirit, no changes, no commotions, no revolutions there, no fluxes and refluxes of the thoughts which may be made interesting by modest combination with the stiller actions of the bodily frame" (*Middle Years* 1:198).

The simplest explanation of what Wordsworth wants from his narratives involves the concept of internalization. The movement away from gross physical action is a movement inward, a turn toward the world of the spirit. This simple explanation should not be ignored. The desire to exchange some of the outward commotion of events for the inward flux and reflux of thought is shared by many later novelists, including prominently George Eliot and Henry James. In *Middlemarch* Dorothea's struggles with her own thoughts are shown to be as decisive as any outward events; and the descriptions of the meditative hours she spends looking out the window of her sitting room are strikingly Wordsworthian (*Middlemarch* 406, 464–5). Henry James takes this same process even farther. The famous Chapter 42 of *The Portrait of a Lady*, in which Isabel Archer does nothing but sit by the fire in her room and think, looks back through the image of Dorothea at her sitting-room window to the Wordsworthian opposition that lies behind them both. In the Preface to this novel, James contrasts "the moving accident, of battle and murder and sudden death" with the mild adventures of his heroine's inner life (*Literary Criticism* 2:1083). When James speaks of the "mystic conversion" of such small events "into the stuff of drama or, even more delightful word still, of 'story'" (2:1083), we might think of Wordsworth's hope to make "the victories in the world of spirit" as interesting as the dramatist's "gross and visible action." This is the Preface, after all, in which James wonders if he "could do so subtle, if not so monstrous, a thing as to write the history of the growth of one's imagination" (2:1076), a project for which Wordsworth is an inevitable precursor.

If internalization represents a useful way of conceiving what is important in Wordsworth's attitude toward narrative, it cannot be the final word on this subject. The very coherence of the process as a psychological phenomenon might prevent us from noticing the difficulties it entails as an aspect of literary structure. If something can be "internalized," it must have once been "external." In the domain of psychology, internal and external refer to the boundaries of the self. But it is not immediately apparent how some aspects of literature can be more external than others. We need to ask ourselves a simple question: External to what? The concept implies that certain literary structures lie inside or at the heart of literature itself, whereas other structures can be thought of as outside literature's true being.[5]

Geoffrey Hartman has occasionally suggested that a phenomenological account of Romantic lyricism would be useful, but the problems he encounters in developing such an account might help us understand the limits of this (and other thematic) approaches to form. In the opening chapters of his book *Wordsworth's Poetry*, Hartman argues that Romantic lyricism might profitably be studied as an extended form of surmise, a traditional rhetorical structure that in Romantic hands "disconcertingly turns all terms descriptive of mode into terms descriptive of mood" (11). He characterizes this mode or mood as reflective, melancholy yet self-aware, and he connects it with the "shock of self-consciousness," which is "a general feature of Romantic lyricism" (12). Finally, he wonders whether "self-consciousness and Wordsworth's lyricism are connected in an intrinsic and more than occasional way" (15). Hartman, however, does not develop these suggestions into a full theory of Romantic (or even Wordsworthian) lyricism; and perhaps there are good reasons for not doing so.

From Hartman's point of view, the chief reason is that we do not need more genre theory. Hartman believes that efforts to classify genres lead to the virtually endless project of distinguishing one form from another; but, he says, "there are too many forms already." We need a history that tells us why the forms that we have are important, why and how they have come to matter to us in the particular ways that they do (*Fate of Reading* 101–13). Instead of elaborating genre systems, he thinks we should relate the forms of literature "to the form of the artist's historical consciousness" (*Beyond Formalism* 366). Hence his discussions of such topics as the "westering" of consciousness, the development of an "evening" mode of poetry, or the purification of romance by Romanticism present themselves as alternatives to traditional ways of defining and delimiting genre categories.[6] Yet he worries about the possibility of such work being confused with the definition of new forms. If his speculations are taken to specify the way certain "kinds" of poetry are organized, then he has failed to differentiate his brand of "history writing" from, on the one hand, a "culture-grammar" of forms (*à la*

Northrop Frye) and, on the other hand, the "histories of topical ideas" by Curtius or Lovejoy (*Beyond Formalism* 112–13). Hartman's project, however, continually seems on the verge of slipping into one camp or the other. And the problem seems to lie in the temptation to equate a poet's forms with his themes.

Wordsworth's tendency to equate lyric with internalization provides both the occasion and the model for Hartman's difficulty. Increasingly, we are discovering that the formal distinction between lyric and narrative seems to court assimilation to other systems of thought – to ontological, religious, or ethical distinctions that may be as figurative as the literary discourses they supposedly ground. We come back to the need to discover a more fundamental way of describing the relationship between lyric and narrative than the phenomenological terms that Wordsworth and his critics have hitherto employed.

NARRATIVE, REPETITION, AND THE UNCANNY

It would be a mistake to treat the opposition between internal and external as a displacement of some other, more fundamental dichotomy: self and other, consciousness and nature, life and "a universe of death" (P.14.160). We need to ask if the dialectical structure so characteristic of Wordsworth's thinking[7] might not conceal a different structure, or more radically, places where the distinctions that create structure are put in doubt. This question is prompted by passages in Wordsworth's poetry where a positive term takes on negative properties. Think about Wordsworth's ambivalence toward the idea of connections or bonds. Usually, any evidence that there is a link joining disparate objects – a bond that unites the individual to nature and through nature to mankind at large – is a source of joy for the poet.[8] In "To My Sister" Wordsworth celebrates such a principle of connection as "Love," a universal birth stealing from heart to heart, "From earth to man, from man to earth" (*Poetical Works* 4:60). In "Tintern Abbey" he rejoices in a "motion and a spirit" that links "All thinking things, all objects of all thought / And rolls through all things" (*Poetical Works* 2:262). Occasionally, however, the feeling of connection can seem only a partial blessing. Sometimes Wordsworth seems to feel overwhelmed by the endless connections among things. The links that free him from his fears of solitude can, in certain circumstances, become the chains that bind his feelings.

These negative moments most often occur in the city, allowing Wordsworth to recuperate them as part of a larger theme, the familiar Romantic creed of nature's superiority to urban life. Again, however, the thematic treatment may be less important than the process which it glosses, for the same unpleasant experience can occur in the midst of nature too. In the sonnet "How sweet it is, when mother Fancy rocks,"

Wordsworth describes being overwhelmed by linked sensations while "saunter[ing]" through a pleasant wood:

> thoughts, link by link,
> Enter through ears and eyesight, with such gleam
> Of all things, that at last in fear I shrink,
> And leap at once from the delicious stream. (*Poetical Works* 3:21)

It appears that the evidence of connection brought to the mind by the senses can be disturbing, unless the mind can discern a law, a meaning, and an end in that connection.

It is easy to see what makes a bond living. Connections are vital when they are filled with "Being," when they seem to possess a consciousness of their own or participate in the feelings of the observer.[9] It is less easy to see what makes a bond unliving. How does any form of connection become arbitrary and unmeaningful? What makes some bonds threaten to overwhelm the powers of the mind? Any evidence of connection to the natural world would be valuable, one would think.

The answer that Wordsworth suggests is that some bonds have the capacity to remind us that our lives are inextricably connected with death. In "We Are Seven" an adult grows strangely frustrated with a little girl who keeps insisting that she is still connected with her two siblings in their graves. At first one wonders why a girl's innocent attachment should so upset a grown man. In the "Preface to *Lyrical Ballads* (1800)," Wordsworth explains that he hoped to show "the perplexity and obscurity which in childhood attend our notion of death, or rather our utter inability to admit that notion" (*Prose* 1:126). And in other places he discusses his difficulty in accepting that life leads to death. In the note on the "Intimations Ode" that he dictated to Isabella Fenwick he confessed that "nothing was more difficult for me in childhood than to admit the notion of death as a state applicable to my own being. . . . I used to brood over the stories of Enoch and Elijah, and almost to persuade myself that, whatever might become of others, I should be translated, in something of the same way, to heaven" (*Poetical Works* 4:463). But the poet's attitude toward the link between life and death is more complex than these simple statements imply. Throughout his poetry he deals with figures on the edge of death: old men "not all alive nor dead," mothers declining to their end, children lost in storms or murdered at birth. The knowledge that life leads to death, that animate things become inanimate, seems to fascinate as well as to disturb the poet.

This mixed response to situations which link life with death might properly be described as "uncanny." According to Freud, the uncanny is provoked when "familiar" things become "strange," when domestic feelings, common incidents, or homely facts suddenly take on a power to shock. This definition of the uncanny seems relevant to a large portion of the poet's best work. Wordsworth has a gift for making ordinary objects – a mound of rocks, a lone sheep, a stunted tree – or homely characters – old men, little children, an idiot boy – seem mysterious and strange. Wordsworth's share in *Lyrical Ballads*, Coleridge tells us, was to "excite a feeling analogous to the supernatural" by giving "the charm of novelty to things of every day" (*Biographia Literaria* 2:7), which sounds almost like a prescription for creating uncanny effects. In light of the "animism" that several commentators have found in Wordsworth's philosophy,[10] it is interesting to note that Freud traces the uncanny back to the primitive belief in animism. "Archaic forms of thought belonging to the past of the individual and of the race" ("The Uncanny" 153) could be said to lie behind the ghostliness, the sense of preternatural presences, that Wordsworth discovers in the rushing wind or in moments of sudden calm. Such archaic forms of thought, according to Freud, induce in adults a tendency toward the "overestimation of subjective mental processes" that is a survival of the child's instinctive belief in the "omnipotence of thought" (147). One thinks not only of the "curse poems" in *Lyrical Ballads* but also of those passages in *The Prelude* that demonstrate the mind's power over the natural world. Even some of the experiences that Freud uses to illustrate the uncanny might have been drawn from Wordsworth's poetry, particularly from the Simplon Pass episode in *The Prelude*. The involuntary return to a haunted spot, Freud writes, is a potent cause of the uncanny, "as, for instance, when one is lost in a forest in high altitudes, caught, we will suppose, by the mountain mist, and when every endeavour to find the marked or familiar path ends again and again in a return to one and the same spot, recognizable by some particular landmark" (144).

This element of repetition, of involuntary return, is the most important aspect of the uncanny, both to Freud's theory and to a consideration of narrative in Wordsworth. Let us look at "We Are Seven" again. Wordsworth tells us that he began the poem with the last line – "Nay, we are seven!" – a fragment of the girl's speech that seems to have little meaning in and of itself. From this peculiarly insistent line, he went on to write the rest of the last stanza:

> "But they are dead; those two are dead!
> Their spirits are in heaven!"
> 'Twas throwing words away; for still
> The little Maid would have her will,
> And said, "Nay, we are seven!" (*Poetical Works* 1:238, lines 65–9).

One can see how this stanza would come first: It is charged with the kind of power that can generate the rest of a story. Two willful figures meet head to head. There is denial on the child's part, though not, in a

Freudian sense, of the hard facts of death but rather of an adult form of logic; and frustration on the man's part, sheer exasperation – "'Twas throwing words away" – that must have prompted his unseemly attack. Out of context, the stanza does not have the light tone, the almost silly air, that it picks up from the rest of the poem. The story that Wordsworth proceeded to write creates a very different kind of effect from the power that we detect in these last lines. It seems as if Wordsworth responded not to the "incident" that the poem recounts, the meeting with the little girl, but to a power in the phrase "we are seven" itself. The insistence of the words, from their very first appearance, makes us suspect that the power in them lies in the fascination of repetition. "We are seven" is repeated with slight modifications – in the title, by the little girl, and once by the man himself – seven times in all. This insistent repetition seems to be the real source of the uncanny in the poem, the element in the girl's innocent attachment that makes it appear so unnatural to the older man.

If repetition can make this harmless bond seem uncanny, then perhaps it is this formal property, rather than any thematic issue, that is the source of Wordsworth's uneasiness about certain forms of connection. In its revised form, the next poem in *Lyrical Ballads*, "Lines Written in Early Spring," has a thematic similarity to "We Are Seven." The final stanza's pantheistic reference to "Nature's holy plan" resembles the girl's simple creed. But in the first edition there is a more significant similarity between the poems, which may be why Wordsworth grouped them together. The last stanza of "Lines Written in Early Spring" originally began not with a reference to "Nature's holy plan" but with an allusion to the power of repetition:

> If I these thoughts may not prevent,
> If such be of my creed the plan. . . .
>
> (*Lyrical Ballads* [1798], lines 21–2)

Wordsworth's revision perhaps reflects his discomfort with a faith founded on thoughts that one cannot prevent from recurring in the mind, and this discomfort might account for what Mary Moorman calls "the shadow [that] lies over the spring landscape" in this poem about the "joy and 'pleasure' of living Nature" (1:381). Be that as it may, the next poem in the volume, "The Thorn," overwhelmingly confirms that Wordsworth associated repetition with disturbing feelings about the connection between life and death.

"The Thorn" is the most uncanny poem that Wordsworth ever wrote, and it is an overt study in the power of repetition.[11] In the 1800 edition of *Lyrical Ballads* the poet thought it necessary to include a three page "Note to 'The Thorn' " defending "repetition and apparent tautology"

(*Poetical Works* 2:513) in poetry. His most striking conclusion, in the context of our current discussion, is that repetition and superstitious beliefs go hand in hand: "Superstitious men are almost always men of slow faculties and deep feelings; their minds are not loose, but adhesive" (*Poetical Works* 2:512). Wordsworth, like Freud, seems to think that "the manner in which such men cleave to the same ideas" (2:512) has a more than casual relation to uncanny subjects. The original inspiration for the piece, Wordsworth tells us, was his observing a stunted thorn in a storm. The story of Martha Ray was a later "invention," created for the purpose of making "this Thorn permanently an impressive object" (*Poetical Works* 2:511).[12] The first draft consists entirely of a description of the thorn, making no mention of Martha Ray or any of the incidents of her tale. Several critics have shown that the association between a thorn and a tale of infanticide was conventional (Gerard 76, Jacobus 241–2). Nevertheless, Wordsworth's strange, repetitious description of the thorn might easily have generated many of the details of the story, and much of the emotion besides. As in "We Are Seven," the poet seems to respond to a structural feature of his own writing as much as to the events of the story he eventually tells.

The first stanza of "The Thorn" will sufficiently reveal the strange force that repetition exerts in this poem, although the five opening stanzas would amplify the point, for they do nothing but circle in fascination around the site of the thorn.

> "There is a Thorn – it looks so old,
> In truth, you'd find it hard to say
> How it could ever have been young,
> It looks so old and grey.
> Not higher than a two years' child
> It stands erect, this aged Thorn;
> No leaves it has, no prickly points;
> It is a mass of knotted joints,
> A wretched thing forlorn.
> It stands erect, and like a stone
> With lichens is it overgrown.["] (*Poetical Works* 2:240–1, lines 1–11)

The denuded thorn looks too old to have ever been young, yet it is not higher than a two years' child. It stands erect, but the lichens and moss that cover it struggle to drag it to the ground (stanza 2). Beside this wretched form, and mysteriously connected with it, lies a mound of earth that "[i]s like an infant's grave in size" (line 52). The bond between life and death has grown close indeed; in the story of Martha Ray, it may come even closer. A child murdered in birth compresses the link between the two to an interval that Wordsworth finds both fascinating and disturbing. With so vivid an example of the uncanny before us, we are prepared to consider why repetition plays such a prominent role in this feeling.

According to Freud, anything that reminds us of our tendency to repeat partakes of what he calls the "death-instinct." Like all instincts, this wish is conservative in nature, striving toward the restoration of an earlier condition. It is hardly surprising that the death-instinct, which is an "expression of the inertia inherent in organic life" (*Beyond the Pleasure Principle* 30), should be associated with the phenomenon of repetition, for the latter reveals the pull of past states of existence, the attraction of the same. Repetition is the most obvious reminder that "the aim of all life is death" or that "inanimate things existed before living ones" (*Beyond the Pleasure Principle* 32). For Wordsworth, the fact that life leads to death is the kind of mundane observation that usually could be acknowledged in a straightforward way but that occasionally would become a source of the uncanny. "To be born and to die are the two points in which all men feel themselves to be in absolute coincidence," the poet writes in his first "Essay upon Epitaphs" (*Prose* 2:57). But, in "The Thorn," the tendency of these two universal points to become absolutely coincident is deeply disturbing. When the link between birth and death becomes so close that one seems the repetition of the other, then the structure of repetition can itself become a source of powerful but unnerving feelings. Or, conversely, the repetitions of life, the tendency of little girls or grown men to "cleave to the same ideas," can make the poet recognize that the bond of life is itself what connects all mortal beings with death.

To return to the problem of connection, we can say that repetition is the element in bonds that can be either a force for life or a kind of death. All bonds necessarily contain an element of repetition. The mind cannot be fitted to the external world, the present cannot be linked to the past, individuals cannot be part of a community, unless each has something in common with the other. The persistence of this common element can seem organic or merely mechanical, the vital preservation of one state in another or the harsh restriction to rigid lines of development.[13] Thus strong bonds by their very nature can provoke ambivalent responses within the same person. If repetition lies behind Wordsworth's ambivalent attitude toward bonds, the categories in which he interprets this problem – internal and external, consciousness and nature – become less fundamental. They represent an attempt to articulate as a *theme* a problem that exists within the *structure* of connection itself. More important, they represent an attempt to overcome the problem, for they reformulate an identity (repetition's uncanny capacity to be positive and negative at the same time) as a dichotomy. To the extent that this uncanniness can be treated in dialectical terms, its power is dispersed and the problem is moot.

As a form of connection that relies upon repetition, narrative always has the potential to become uncanny for Wordsworth. All stories involve a measure of repetition. Without a common thread connecting one action to another, the events of a piece would be no more than random occurrences, arbitrary incidents without pattern or form. No set of events, of course, can ever remain truly random. As has often been observed, the mind struggles to make coherence out of any series, no matter how disconnected. The observance of repetitions, of similarity in difference, is one of the chief ways that the mind discovers (or imposes) order. As an aspect of narrative, repetition can remind us of the unity in our experiences, the organic growth of our lives, or alternatively of the frightening tendency of experience to repeat itself, of the eternal recurrence of the same.

Wordsworth tries to preserve both possibilities simultaneously, again through the theme of internal and external modes of action. When repetition is an internal process, an aspect of the mind's power to create order, it is viewed positively; it becomes part of a story about the poet's inner life, a tale that records the growth of the imagination. Explaining how certain scenes remained "in their substantial lineaments / Depicted on the brain," he writes that "pleasure and repeated happiness, / So frequently repeated" made them "[h]abitually dear, and all their forms / And changeful colours by invisible links / Were fastened to the affections" (*P*.1.600–12). As part of a tale filled with "moving accidents," however, repetition is the thing that makes narrative's connections too "palpable," its links too "physical" and "gross." But we must emphasize that the terms of this opposition dispel the real uncanniness of repetition even as they seem to pose repetition as a problem for dialectical resolution. The structure of repetition remains the same, whether it is viewed as an internal or an external mode of experience. Internal and external are only metaphors for the conflicting effects of a single property of narrative: its dependence on repetition for much of its life.

For Wordsworth, the dependence of narrative on the principle of repetition is its most disturbing characteristic. The more "moving" the "accident" of a tale, the more quickly it will reach its inevitable end. In the Lucy poems the poet verges on the conclusion that those people who are most alive are in the greatest danger of death. In his thinking about narrative this tentative equation becomes a terrible certainty. The violence of strong action, which in the popular mind goes hand in hand with a good story, seems in Wordsworth's mind to uncover a violent tendency within narrative itself. The "life" of one kind of story – the story of gross, visible action – means the actual "death" of another kind of story, the tale of inward suffering.

Geoffrey Hartman discusses Wordsworth's turn from narrative to lyric as a movement from the outward world of nature to the more internal realm of consciousness. According to Hartman, the theme of the "halted traveller" in Wordsworth's stories signals "a real deepening of mind-time or self-consciousness" (*Wordsworth's Poetry* 12). It is important to recognize, however, that this desire to slow down the flow of events responds as much to a threatening quality in narrative itself as to the poet's thinking about the relation between the mind and the external world.

LIMINAL FIGURES

In the Introduction we discussed the liminal structure of Wordsworth's visionary moments, relating these moments to the poet's practice of disrupting his narratives. We discovered that the process of transcendence, in Wordsworth, acts as the self's defense against otherness. What the poet calls the "visionary power" opposes any force that seems to deny the autonomy of the self, even if that force is the narrative of a poem that he himself is writing. To this account, however, we must now add that the thematic uses to which a writer puts transcendence may differ greatly from the structure of the experience. Hence we should look again at the liminal moment in Wordsworth's poetry in order to discover how it relates to the problem of repetition in narrative rather than to the subject of the poet's self-consciousness.

When we look at a lyrical ballad such as "The Thorn," we discover that the interruption of the narrative does not visibly augment the narrator's identity, although it does preserve him from something that he fears. The disruption in this poem occurs at a critical point in the narrative, the point that Aristotle designates as the crux of a plot – the point of recognition, the moment when a "discovery" would ordinarily lead to a "reversal" of the action.

The narrator has gone climbing one afternoon, hoping to gain a view of the ocean through his telescope; without warning, a storm comes on and the man can see no object higher than his knee. In the midst of this storm he stumbles upon what he thinks is the form of Martha Ray, crouched on the ground beside the thorn.

> ["]I looked around, I thought I saw
> A jutting crag, – and off I ran,
> Head-foremost, through the driving rain,
> The shelter of the crag to gain;
> And, as I am a man,
> Instead of jutting crag, I found
> A Woman seated on the ground.["] (lines 181–7)

This moment is the crisis of the poem; it conveys all the uncanny power that the repeated descriptions of the thorn have built up. But instead of a recognition scene, in which the narrator discovers the truth or falsity of all his conjectures about this spot, the moment is interrupted by a turn away from the action:

> "I did not speak – I saw her face;
> Her face! – it was enough for me;
> I turned about and heard her cry,
> 'Oh misery! oh misery!'["]]   (lines 188–91)

The next seven lines record a visionary experience, in which the narrator imagines the woman sitting by this spot night after night, crying her mournful refrain. In a manner wholly characteristic of Wordsworth's best works, the poem turns from a scene of external action to a visionary realm within the mind.

If this were a more self-conscious poem, we would be justified in saying that thematically the turn from the otherness of narrative to the inward solace of Imagination testifies to the self's dominion over external circumstance. Such clearly is the pattern in those Wordsworthian "turns" in *The Prelude*, when the protagonist of the poem recoils from a shocking incident in the external world to a moment of internal visionary power. One thinks of the Penrith Beacon episode or the meeting with the Blind Beggar. In "The Thorn," however, there is little sign of increased interiority. The narrative is stopped, but without any new consciousness of self. The reason this experience does not open up new realms of being is easy to state. Wordsworth's great theme of Imagination's compensatory value is available only to the character of the Poet as semidivine creator, not to the character of a credulous and nosy Captain. The absence of this theme, however, allows us to see how the structure of a visionary experience, which tends to disrupt narrative, can be dissociated from the various terms in which the experience is conceptualized.

Despite the absence of any significant form of self-expansion, a liminal structure is as prominent in "The Thorn" as it is in the visionary passages of *The Prelude*. The moment of encounter is a powerful threshold experience. The doubling in the lines " – I saw her face; / Her face! – " seems to mark the actual moment of crossing. On one side lies the only chance the narrator will ever have to get to the root of Martha Ray's story; if he had stopped to help her, then perhaps he would know what really had happened to this woman and her baby. On the other side lies the man's adventures in vision, the superstitious conjectures that he and his neighbors so relish. We need to make two points about this experience. First, the liminal moment successfully turns the power of repetition against itself. By dividing "her face," as a descriptive element in a narrative, from "her face!" as a cry announcing the onset of vision – a gesture equivalent to the lyric "O" – the words are set on different levels of discourse. Hence the uncanniness of a continual return to the same place, the same words, the same end is disrupted. Second, and closely related, the liminal moment signals a decisive shift in modes. By refusing to remain an episode in the ballad-story of Martha Ray, the passage participates in a more intensely lyrical impulse. We hear this in the refrain "Oh misery! oh misery!" – words that approach the status of pure song as they echo through the poem.

Having established that a visionary moment in a poem may involve a shift from narrative to lyric without involving an increased sense of self, we should next inquire why the disruption occurs where it does. What is it about the moment of recognition that makes Wordsworth's narrator turn and flee? The answer returns us to the problem of repetition in narrative. The point of recognition is the place in narrative where the element of repetition is most apparent. According to Aristotle, "discovery" is the act of seeing something in the story of one's life that was there all along. The moment stages a critical re-viewing, in which the protagonist sees an old event in a new light. Hence it reveals that our end lies in our beginning, that our progress toward a goal is but a circuitous return to a place where we have been before. For Aristotle, this moment has a wholly positive value. It is what gives unity to narrative and what makes that unity instructive to others. That the scene of recognition acts in accordance with what Freud would call the death-instinct and what Aristotle calls fate is no impediment at all. Rather, it serves to make the structure of narrative reflect, in and of itself, the shape of men's and women's lives. In his recent book *After Virtue*, the philosopher Alasdair MacIntyre nicely captures Aristotle's sense of the intrinsic relation that exists between the structure of narrative and the shape dictated to life by fate: "The man therefore who does what he ought moves steadily towards his fate and his death. It is defeat and not victory that lies at the end" (117).

Writers who may not share Aristotle's assumptions about the meaningful coincidence of fate and form can still view the inevitable course of all narratives toward their ends as a source of value and strength. Frank Kermode speaks of the "benefaction" of meaning that the inevitability of an ending bestows on the otherwise random course of events. Even if our lives do not have the shape and value that Aristotle accords them, stories do; and it is this truth, if no other, that a scene of discovery forces us to recognize: "In a novel the beginning implies the end: if you seem to begin at the beginning . . . you are in fact beginning at the end; all that seems fortuitous and contingent in what follows is in fact reserved for a later benefaction of significance in some concordant structure" (*Sense of an Ending* 148).

Wordsworth, too, understands that the structure of narrative links our beginnings to our ends, never more than at the moment of recognition when the "concordant structure" that has been there all along is revealed. Unlike Aristotle, and unlike Kermode as well, Wordsworth finds this property of narrative less than a "benefaction." The poet views the "profound and sombre fatalism" that Karl Kroeber says is a feature of traditional ballads (*Romantic Narrative Art* 37) as a property of all stories that contain a strong recognition scene. Such works truly "convey the sense of being trapped in circumstances against which [one's] struggles are futile" (Kroeber 37). Thus Wordsworth characteristically interrupts his narratives at (or just before) the point of discovery. This is his central strategy for lessening the uncanniness of narrative. In place of a scene of recognition, he substitutes a liminal moment. Through the shift from one level of discourse to another, he hopes to postpone the conclusion of all discourse found at narrative's end.

In "The Thorn" the liminal moment offers only a brief reprieve, a momentary escape to the realm of vision. In other poems the liminal experience receives more extended treatment, and the shift from narrative to lyric is correspondingly more pronounced. Often a larger structure – a central episode, a crucial image, a major character – serves as a figure of liminality. Jonathan Wordsworth has called these figures "borderers," characters or forms that haunt the "border-line which is the entrance to another world" ("Wordsworth's 'Borderers'" 173). Such figures can be found throughout the poetry. Jonathan Wordsworth connects them to the poet's preoccupation with marginal states of existence – with the Leech-Gatherer "not all alive nor dead," with solitaries such as the Blind Beggar or the Old Man Travelling, with the heroine of the Lucy poems, even with a horse standing motionless under a moonlit sky, "A borderer betwixt life and death / A living statue or a statued life" (171).[14] These figures mark the boundary where two incompatible realms meet, especially the border between life and death. We say they "mark" the boundary, because it is hard to speak in more precise terms. Nevertheless, in a difficult yet important way, they seem to *be* the line itself. As figures for the possibility of transformation, a kind of embodied virtuality, they strive to give expression to the principle of liminality itself.

When we turn to the work of novelists in the next two chapters, we shall discover that liminal figures are not an exclusive property of Wordsworth's poetry. They play an important but rarely understood role in much nineteenth-century fiction, particularly in the novels of Charles Dickens. As an aspect of fiction, characters who inhabit a transitional space seem to present certain conceptual difficulties. What are we to make of a person who is neither one thing nor another, who always falls between the categories that locate a man or woman within a recognizable framework? Such characters are a familiar concept in anthropology. Victor Turner describes "threshold people" as "necessarily ambiguous" since "these persons elude or slip through the network of classifications that normally locate states and positions in cultural space":

> Liminal entities are neither here nor there; they are betwixt and between the positions assigned and arrayed by law, custom, convention, and ceremonial. . . . Thus, liminality is frequently likened to death, to being in the womb, to invisibility, to darkness, to bisexuality, to the wilderness, and to an eclipse of the sun or moon. (95)

In Wordsworth's short lyric, "Lucy Gray or, Solitude" (*Poetical Works* 1:234–6), the character of a little girl is given virtually all of these attributes of liminality. Lucy Gray can be seen at "break of day," the moment of transition between two realms. Before her death, she seems a creature of the wild, more akin to "the fawn at play" or "the hare upon the green" than to a human child. She notices the "day-moon" in the sky, a sign of her sensitivity to natural phenomena that Wordsworth thought especially important to her character.[15] Her blithe solitude contrasts with the socially engaged pursuits of her mother in town or her father plying his trade with raised "hook" and "faggot-band." She even seems to live in two different time frames. Jeffrey Baker puts this last point nicely: "By the social calendar Lucy is a child, but by the calendar of natural circumstances she is on the brink of death – 'the storm came on before its time'" (38–9).

As a character in a narrative, Lucy occupies a peculiar position. At first she seems to be the heroine of a "moving accident." The story is simple but dramatic. A solitary child is sent across the wild moor to fetch her mother from town. While she is gone, a storm blows up and Lucy loses her way. Her parents search for her all through the night, but in the morning they find her tracks in the snow, leading to a wooden bridge that lies only a furlong from their door. In the very middle of the bridge, the footprints disappear. Even today, the poem concludes, some people maintain that you can see Lucy Gray on the lonesome wild and hear her solitary song whistling in the wind. At the very crisis of this story, however, Lucy seems to disappear as a recognizable character. The natural end to such a "moving accident" would be the discovery of her body in the stream below. In the incident upon which this poem was based, Wordsworth tells us, the girl's body was discovered in the canal (*Poetical Works* 1:360). Here, however, we learn nothing more about the fate of a real child. Lucy becomes a figure for solitude, the spirit of the wind as it is embodied in sound.

This transformation becomes all the more remarkable when we notice how prominent a role sequence plays in the story of the little girl's "death." Lucy's footprints form an inexorable trail, a sequence that moves steadily toward a conclusion that her parents would do anything to deny. The poem takes special care to emphasize the inevitability of this process. For three stanzas, Lucy's parents track her "footmarks small" (line 46) across the winter landscape. Repeatedly, the poem tells us that "the marks were still the same" (line 50), that the parents never lost sight of the tracks, that the trail lay clear and unbroken. Here is the last of these three stanzas:

> They followed from the snowy bank
> Those footmarks, one by one,
> Into the middle of the plank;
> And further there were none! (lines 52–6)

Her story has led, step by step, to an inevitable conclusion. But at the precise point when that end must be acknowledged, we encounter the image of a threshold. The middle of the bridge ends Lucy's story rather than her life.

In the Introduction, we noted that Wordsworth's own liminal experiences could be viewed as form of sublimation, in which a lower state is exchanged for one that seems spiritually "higher." In this poem, however, it is as if Lucy is "sublimed" out of existence entirely. Hence there cannot be any reference to the theme of consciousness, which the notion of sublimation would ordinarily suggest. In order to become a higher spirit, a figure beyond the touch of death, she ceases to be an ordinary character at all. Because the mode of her story precludes any access to a dimension of increased interiority, Lucy's translation to a higher state can be effected only by a modal change. If her life in narrative was tinged with a profound and sombre fatalism, the death of narrative will give her a new mode of existence. This new mode is more "spiritual," in an atavistic sense of the word. It is "disembodied," the ghostly trace of a prior form. By its very nature, this mode is less palpable and gross than narrative, because it scarcely possesses "bodily form." Instead, it participates in the invisible power of sound. Lucy's new mode of existence, of course, is the mode of song. In her pure, wordless singing, a sound that can be heard in the whistling wind, we encounter the life of lyricism itself. Through the death of narrative, Wordsworth hopes to keep his lyric alive.

In this chapter we have sought to describe the literary modes in a way that does not elaborate them as thematic categories. Even when stripped of their figurative dimensions, when distinguished from such interpretative categories as externality or self-consciousness, narrative and lyric still possessed characteristics that led Wordsworth to attribute distinctive values to each. We undertook this task in response to the challenge of Emily Brontë's work, which suggested that, while all specific representations were necessarily inadequate, there existed a power behind or within the literary act that could not be reduced to any of the text's representations. Emily Brontë conceived of this power as an "otherness," which she called Imagination, but which was neither a psychological faculty nor a textual feature. This otherness could be thought of as a drive within a text, rather than any specific meaning or interpretation of the text. Our discussion of Wordsworth leads to the conclusion that, for the mode of narrative, the source of this otherness, the source of a drive that is independent of the meanings we attribute to it, is repetition. This conclusion fits well with our understanding of Jane Austen. The fact that repetition plays a part both in constituting a community and in creating a narrative helps explain Austen's belief that there is a privileged relation between narrative and society. Her faith that narrative can be "curative" because it reflects a special care for the order of the social world might be based, then, on the principle of repetition common to both. Equally, Austen's avoidance of lyrical moments can now be seen as a rejection of liminality (think of the gate scene at Sotherton, the window scene at Mansfield Park). But we have only begun to explore the relation of such moments to narrative. Let us turn to a Wordsworthian novel that contains a number of liminal figures, Charles Dickens's *Little Dorrit*.

6

LITTLE DORRIT

In *The Old Curiosity Shop,* the novel by Dickens most often identified as Wordsworthian,[1] Little Nell has an encounter that mirrors the incident of "We Are Seven." It is a beautiful autumn morning, a morning when Nature herself seems to bless her children, even in the midst of a graveyard: "The dew glistened on the green mounds, like tears shed by Good Spirits over the dead" (490). As Nell passes the cemetery, she meets a group of children playing among the graves, one of which is clearly recent. Nell herself is already drawing near to death, but she does not hesitate to ask about the new grave. As in Wordsworth's poem, the spot is the resting place of one of the children's brother, but the child whom Nell questions insists that the place should not be called a grave: "The child answered that that was not its name; it was a garden – his brother's. It was greener, he said, than all the other gardens, and the birds loved it better because he had been used to feed them" (490). Dickens seems to have found Wordsworth's poem irresistible; its conjunction of childhood, death, and the belief in a survival after death in nature runs through this entire chapter and the next as well.

It is easy to recognize the Romanticism of such moments in Dickens but less easy to know what to make of it.[2] Unlike the adult in Wordsworth's poem, Nell feels no need to argue with the child's unrealistic view of the grave; she herself seems half in love with such an easeful vision of death. Only a few pages later, she will sit among the more richly figured tombs in the chapel and reflect, "It would be no pain to sleep amidst them" (494). As soon as one starts to think about the Romantic children in Dickens, one realizes how often the novelist associates their longing for a better, more innocent world with the realm of death.[3] Paul Dombey's vision of the sea is the most obvious example, but Nell also has a glimpse of a realm of peace and happiness available only in the life after death. Following her meditation among the tombs, she climbs the winding stairs of the church tower until "she gained the end of the ascent and stood upon the turret top" (494). As so often in Wordsworth's poetry, the onset of vision is signalled by a sudden burst of light from above: "Oh! the glory of the sudden burst of light. . . . It was like passing from death to life; it was drawing nearer Heaven" (495–6).[4] From the evidence of *The Old Curiosity Shop* and *Dombey and Son*, it would seem that death is the price that a character must pay in order to gain access to a transcendent realm.

There are, however, other ways that the transcendent aspirations of Dickens's characters can be fulfilled. In the late novels we find characters who are associated with a more than natural power, yet who do not die. One such figure is Jenny Wren; another is Little Dorrit. Both of these characters are diminutive child-women; both prefer their self-chosen or self-retained nicknames; both dream dreams and have transcendent visions.[5] Significantly, the visionary power of these characters is deployed for the benefit more of others than of themselves. At a crucial moment, each of these women finds herself ministering at the sickbed of the hero; and each seems to aid the hero merely by her presence. Perhaps their immunity from the death that claims Nell and Paul Dombey has to do with this ministering function.[6]

Whereas Nell's preoccupation with the transcendent world of death changes *her* – "A change had been gradually stealing over her, in the time of her loneliness and sorrow" (*Old Curiosity Shop* 484) – the power of Jenny Wren and Amy Dorrit changes *others*. The latter characters are mediators in the process of transformation; they help someone else to gain a purified and altered mind. Jenny's "secret sympathy or power" (*Our Mutual Friend* 809) is explicitly described as a form of mediation. At the bedside of the hero, it seemed "as if she were an interpreter between this sentient world and the insensible man" (*Our Mutual Friend* 809). In the terms developed in the prior chapter, Jenny seems to possess many of the attributes and the functions of a liminal being; and so, as we shall see, does Amy Dorrit. The difference between Little Nell and Little Dorrit – the reason the latter remains interesting to us today, while the former has become a symbol for all that is sentimental in the novelist's vision of childhood – is the social function (ministering, transformative of others) that Dickens discovers in his visionary figures.

LIMINAL FIGURES

Little Dorrit begins with a striking image of a threshold. A number of the principal characters in the novel are either in prison or in quarantine in the port of Marseilles. This period of enforced idleness is a time out of time, a span forcibly removed from the continuum of their ordinary lives. Those in quarantine have little to do but stare at the blank sky, the blank buildings, and the blank harbor, while the sky, buildings, and harbor stare blankly back.[7] Here is the description of the harbor in the second paragraph of the novel: "There was no wind to make a ripple on the foul water within the harbor, or on the beautiful seas without. The line of demarcation between the two colors, black and blue, showed the point which the pure sea would not pass; but it lay as quiet as the abominable pool, with which it never mixed" (1).

Dickens's late novels often begin with figures of liminality, images of the uncertain zone between two orders of existence. These figures are inherently ambiguous, because they partake of the contradictory attributes of the two realms they divide. In *Our Mutual Friend* Dickens opens with the character of Mr. Hexam, whose uncanny boat is "allied to the bottom of the river rather than the surface, by reason of the slime and ooze with which it was covered" (43). The River Thames serves as a crucial figure throughout the novel, a region in which categories become unclear, in which the dead and the living are confused and identities are exchanged. The most famous liminal figure in Dickens appears at the beginning of *Great Expectations*. The graveyard where Pip goes to search for some indication of his origin is uncanny enough even before the convict Magwitch rises suddenly from among the graves. We have come far indeed from Little Nell's quiet questions in the graveyard; the terrifying incident that begins this late novel shapes the psychology of a child whose guilt and uncertainty represent the opposite extreme from Nell's self-confidence and assurance of grace. Pip's "fancies" regarding the tombstones of his parents and siblings seem a cruel parody of the innocent faith held by the children in *The Old Curiosity Shop* and "We Are Seven." It is as if the naïveté of Wordsworth's child and the doubts and fears of her adult questioner had been combined in the single, vulnerable character of Pip.

When we turn from preliminary images of thresholds to fully rendered liminal experiences, we discover that the liminal moment in Dickens often provokes a crisis in a character that is like the onset of madness. One of the most striking of these episodes occurs in the second half of *Little Dorrit*. Mr. Dorrit, an old man who had been confined for years in debtor's prison until a sudden discovery made him a rich man, has moved with his family to Rome, where he has established himself in palatial quarters. In the Marshalsea prison, Mr. Dorrit had been known as the Father of the Marshalsea and had been waited on constantly by his daughter, Amy. Now that he is rich, he expects and receives exactly the same treatment. His daughter continues to attend to his every whim. She devotes herself to his comfort so completely that she hardly has time for a life of her own. In the incident in question Mr. Dorrit has returned to his house in Rome from a long trip, expecting to be welcomed with great ceremony. Instead, he finds the rooms dark, his daughter, Amy, and his brother, Frederick, absent. As he wanders through the great empty chambers, an anxiety, born of weariness but nourished by his more habitual self-doubts, grows within him. Finally he sees a light in a small anteroom:

> It was a curtained nook, like a tent, within two other rooms; and it looked warm, and bright in color, as he approached it through the dark avenue they made.
>
> There was a draped doorway, but no door; and as he stopped here, looking in unseen, he felt a pang. . . . There were only his daughter and his brother there: he, with his chair drawn to the hearth, enjoying the warmth of the evening wood fire; she, seated at a little table, busied with some embroidery-work. (618)

Standing literally on a threshold, Mr. Dorrit experiences a profound shock. What he sees seems like a scene from his own past: "The figures were much the same as of old; his brother being sufficiently like himself to represent himself, for a moment, in the composition. So had he sat many a night, over a coal fire far away; so had she sat, devoted to him" (618).

As a recognition scene, the incident constitutes a nice, if somewhat simple, instance of Dickens's remarkable dramatic gift. The darkened rooms place the domestic tableau before Mr. Dorrit as if on a lighted stage. Watching this private play, he cannot avoid its message. The truth about his past is acted out before his very eyes. He comes to himself, in a literal sense characteristic of Dickens, by coming upon himself.

As a moment of vision, the incident participates in a more complex structure. Mr. Dorrit witnesses a moment out of time, an instant that seems to have lost its proper place in the sequence of events. The visionary group "represents" his life as it might have been had he abjured all the fictions that prop up his current identity. Had Mr. Dorrit continued to live much as he did before he was liberated from prison, he would have possessed all the peace and fulfillment that he perceives in these two figures. Disengaged from the old story of his life, the fiction of the "Father of the Marshalsea" that had sustained him in "Poverty," but unassimilated to any of the new fictions supplied by the plot of "Riches," he would have become a purely visionary figure, would have attained a state of being beyond any of the realistic possibilities presented in his character. This, of course, is not what has happened. The entire novel documents Mr. Dorrit's inability to transcend the limits of his old character. Yet, for one shattering moment, he *sees* what the transformation would have been like.

Amy and her uncle have no place in the new world of Rome, but they do not merely recreate the old world of the Marshalsea. Rather, they seem suspended in a time and place all their own. Their happiness is too perfect for any ordinary world. They inhabit a magical, or at least protected, realm – one that in a less dark novel we should identify as the happy world of romance found in some of Dickens's early books. Frederick's passivity in the picture images the settled quiet of a man beyond the concerns of ordinary existence, a figure to whom "all effort seems forgotten," to borrow Wordsworth's line about another old man ("Animal Tranquillity and Decay," *Poetical Works* 4:247). Even the conversation that Mr. Dorrit overhears seems to deny the laws of the ordinary universe, the sequence of growth and aging that governs life as well as narrative. "Do you know, uncle, I think you are growing young again?" Amy says. "I think . . . that you have been growing younger for weeks past" (618). Their moment together has a lyrical charm. To Mr. Dorrit, however, this charm proves strangely disturbing. Amid the rush of all his present plans, the shock of this vision comes as an unwelcome disruption.

At first Mr. Dorrit attempts to deny the implications of what he has seen, employing his usual defense – to blame his brother for all the weaknesses and faults he has just discovered in himself. But the shock of this revelation has been too great. The scene continues to haunt him. Twice during the supper that follows, Mr. Dorrit "looked about him, as if the association were so strong that he needed assurance from his sense of sight that they were not in the old prison-room" (621). Worse, Mr. Dorrit keeps lapsing into strange fits of unconsciousness:

> After dismissing his brother . . . he fell into a doze again, before the old man was well out of the room: and he would have stumbled forward upon the logs, but for his daughter's restraining hold.
>
> "Your uncle wanders very much, Amy," he said, when he was thus roused. "He is less – ha – coherent, and his conversation is more – hum – broken, than I have – ha hum – ever known.["] (620–1)

A similar confusion follows many of Wordsworth's visionary experiences. For days after the episode of the stolen boat, Wordsworth tells us, a "darkness" or "blank desertion" hung over his thoughts and "no familiar shapes / Remained" (*P*.1.394–6). In Mr. Dorrit, these fits grow worse and worse – a kind of galloping narcolepsy – preparing us for his complete breakdown the next evening at a dinner party given by Mrs. Merdle. There, in the midst of the most glorious assemblage of English society the city of Rome has ever known, Mr. Dorrit begins what the illustration drolly titles "An unexpected After-Dinner Speech" (627). He welcomes Mrs. Merdle's guests to debtor's prison, with all the pomp attendant upon his former high position as the Father of the Marshalsea. After this collapse Mr. Dorrit can recognize nothing from his new life. All his present plans are forgotten. Mrs. General, the woman he had recently decided to marry, no longer exists for him. He loses the power to act for himself, ceases to speak coherently, dozes and awakes by starts, and raves for hours in a final mad fit. Within a very few days Mr. Dorrit is dead.

The most interesting and complex liminal figure in Dickens, however, is neither an image nor a disturbing experience, but a character, the figure who gives her name to the novel in which she appears – Little Dorrit. Amy Dorrit resembles any number of Wordsworth's children.[8] She is as innocent as the child in the "Intimations Ode" and as solitary as Lucy Gray; she possesses as much independence as the girl in "We Are Seven," but, to protect her father, she will even stoop to lying, like Edward in "Anecdote for Fathers"; in crowded city streets, she has reveries of trees and fields, just as does Poor Susan; like Lucy, she is "A Maid whom there were none to praise / And very few to love"; but she is exempt from time, as Lucy only appeared to be: "She seemed a thing that could not feel / The touch of earthly years."

Dickens pronounces Amy Dorrit a "Good Angel!" in one of the running titles that he added in 1864 (see Appendix C, *Little Dorrit* 835). He suggests that she is divinely inspired: "Shall we speak of the inspiration of a poet or a priest, and not of the heart impelled by love and self-devotion to the lowliest work in the lowliest way of life!" (70). He glorifies her with the imagery of the resurrection: "From a radiant centre, over the whole length and breadth of the tranquil firmament, great shoots of light streamed among the early stars, like signs of the blessed later covenant of peace and hope that changed the crown of thorns into a glory" (771). He dresses her in rags, like Wordsworth's Alice Fell, then overwhelms her with riches, like the Princess in Amy's own fairy tale. He introduces her to care and hardship, yet preserves her innocence in every other way. He gives her the body of a child and the heart of a woman. So innocent-appearing that a prostitute mistakes her for a little girl, she is woman enough to love a mature man. "If you loved any one," she explains to her sister, "you would no more be yourself, but you would quite lose and forget yourself in your devotion to him" (572–3). Finally, she devotes herself to her father with an excessive yet pure passion, like the Romantic figure of Père Goriot in reverse. Often she will spend the entire night with her father: "As if she had done him a wrong which her tenderness could hardly repair, she sat by him in his sleep, at times softly kissing him with suspended breath, and calling him in a whisper by some endearing name" (224).

It is not surprising that Amy Dorrit, a complex and contradictory figure, has provoked more debate among critics than any other aspect of the novel. Lionel Trilling speaks of her "untinctured goodness" and calls her "the Beatrice of the *Comedy*, the Paraclete in female form" ("*Little Dorrit*" 57). J. Hillis Miller agrees, comparing her to Dostoyevsky's

Prince Myshkin and speaking of "the mystery of divine goodness incarnate in a human person" (*Charles Dickens* 240, 242–3).[9] Janice Carlisle, on the other hand, points to Amy's many lies, her frequent recourse to "necessary fictions," as implicating her in the real world. Finally, Robert Garis argues that Dickens tries to have matters both ways, that he wants Amy at times to inhabit a pure, spiritual realm, and at other times to dwell in the realm of social and sexual desire (182–5).[10] Even within the novel characters cannot decide how to think of her. In addition to the prostitute, Flora Finching and Arthur Clennam are confused about her status. Arthur, for example, cannot decide whether she inhabits the real, everyday world or some Romantic fairy-tale realm:

> He had come to attach to Little Dorrit an interest so peculiar – an interest that removed her from, while it grew out of, the common and coarse things surrounding her. . . . On the other hand, he reasoned with himself . . . that to make a kind of domesticated fairy of her, on the penalty of isolation at heart from the only people she knew, would be but a weakness of his own fancy, and not a kind one. (252)

In truth, Amy stands between the two realms. She is the end of one and the beginning of the other. It is difficult for us to visualize a human being in such a role, but as a structural component in the literary work her function is clear. She is the gap itself between the two conflicting realms, and she acts as the interface between utterly discontinuous orders. The abstractness of such a definition illustrates the difficulty novelists encounter in trying to write about a liminal character in the context of a modern, realistic novel. Such figures nevertheless play an important role in many structures, both social and literary, for they mediate the difficult passage between different levels of a hierarchy. In Chapter 5 we quoted the anthropologist Victor Turner on the necessary ambiguity, even indeterminacy, of these figures who "elude or slip through the network of classifications" that locates most people within a cultural space. In addition to the characteristics of liminality that we discussed earlier – association with death, structural invisibility, and marginality – other attributes of the condition are even more applicable to Amy Dorrit. Turner writes of liminal figures that "their behavior is normally passive or humble; they must obey their instructors implicitly, and accept arbitrary punishment without complaint" (95); they blend "lowliness and sacredness" (96); they are "submissive," "silent," and have a kind of "anonymity" (102–3); above all, they appear "sexless," as if cut off from the normal process of physical development (102), and they seem to dwell in an altered temporal frame, a "moment in and out of time" (96).

There are numerous advantages to conceiving of Amy Dorrit as a liminal entity. To begin with, it explains her peculiar status as a child-woman, her apparent sexlessness, her humble and submissive attitude toward the demands of others, especially her father, and her sometimes infuriating passivity. Perhaps even more important, it helps to clarify her status as a spiritual being. Amy is a religious figure, right enough, but not of the sort that Trilling, Miller, and others have thought her. She has been much misunderstood as a paragon, a saint, the incarnation of divine goodness. Such an interpretation reduces the human dimension of her character, minimizes the very real, personal costs of the role she is required to play in her world. Her sacredness is not that of a purely spiritual being – the terrible, eternal attributes of divinity – but the transitory holiness that belongs to the *position* she occupies within the social system, the aura of dangerous purity that accompanies any radical moment, state, or figure of transition.

Viewing Amy as a liminal figure can also clarify one of the most troubling problems with the novel's theme. Many readers are perplexed by what Amy is supposed to "mean," what values her character is intended to embody. If she is regarded as a purely "good" figure, then she must be thought of as representing some fundamental truth or reality behind the world of appearances, which authorizes all the meanings of the work. Janice Carlisle, however, has effectively disposed of this reading. Amy, with all her roles, fictions, even lies, is presented by Dickens as no more immune from contingency than the people around her. If we view Amy, however, not as the content of a vision, not as the Truth that Dickens hoped to incarnate in a character, but as its liminal medium, then many of these difficulties disappear. We should not suppose that Dickens is advising his readers to become like Amy Dorrit or even that he is advising the characters in his novel to emulate her submissive and sexless behavior. The whole burden of the famous ending lines of the novel is that Amy herself leaves behind the old role she has been performing. With the death of her father and the cure of Arthur's illness, it is no longer necessary for Amy to occupy the ambiguous and uncomfortable position into which she had been forced. Amy's character should not be reduced to a meaning at all. She does not represent goodness, innocence, duty, or truth.

In this respect, Amy resembles many of Wordsworth's characters who have been misunderstood in a similar manner. The power of "Resolution and Independence," for example, cannot be explained by the "moral" that the poet derives from his encounter with the Leech Gatherer. This simple old man is a figure who provokes vision; he is not the meaning or content of that vision. His importance lies in the transformation he makes possible, the change in the poet that he occasions. His "sacredness," as well, belongs to the state of transition; he is a symbol of the power that changes others. Those readers who accept Wordsworth's moral at face value, thinking that the Leech Gatherer's "lesson" about fortitude in adversity is what makes him powerful, entirely misunderstand how such figures work in visionary literature. Amy, too, possesses a power greater than any of the novel's formulations about her. She represents the threshold to transcendence, not the transcendent vision.

Amy Dorrit's special status as a character is emphasized by an unusual verbal figure. Amy is always associated with the power of a metaphor; its influence, in fact, extends over the entire novel. It is a figure for liminality, one that implies a threshold, a narrow or little gate, even as it names a woman: it is her nickname, "Little Dorrit." The illustration that appeared on the cover of the monthly parts emphasizes the liminal character of this title (it is reprinted as the flyleaf in the new Oxford edition). Amy is portrayed in the act of entering the Marshalsea gates, which are barely open wide enough for her small form to squeeze through, while a last beam of light from the setting sun illuminates her (daily) transition from the huge, open world of the city to the confined space of the prison. Her figure in the gate is set off, framed and given its own space, both by the stone lintel of the door and by the large letters of the novel's title that circle the picture. In case even more imagery of thresholds were needed, the letters of Amy's surname are split apart, like a door half opened, directly before the path that her feet must take. The first three capitals, D-O-R, are held together by the links of a chain, as are the last three, R-I-T, but the bolt barring the gate between the double letters is thrown back.

Her name differs from all the other nicknames in the novel. It does not adequately "represent" her, as even Flora Finching is able to see: "and of all the strangest names I ever heard the strangest, like a place down in the country with a turnpike, or a favorite pony or a puppy or a bird or something from a seed-shop to be put in a garden or a flower-pot and come up speckled" (265).[11] Flora's profusion of similes illustrates the indeterminacy of this figure, its refusal to submit to the definitive, one-for-one correspondence between tenor and vehicle characteristic of so many other names in the novel: Bar, Bishop, Physician, Barnacle, Pet, Tattycoram, Doyce-and-Clennam, the Clever Ones, Mrs. F.'s Aunt, and the Patriarch. By not adequately defining her identity, the figure of her name opens her character to the liminal role it must play. Thus Amy welcomes the nickname, even while recognizing that, like all thresholds, it can bar access to her character as well as serve as an opening for the man she loves. Until Arthur is ready to see beyond the barrier that this diminutive figure presents, her name will be one of the very things that prevents him from appreciating her. But once he is ready to "read" her name properly, the words themselves, "Little Dorrit," will form the best possible entrance to the realm of happiness and spiritual redemption. As

Arthur rises from his illness, near the end of the novel, he tries to tell Amy how much she has come to mean to him, but he does not know how to address her:

> "I have thought of you – " he hesitated what to call her. She perceived it in an instant.
> "You have not spoken to me by my right name yet. You know what my right name always is with you."
> "I have thought of you, Little Dorrit, every day, every hour, every minute, since I have been here." (736)

Dickens's choice of the name "Little Dorrit" as the title for his novel (he rejected the working title "Nobody's Fault") suggests that the greatest liminal figure is in a sense the text of the novel itself. The work as a whole can be viewed as a kind of liminal space, an ambiguous threshold that opens as well as challenges the reader's passage to a vision beyond any of its figures.

THE VANISHING POINT OF NARRATIVE

Why should Dickens find a character such as Amy Dorrit interesting? If her importance lies not in the representation of a particular theme, does she satisfy an identifiable structural need? If so, how does this structural requirement correspond to larger social patterns? To answer these questions, we must enlarge the field of our inquiry, looking not only at the visionary aspects of Dickens's fiction but also at the narrative context within which they appear. Amy's liminal status, it will be discovered, mediates the complex relation between two opposed modes of discourse. In doing so, she serves as the transition between two different ways of organizing experience.

In *Little Dorrit* the theme of connections receives even more emphasis than it does in Wordsworth's poetry. And, once again, the principle of connection is given two diametrically opposed interpretations. John Holloway has noticed the two ways of viewing bonds in the novel, and he has related the motif to a passage in Carlyle's *Sartor Resartus*. Carlyle, like Wordsworth before him, contrasted a harsh, coercive bond with the gentle bond of love: "Wonderous are the bonds that unite us one and all; whether by the soft binding of Love, or the iron chaining of Necessity" (Carlyle, quoted in Holloway 16). As we saw in the prior chapter, these different ways of thinking about bonds could easily be associated with different formal modes. The concept of destiny lends itself to an association with narrative, whereas the bond of love suggests the more elliptical – the unseen, the visionary – affinities of lyric. Dickens, however, values the iron chaining of narrative. His late novels do not turn from an association of connection with "Necessity," because he sees the principle of inevitability (in stories and in life) as a potent force for good.

If the bond of narrative can seem inescapable, this iron chaining has the dual virtues of forcing characters to acknowledge their relationship with one another and to face the consequences of their deeds. Dickens embraces the very aspect of narrative that disturbed Wordsworth, because it teaches that the action of an individual or of a group carries its own destined outcome.

In a letter to his friend John Forster, Dickens reveals that exploring the mystery of "connections" was one of his principal motives for writing *Little Dorrit*: "It struck me that it would be a new thing to show people coming together, in a chance way, as fellow-travellers, and being in the same place, ignorant of one another, as happens in life; and to connect them afterwards, and to make the waiting for that connection a part of the interest" (*Letters* 2:685). The novelist is relying on a fundamental convention of narrative, the expectation that different characters in the same story will have a connection to one another. He regards this feature of narrative as a realistic, not a visionary property, even though the links that draw people together may be hidden for long periods and seem marvelous when they finally emerge. The marvel will be produced by the turns of a plot, whose surprising connections must be rendered probable. The moment of insight will be a narrative moment, not a transcendent vision of a bond that lies beyond all visible forms of connection. The "recognition" will be exactly that, a dramatic scene of discovery that leads to a "reversal" in an intricate yet unbroken chain of events.[12]

In the "Preface to the 1857 Edition" Dickens alerts his readers to the care he has taken to weave the various threads of his book into one seamless narrative: "As it is not unreasonable to suppose that I may have held its various threads with a more continuous attention than any one else can have given to them during its desultory publication, it is not unreasonable to ask that the weaving may be looked at in its completed state, and with the pattern finished" (lix).[13] The first two chapters of the novel contain many details designed to announce the author's intention. The parallel confinement of the prisoners and the travelers, the pointed imagery of the journey and the labyrinth,[14] and the frequent hints made by the narrator and by characters such as Miss Wade, all signal Dickens's ultimate intention. "In our course through life we shall meet the people who are coming to meet *us*, from many strange places and by many strange roads," Miss Wade states, "and what it is set to us to do to them, and what it is set to them to do to us, will all be done" (24).

Miss Wade herself will be responsible for many of these later meetings, as will Rigaud, but the figure whose actions lie behind the most menacing connections in the plot is Mrs. Clennam. Early in the novel, the narrator alerts us to the role this grim woman is to play in the destinies of the other characters. Speaking of the room in which Mrs. Clennam is confined, the narrator echoes the words with which the second chapter ended:

> Strange, if the little sick-room fire were in effect a beacon fire, summoning some one, and that the most unlikely some one in the world, to the spot that *must* be come to. . . . Which of the vast multitude of travellers . . . journeying by land and journeying by sea, coming and going so strangely, to meet and to act and re-act on one another, which of the host may, with no suspicion of the journey's end, be travelling surely hither? (173)

The immediate answer is Rigaud, but most of the characters in the novel are "travelling surely hither" in their own ways; each member of the host is destined "to meet and to act and to re-act" until the appointed event should be watched out. Mrs. Clennam's house is both beginning and end, center and circumference, of all these meetings. Here is Arthur's description of her in her house: "At the heart of it his mother presided, inflexible of face, indomitable of will, firmly holding all the secrets of her own and his father's life, and austerely opposing herself, front to front, to the great final secret of all life" (526).

The figure of Mrs. Clennam presides over a vast network of connections. As a symbol of one kind of order, this woman represents the power of bonds to be inescapable, and ultimately tragic. Arthur is confused about his relation to this mysterious network. His confusion results first in passivity, a desire not to act at all, so as to avoid the responsibility of participating in a story whose beginning antedates his birth and whose crisis he can only fearfully anticipate. Later, his confusion leads him to value a distinctive form of vision, a way of "seeing" that can perhaps best be called spying. Because of his suspicion that some injured party has a claim upon him for reparation, Arthur makes no effort to establish himself in life, but instead watches and waits, searches for a clue to a mystery he is hardly certain exists. His first curiosity about Amy is heightened by the possibility of her being in some way associated with his "predominant idea" (58). The mere chance of such an association leads him to watch her. He follows her to her home, as unobtrusively as an experienced sleuth. But this first bit of detective work is not his last. After accidentally observing Tattycoram in the street, he trails her to a rendezvous with Miss Wade and Rigaud. There he unashamedly eavesdrops on their conversation. Later he follows Rigaud to Mrs. Clennam's house. The important point is that the novel establishes a logical relation between Arthur's mode of vision and the harsher connections of narrative. His curiosity leads him to search out the hidden links between events. He looks for a coherent pattern of cause and effect, for some metonymic principle of explanation, which seems to be the only form of order that he acknowledges. In the end, Arthur's confusion about his place in such a pattern will make him think he is implicated in a network of guilt that stretches far beyond any individual capacity for reparation, a narrative that seems to encompass the largest crimes, the most enduring injustices of his society.

Part of Arthur's problem is that he has an exaggerated respect for the visible, for the kind of connections that can be traced by the bodily eye. While consistently overestimating the clues that come before his senses, he neglects the evidence of his own feelings, first in regard to Pet, then to Amy. In a chapter titled "More Fortune-Telling," Arthur quizzes Amy about her connection to a "secret," the mystery that surrounds his own identity, never guessing the secret of her love for him: "The light of her domestic story made all else dark to him" (374). The light of a certain kind of narrative seems able to occlude the vision of the inner eye. Arthur's tendency to trust only the outward signs of connection comes as a direct consequence of his acceptance of Mrs. Clennam's view of the world. There seems to be an intrinsic relation between his acceptance of this attitude toward connections and a mode of vision that emphasizes the importance of the external and observable. So long as Arthur believes that the only important account of his life is the kind of story ruled over by the figure of Mrs. Clennam, he is doomed to the role of a mere observer, waiting for the visible connections of his life to be revealed.

Arthur's preoccupation with visible connections leads him ultimately to confuse the kinds of action appropriate to the world in which he lives. Near the end of the novel, when he has come to believe that he is somehow responsible for a crime that other people have committed, he makes the wrong form of expiation. He attempts to repay a purely visionary debt – a "fault" over which he could have had no control – with a real physical action. In effect, he takes the Romantic model of compensation literally. He confuses a form of personal consolation with a real, effective means of redressing an earthly ill. The psychic economy in which one state of consciousness serves as recompense for the loss of another was never meant to be a remedy for the actual monetary losses of a multitude of strangers. It takes his level-headed partner, Daniel Doyce, to explain to Arthur that "there was an error in your calcula-tions" (797).

There is an error in Mrs. Clennam's calculations too. She attempts to compensate for a physical act of cruelty by making purely spiritual amends. Because she has condemned another person to a literal prison, she locks herself within the figurative prison of her house. Arthur understands at least this much of his mother's secret: "A swift thought shot into his mind. In that long imprisonment here, and in her long confinement to her room, did his mother find a balance to be struck? I admit that I was accessory to that man's captivity. I have suffered for it

in kind. He has decayed in his prison; I in mine. I have paid the penalty"
(86). But Mrs. Clennam is wrong. Her "payment" in no way compensates the Dorrits for their suffering. She has confused the kind of action
appropriate to the realm in which she lives. Mrs. Clennam's error is just
the reverse of Arthur's; she mistakes the spiritual recompense afforded by
an inward mode of action for the external redress required by her
injustice.

Mrs. Clennam's error is corrected and her wrongs are righted by the
very chain of circumstances that her actions have set in motion. Actual
redress is accomplished by the plot itself. At the climax of the story,
Rigaud and the Flintwinches force Mrs. Clennam into a recognition that
initiates the long-awaited reversal of the characters' fortunes. Robert
Caserio has excellently described the function of such scenes in Dickens's
fiction:

> Dickens usually does not demean reversal to the status of convenience
> because he believes in the power of reversal to focus the particular
> narrative reason and moral of a particular, undisplaced plot, and because
> he wants his readers to feel that the action pointed up by reversal is a
> hazardous, crucial, and "real" development for his readers as well as for
> his story's characters. (67)

Caserio does not discuss the recognition scene in *Little Dorrit*, but his
belief that such scenes are meant by the author to be "real" and important
events certainly holds true for this novel.

One of the ways in which Dickens attempts to insure that the reversal
will have an authentic power, will be a meaningful point in the text
rather than a mere convenience, is by subverting the disruptive potential
of a false liminal figure. Mrs. Clennam had long regarded herself as the
servant and minister of an appointed destiny, the sacred emissary of a
power to punish others for their sins. The symbols of her mission were
the letters "D.N.F.," which stood for "Do not forget." In her unnatural
reading, however, these letters do not form a call to action, a reminder
to make restitution for the suppression of the codicil to the will, but a
divine injunction to do nothing. She thinks that through her inaction she
allows a stern Providence to exact retribution from those who have
sinned. The letters serve, for her, as liminal figures, for they effect a shift
from the realm of human action to the mysterious agency of the Creator.
Notice the religious aura with which she invests the words: "'Do not
forget.' It spoke to me like a voice from an angry cloud. Do not forget
the deadly sin, do not forget the appointed discovery, do not forget the
appointed suffering. . . . I was but a servant and a minister" (753–4).

In the novel's recognition scene, her interpretation of the letters is
revealed as "her old impiety" (754), for in regarding the words as a
divine call to let judgment take its course, she "reversed the order of
Creation, and breathed her own breath into a clay image of her Creator"

(754). To undo her error, to reverse her "reversal," Rigaud undertakes to tell the true "history" behind the letters, and he gives his narrative a proper name, "Shall I name it the history of this house?" (750). Whereas Wordsworth had attempted to avoid the crisis of recognition by substituting a liminal moment, Dickens precipitates a violent recognition scene by disclosing the impiety that lay behind Mrs. Clennam's religious pretensions. Dickens's strategy of inverting the structure of visionary experience is comically underlined by Mrs. Flintwinch's "dreams." This old family retainer has a "genius for dreaming" (750), a "visionary" talent that consists of nothing more than observing *real* incidents and *real* conversations that contain the essential clues to solve the mystery of the entire story.

The exposure of Mrs. Clennam's false religious economy reverses the inequity in her scheme of recompense. Arthur, however, is still caught in his confusion. Even after the fall of Mrs. Clennam's house, he remains in the Marshalsea prison, suffering from his sense of guilt and despair. The recognition scene, then, does not solve his problems. What does this imply about the unity and singleness of the narrative? Caserio has rightly emphasized the importance of the point of recognition in Dickens's sense of plot; it is the crucial moment in the narrative organization of his novels. In *Little Dorrit*, however, there is another system of order, another way of viewing connection, that has very little to do with the primary plot. Carlyle would call this alternative organization the bond of Love. The links of this bond do not really form a part of the iron chain of Mrs. Clennam's story. Hence this other way of viewing connections challenges Arthur's notion that Mrs. Clennam's story is the only way to understand experience. It suggests that the *anagnorisis* and *peripeteia* of her story are not the only important elements organizing the literary work.

The links of this second bond are so delicate as to be almost invisible. It is difficult, in fact, to point to any real evidence of its existence. The reader can only trace its influence in those passages of the text where the rival bond of the narrative does not seem to exercise a complete control over the direction of the work. There is one point, however, where this alternative mode makes an overt appearance in the novel. Significantly, it directly challenges Mrs. Clennam's authority over the text. It comes at the end of the book, while Arthur is still crushed by the course of events. Looking back over the story of his life, he decides that he has mistaken its true meaning, missed the real principle that has organized and directed its course. In his room in the Marshalsea prison, Arthur decides that Little Dorrit, not Mrs. Clennam, has always been at the center of his experience:

> Looking back upon his own poor story, she was its vanishing-point.
> Everything in its perspective led to her innocent figure. He had

travelled thousands of miles towards it; previous unquiet hopes and doubts had worked themselves out before it; it was the centre of the interest of his life; it was the termination of everything that was good and pleasant in it; beyond there was nothing but mere waste, and darkened sky. (714)

This passage contrasts with the earlier image of Mrs. Clennam, the image of her sitting at the heart of a vast web of connections, controlling the destiny of a multitude of unknown, mysterious figures. Both women, Amy and Mrs. Clennam, are described as the terminal point of a lifelong journey. Everything in Arthur's story leads up to them; everything ends in them; they are the center and circumference of his being. But the images of the two women are utterly opposed. Amy and Mrs. Clennam represent completely incompatible versions of Arthur's experience, and by extension, rival ways of viewing the novel as a whole. The work does not move sequentially from one image to the other; rather, the tension between them remains constant. They inhabit entirely discontinuous orders, and a faith in the validity of one image constitutes a rejection of the other. These different perspectives can never come together, just as parallel lines can never intersect. To see one as the only valid way of comprehending the events in Arthur's life is to make the other vanish entirely.

It is possible to view the two figures as emblematic of the contrasting claims of two different modes of literature. This idealized vision of Amy gives her a gentle form of power, a subtle influence, that might be described as lyrical.[15] Her charm is that of a refuge, an escape from the flood tide of events. Arthur's awareness of this charm depends upon his being cut off from the plot, isolated from the course of the action. "None of us clearly know to whom or to what we are indebted," the narrator comments, "until some marked stop in the whirling wheel of life brings the right perception with it" (700). The "unnatural peace" (699) that descends on Arthur after his arrest prompts a kind of retrospective understanding that is distinctly Wordsworthian, even in its reference to the authentic effect of transcendence: "He could think of some passages in his life, almost as if he were removed from them into another state of existence" (699). It has taken this "marked stop" – a lyric pause in the rush of narrative – to bring about such a radical transformation. As in the Romantic poetry we have examined, Arthur's new appreciation of Amy comes not from a development in her character, but from a change in his way of perceiving her: "The same deep, timid earnestness that he had always seen in her, and never without emotion, he saw still. If it had a new meaning that smote him to the heart, the change was in his perception, not in her" (737). The great, renovating virtue that Arthur now is able to find in her small figure is described in phrases that

repeatedly echo lines from Wordsworth's poetry. In the last chapter of
the novel, the sound of Amy Dorrit reading possesses all the power of
Wordsworth's healing, lyrical voice:

> Clennam, listening to the voice as it read to him, heard in it all that great
> Nature was doing, heard in it all the soothing songs she sings to man.
> At no Mother's knee but hers, had he ever dwelt in his youth on hopeful
> promises, on playful fancies, on the harvests of tenderness and humility
> that lie hidden in the early-fostered seeds of the imagination; on the oaks
> of retreat from blighting winds, that have the germs of their strong
> roots in nursery acorns. But, in the tones of the voice that read to him,
> there were memories of an old feeling of such things, and echoes of
> every merciful and loving whisper that had ever stolen to him in his life.
> (790)

The influence of Wordsworth is felt in the reference to Nature's
healing power, its ability to console us for the losses we have suffered;
even more, it is present in an echo of a passage from *The Prelude*, lines
which acknowledge Nature's power in the "seed-time" of youth to
"foster" the imagination. There are, however, parallels of another sort to
be found in this passage. Arthur's mother had denied him all "hopeful
promises" and "playful fancies," but in the tones of Amy's voice, Arthur
finds "memories" and "echoes" of such things. The lyric moment
retrospectively locates its own power in a fictional moment in the past.
The harsh, unloving bonds that had held the events of his life together,
that had given him a character and a story, are now, after the fact,
"seeded" with a talent for love, planted with the feelings that make a
lyrical bond possible. If nothing in the narrative of Arthur's life could
have led up to this moment of transcendence, the visionary power of the
experience will cast its own spell back over the past, will revise that story
in the light of the new vision.

The lyric interlude has been allowed to pass a conscious fiction on the
self. We can understand the effect of this fictionalizing of the past by
comparing its working with the process that Freud called "deferred
action." Freud's term refers to the capacity of a memory-trace to act in
the present in ways that could not have been foreseen at the time the
original memory was formed. Arthur creates an imaginary memory-
trace that is then credited with a "deferred" power, the power that
enables him to respond to the voice of Nature.[16]

It would be a mistake, however, to suppose that this passage is held up
as the final solution to Arthur's long difficulties, that his lyrical "memory" of Nature is proposed as an answer to the guilt and corruption that
Mrs. Clennam's story represents. This imaginary world has its own
drawbacks. First and foremost, it isolates one from the world at large. At
Amy's knees, Arthur inhabits a protected realm; like Frederick Dorrit in

Rome, he appears to be growing younger all the time. Such an infantilized figure can scarcely be thought capable of independent action. Hence we might say that Arthur has lost the very quality that makes character *ethos*; he has become a figure of *pathos* alone. Harold Bloom has remarked that "*ethos* results from the successful translation of the will into an act, verbal or physical, whereas *pathos* ensues when there is a failure to translate will into act" (*Poems of Our Climate* 382). If Dickens had been content to allow Arthur to remain under the sway of such soothing songs, Arthur would have been separated from the ethical scheme of narrative entirely. Amy's refusal to tell him of the codicil works to keep him in this protected realm, but the lovers' final movement down into the bustling streets of London implies that they cannot remain in a sheltered world forever. The ethical demands of life, the demands of a world ordered by causality and fault, must be met. The appeal of Arthur's character must become *ethos* again, not the *pathos* of this single, lyrical moment.

The mode of lyric always appears as the vanishing point of narrative. Dickens recognizes the need for lyric in a world that misuses the structure of narrative, a world that manipulates the very bond that connects us to our deeds to keep us in ignorance of our own lives. A character such as Arthur is so busy trying to discover the plot of his past that he is unable to perceive the meaning of his present. Without a pause in the whirling wheel, he might never have lost his preoccupation with the secret connections, the deceptive relations, that were turning his world upside down. But Dickens also values the stern, ethical commitments of narrative. The novelist will not let his characters remain in the "unnatural peace" of lyric forever. He believes that the claims of narrative, for better or for worse, are the claims of life. Lyric can only be a moment to recoup the forces of the individual self, to recover – or, if necessary, to create – the quality of feeling and the sensitivity of vision needed to continue with the story of one's life.

In the next chapter we shall look at the major English novelist of the nineteenth century who most explicitly acknowledged and explored the legacy of Wordsworth. George Eliot's first novel, *Adam Bede*, treats the problems of narrative and vision that we have been discussing more directly than Dickens ever did. Unlike the latter novelist, she thought in theoretical terms about the problematic relationship between transcendence and narrative. We shall find that her formulations of the problem emphasize both the role of repetition in forging an iron chain of narrative and the importance of a liminal figure in disrupting that chain. But her special consciousness of the issue makes apparent certain aspects of the problem that the texts of other novelists have obscured.

7

ADAM BEDE

"I know you are fond of queer, wizard-like stories. It's a volume of poems, 'Lyrical Ballads:' most of them seem to be twaddling stuff; but the first is in a different style – 'The Ancient Mariner' is the title. I can hardly make head or tail of it as a story, but it's a strange, striking thing." So Arthur Donnithorne prefaces his gift to Mrs. Irwine in George Eliot's *Adam Bede* (1:94). We can be sure that Arthur's casual preference for Coleridge's "queer, wizard-like stories" lowers the dutiful godson in the eyes of George Eliot. After all, the novelist begins *Adam Bede* with an epigraph from Wordsworth, and her essays, letters, and other novels attest to her admiration for what Arthur calls "twaddling stuff." As has been frequently noted, George Eliot's little joke at Arthur's expense records a serious intellectual debt.[1] The novelist's views on nature, language, and memory, as set forth in her essay "The Natural History of German Life" (*Essays* 266–99) and embodied in her fiction, repeatedly echo views Wordsworth expressed in the "Preface to *Lyrical Ballads.*" The story of Hetty's journey in Book 5 of *Adam Bede* closely resembles the tale of Martha Ray in "The Thorn," and the treatment of Dinah's Methodism emphasizes spontaneous emotion fully as much as does Wordsworth's religion of nature.

This familiar case of influence is relevant to our current discussion for two reasons. In theoretical terms, an awareness of George Eliot's interest in the disruptive power of visionary experience can help us to perceive the element of conflict that lies behind – is hidden by – the novel's presentation of spiritual growth as a continuous, natural, and "narratable" process.[2] The conflict of modes in *Adam Bede* is just as urgent as in *Little Dorrit*, but George Eliot is more adept at recuperating this conflict in terms of the *theme* of transcendence. This brings us to the second point. Adam Bede's development of a "larger" sympathy and a more inclusive state of consciousness has distinctly Wordsworthian overtones. But an understanding of the difficult compromises, the complex economic balancing, that is involved in the structure of Wordsworthian compensation should lead us to doubt the adequacy of Adam's final consolation. The long-standing problem of the novel's happy ending (James, *Literary Criticism* 1:921–2; Diekhoff) poses once again a question about the value of transcendence. To understand the balancing of loss and gain in the story of Adam's two loves, we must confront the issue of whether the Wordsworthian structure of transcendence represents a spiritual triumph or a psychological defense.

ADAM'S "HARDNESS"

Adam has a heart of oak. Strong as a beam, straight and true as a fresh-cut board, the best worker in Hayslope is its finest work as well. The simple values of Adam's world stand out in him like a polished grain. He is honest, practical, and diligent; he has raised himself by his own industry and the local night school; he likes the church, respects his betters, and worships his duty. Yet Adam's heart is too hard. Like the strongest center-wood, he is not pliant enough for day-to-day use. His strength has "its correlative hardness" (*Adam Bede* 1:316), his honor its severity. Bartle Massey, Adam's best friend, calls him "over-hasty and proud" (1:367), and Adam himself admits, "When I've said a thing, if it's only to myself, it's hard for me to go back" (1:259). When the novel opens, we find Adam's fellow carpenters working as much on his willfulness as on their doors and windows. "You know Adam will have his way," Seth says. "You may's well try to turn a waggon in a narrow lane" (1:7). Throughout the novel, events sound Adam's heart of oak, testing both its strength and its correlative hardness.

The first crisis strikes with an audible rap. At work one night on a coffin, Adam hears, or thinks he hears, a ghostly willow wand give his door a "strange rap" (1:71). We learn at the end of the chapter what we suspect at the time: Thias Bede has drowned on the way home from a pub. Consequently, we watch Adam, at the very moment of his father's death, recalling the vanished days when Thias could build a wonderful pigeon-house at Broxton parsonage or could give his son "an uncommon notion o' carpentering" (1:68). Then we see Adam thinking of the present and complaining, "Father's a sore cross to me, an's likely to be for many a long year to come" (1:69). Thus by the end of the chapter, Adam's ambivalent response to his father's death comes as no surprise.

Awe and guilt rise in him with equal force. Adam's awe is part of his strength, and George Eliot praises him for being "humble in the region of mystery" (1:70). His guilt, on the other hand, comes from his hardness and responds to Oedipal pressures. Adam has resented his father for standing in the way of his marriage to Hetty. This resentment has occasionally turned to jealousy, though of other men, not of his father. The day after the funeral, Adam finds himself counting the blessings of his father's death: "He could not help saying to himself that the heaviest part of his burden was removed, and that even before the end of another year his circumstances might be brought into a shape that would allow him to think of marrying" (1:315). The title of the chapter, "Home and Its Sorrows," places the entire experience in the context of what Freud would later call the "family romance," as does this powerful comment by the narrator of the novel: "Family likeness has often a deep sadness in it. Nature, that great tragic dramatist, knits us together by bone and muscle, and divides us by the subtler web of our brains; blends yearning and repulsion; and ties us by our heart-strings to the beings that jar us at every movement" (1:55).

Because of Nature, then, that great tragic dramatist, and because of George Eliot's deep understanding of the power of the unconscious,[3] we hear the full resonance of an Oedipal conflict in the sound of rapping that haunts Adam. When the willow wand strikes, the son thinks immediately of his father, but something prevents Adam from acting on the portent: "To Adam, the conception of the future was so inseparable from the painful image of his father, that the fear of any fatal accident to him was excluded by the deeply-infixed fear of his continual degradation" (1:71). The sentence is ruthlessly honest. The thought of his father reduces Adam's fear of his father's death. One painful image blanks out the other, and an equilibrium is established. The violence of Adam's emotional economy is enough to create any number of poltergeists. The strange rap comes like a sudden discharge of energy, a random clap emitted by mental strife.

Uncanny experiences of this sort, according to Freud, occur whenever something revives in us a repressed impulse ("The 'Uncanny'" 157). Adam's resentment of his father had been simmering all night. Working on the coffin his father was supposed to have built seems to have brought that resentment to a boil. It is not farfetched to conclude that the impulse that causes the uncanny rapping is Adam's unacknowledged wish for his father's death. In the past, Adam had often wished to be free of his father. At the age of eighteen, feeling that he could no longer bear the "shame and anguish" (1:68) of his father's drunkenness, Adam had run away from home. Although he came back the next day, he knew the situation would get no better: "So it will go on, worsening and worsening," Adam thought; "there's no slipping up-hill again, and no standing still when once you've begun to slip down" (1:68). The very night of his father's death, Adam had angrily renewed an old threat: "I shall overrun these doings before long. I've stood enough of 'em" (1:57). Our conclusion is further borne out by Adam's first reaction to his father's corpse. Even before sorrow, Adam feels the bitterness of self-reproach:

> This was what the omen meant, then! And the grey-haired father, of whom he had thought with a sort of hardness a few hours ago, as certain to live to be a thorn in his side, was perhaps even then struggling with that watery death! This was the first thought that flashed through Adam's conscience, before he had time to seize the coat and drag out the tall heavy body. (1:74)

Adam regains his peace of mind only by another act of repression. The sense of the uncanny disappears only when Adam is able to banish his harsh feelings toward his father.

The mental balance attained by such means depends upon an element of blindness. Adam's conflicting thoughts, in fact, produce an actual moment of blindness, although of a humorous not a harmful sort. "It's no use staring about to catch sight of a sound," he reflects. "Maybe there's a world about us as we can't see, but th' ear's quicker than the eye, and catches a sound from't now and then" (1:72). This world, trivial as it appears in Adam's commonsensical[4] language, is what Wordsworth calls the "invisible world." In Adam's case, the unusual power arises from a state of mental stress, occasioned by the thought of his father's death. Adam catches intimations of the visionary world now and then, but later, when suffering and death have further softened his heart, he will live in it with a passion. In this early passage, the nearly imperceptible crossing from one level to another – from sight to sound, from a visible workroom to an invisible realm – looks forward to the greater crossing Adam will make from one level of existence to another.[5]

Adam's visionary experience brings him definite, if limited gains. A new, heightened awareness of the composition of his self follows closely on his guilt: "'Ah! I was always too hard,' Adam said to himself. 'It's a sore fault in me as I'm so hot and out o' patience with people when they do wrong, and my heart gets shut up against 'em, so as I can't bring myself to forgive 'em'" (1:303). This passage announces the subject that will be the novel's overt theme. Adam moves from hardness toward sympathy with others. This "sympathy," which is George Eliot's "one poor word" for "all our best insight and our best love" (2:302), will be the result of Adam's spiritual renovation. At the time of his father's death, however, Adam has "only learned the alphabet of it" (1:316), for he has not fully internalized the lesson.[6]

The second crisis in *Adam Bede* comes less abruptly than the first. Adam first learns that Hetty has betrayed him, then that she has murdered her child, and finally that she has been sentenced to hang. When Adam initially hears the tidings of Hetty's fall, he sinks into a numb "semi-idiocy" (2:176), as if he himself had been struck down. On the morning of her trial, he takes her suffering further to himself, internalizing her pain as if it had been his own. Although she is reprieved at the eleventh hour, Adam's experience of "inward suffering" (1:316) remains the same. The pain becomes a permanent presence within him, a part of his character from that day forward. "Let us rather be thankful," the narrator comments, "that our sorrow lives in us as an indestructible force, only changing its form, as forces do, and passing from pain into sympathy" (2:302).

This change takes the psychological form of sublimation.[7] The sorrow lives on, but transformed – purified and exalted. Adam turns his experience of suffering to good account, learning to love the Methodist preacher Dinah with a "higher feeling" (2:365) because of what he has been through with Hetty. His feeling is "higher" in the technical sense of sublimation, for he has redirected an "indestructible force" from its "lower" aim, Hetty, to one that is presented as ethically and spiritually higher, Dinah. The important point about the structure of sublimation is its economic nature – the energy of Adam's sorrow is not lost, but only redistributed. The pain of Hetty's loss becomes a part of Adam's love for Dinah: "Dinah was so bound up with the sad memories of [Adam's] first passion, that he was not forsaking them, but rather giving them a new sacredness by loving her" (2:325). The joys of sublimation, moreover, enable Adam to develop his own personal theory of compensation: "I should never ha' come to know that [Dinah's] love 'ud be the greatest o' blessings to me, if what I counted a blessing hadn't been wrenched and torn away from me, and left me with a greater need, so as I could crave and hunger for a greater and a better comfort" (2:344). The words "so as" are telling. What Providence orders the world so that suffering is given to one for the purpose of allowing one to "crave and hunger" for a better comfort? The psychic balancing of accounts here is stark. Adam's loss becomes his gain. As recompense for the pain that lives on within him, indeed *because* of that pain, he receives the greatest of blessings.

Nevertheless, the original loss remains great. For Adam's consolation, *Hetty* pays with her home, her honor, and her newborn child. This seems a cruel compensation, although we cannot accuse Adam of the cruelty.[8] Hetty's sorrows were of her own and Arthur's making. But many critics do blame George Eliot, objecting to her harsh treatment of Hetty's sexual desires. We need not go into George Eliot's "prudery," as Leavis and Pritchett have done, but we must confront the other question raised by Adam's new love. Can his "higher feeling" really be an adequate recompense for so much suffering? As we have seen, this question rephrases crucial Romantic issues: Does knowledge repay one for lost power? Does consciousness suffice in place of a diminished external world? George Eliot herself views the issue in almost exactly these terms. Adam's love for Hetty springs unbidden and free, like a natural growth of the rich Loamshire soil; and the feeling that replaces it is a sadder but a wiser love,[9] for as Adam says, "feeling's a sort o' knowledge," and "the more we know of it the better we can feel what other people's lives are or might be" (2:336).

In psychological terms, Adam's mature act of sublimation undoubtedly represents an effective means of adapting to the cruel accidents of his life. Thematically, as well, the novel presents Adam's second love as a decided triumph. George Eliot writes, "Tender and deep as his love for Hetty had been . . . his love for Dinah was better and more precious to him; for it was the outgrowth of that fuller life which had come to him from his acquaintance with deep sorrow" (2:365). But countless readers have been dissatisfied with the happy ending of *Adam Bede*. When we look at the formal difficulty of the novel's conclusion, we realize that Adam's "higher feeling" has problems that the psychological model of sublimation and the theme of spiritual growth conceal.

Adam's higher feeling is a radical departure from his first love. The gap between them is absolute. To express the degree of difference, George Eliot turns to the vocabulary of transcendence. Through his suffering, Adam undergoes "a baptism, a regeneration, the initiation into a new state" (2:209). Adam is born again, brought to life on a new plane of existence, so that he looks "back on all the previous years as if they had been a dim sleepy existence, and he had only now awaked to full consciousness" (2:209). Adam moves from "hardness" to a state of "enlarged being" (2:365). It is as if his character has acquired an entirely new dimension. As the narrator explains, "The growth of higher feeling within us is like the growth of faculty, bringing with it a sense of added strength" (2:365). Yet the structure of narrative and the psychological model of sublimation both imply that a character's life is one uninterrupted whole. Hence George Eliot is forced to confront directly the formal problem that we have considered throughout this study. All that is "higher" in Adam's feeling depends upon the structure of transcendence, a structure that threatens the unity of character and continuity of events indispensable to the narrative component of her novel.

THE HARDNESS OF NARRATIVE

The dilemma of Adam's character offers a way to approach the troubling fissure in the novel's story. Just as Adam's strength has "its correlative hardness" (1:316), so some of the best aspects of George Eliot's story unavoidably create what we might call a narrative "hardness." Like Adam in his early pride, events seem to know where they are heading and to have little sympathy for the weakness of characters. "Consequences are unpitying," George Eliot tells us through the good Mr. Irwine. Just as Adam has trouble going back when once he has "said a thing," so there is no turning back from an event in *Adam Bede*. The story charts an inexorable, even deterministic course. "It's well we should feel as life's a reckoning we can't make twice over," Adam says; "there's no real making amends in this world, any more nor you can mend a wrong subtraction by doing your addition right" (1:304).

George Eliot's Law of Consequences, as it has come to be known, contains an implicit law of narrative "hardness": "Consequences are unpitying. Our deeds carry their terrible consequences, quite apart from any fluctuations that went before – consequences that are hardly ever confined to ourselves" (1:258). According to this law, events have a power of their own, actions work themselves out with an energy independent of human will. One deed leads to another, one action creates the next, forging a chain of "consequences" that has a terrible, unpitying strength.[10] Within such bonds, character becomes an agent of the action, and the "fluctuations" of consciousness, though of vital importance both to the individual and to the theme, have little effect on the story's brute facts.

Arthur, to fix on a single example, faces but one real decision in the novel – whether or not to seduce Hetty – and by and by he finds himself seduced into the seduction. This much of the story flows from his character and takes its moral from the useless flailing of his spirit. But the consequences of his act do not proceed from what he thinks of as his identity. He never meant to inflict shame, imprisonment, and exile on Hetty, yet these are the results of his single act. Despite the first principle of his being – that "I always take care the load shall fall on my own shoulders" (1:184) – the weight of consequences crushes another. Furthermore, events trap Arthur himself, forcing him to lie to Adam, although it goes against his self-conception: "His deed was reacting upon him – was already governing him tyrannously, and forcing him into a course that jarred with his habitual feelings" (2:26).

For an action to govern an individual, forcing him one way or another against his will, suggests a threatening aspect of narrative itself. The progress of narrative can possess a stubborn, autonomous power, a movement that lies, to a certain extent, beyond the control of character or theme. "Our deeds determine us, as much as we determine our deeds," George Eliot says. "There is a terrible coercion in our deeds which may first turn the honest man into a deceiver, and then reconcile him to the change" (2:37). Furthermore, the story's theme has no sure way of controlling events. The author can stoop to truth and moralize her tale, but books such as Gregor's *The Moral and the Story*, with its opening criticism of *Adam Bede*, show that George Eliot's theme does not always suit her tale.

The novelist recognizes this "hardness" in events, and she gives it a fitting name, "Nemesis." As her borrowed word reminds us, the belief that there is a "terrible coercion in our deeds" is neither unusual nor new. The Greek tragedians called this power "fate," and more than one critic has viewed George Eliot's novel as a tragedy in the Greek manner (Hardy, *Novels of George Eliot* 32–46). Other critics, preferring a more philosophical account of this "hardness," call attention to George Eliot's "determinism" (Levine, "Determinism and Responsibility"; Bonaparte, *Will and Destiny* 24–6). When Alfred North Whitehead compares the Greek conception of fate with the scientific world view, he gives us one of the best descriptions of this power's effect: "Their vision of fate, remorseless and indifferent, urging a tragic incident to its inevitable issue, is the vision possessed by science. Fate in Greek tragedy becomes the order of nature in modern thought" (15). Thomas Hardy carried his belief in the "hardness" of events so far that he personified it in *Tess of the d'Urbervilles*, a novel partially modeled on *Adam Bede*; and Hardy's "President of the Immortals" scarcely sports more cruelly with Tess than George Eliot's Law of Consequences does with Hetty. But by listing these analogues we have only described the phenomenon, not explained it. How can narrative have an autonomous power? How can deeds err, in the double sense of wander and go wrong? What is the "hardness" in events, so variously denominated determinism, Nemesis, and fate?

George Eliot hints at an answer to these questions when she says of Arthur that a "deed was reacting upon him." Once an act begins to re-act, then action itself has become a protagonist – the story has taken on a "life" of its own. The "hardness" of narrative is nothing other than the stubbornness of being, the pressure to exist; and a story "lives" only so long as it gives us one thing after another. The movement of narrative is its life. But movement alone – the mere flow of events – constitutes the most primitive of life forms. As E. M. Forster puts it, narrative "is the lowest and simplest of literary organisms" (27–8). Its ongoing pulse creates a life of accretion, not essence; of quantity, not quality. Each moment is finally subsumed in momentum. "Our deeds carry their terrible consequences," George Eliot says. No act is ever complete in itself, no deed stands free and pure, cleansed of successiveness. Rather, each becomes the agent of another. In every act, there is something extra, something unintended by the actor, which the deed itself must "carry" like a burden. This unintended weight is the burden of causality. On our shoulders, such a weight would be a terrible responsibility; and, instinctively, we want it to trouble events too. Thus we resurrect ancient goddesses and malignant fates – we humanize the course of action. But Whitehead was right: action is "remorseless and indifferent." It carries but does not feel the awful burden. "Consequences are unpitying," as Adam learns. The power of sympathy belongs only to those who can suffer.

George Eliot's task in *Adam Bede* is to raise a "hard" or unsympathetic narrative into a vehicle for visionary sympathy. This elevation would reenact structurally Adam's rise from "hardness" to "enlarged being." It would constitute an enlargement or opening of the narrative order, an undoing of the hard bond between deed and consequence. We might call this new sort of story a humanized or sympathetic narrative. But would it be the same kind of narrative that governs the rest of the novel? Just as Adam has to be split in two almost in order to be transformed, so the chain of consequences must be broken in order to be humanized. The final book of George Eliot's novel proceeds by meditative stages rather than by cause and effect, strives for "full consciousness" (2:209) and self-knowledge rather than for a dramatic presentation of *ethos* through action. The closest parallel to this project is to be found in Wordsworth's *Lyrical Ballads*, where the conflicting claims of consciousness and nature find their correlative in the conflict between lyric and narrative modes. In the poet's attempt to let feeling give "importance to the action and situation, and not the action and situation to the feeling" (*Prose* 1:129), we can observe a subtle loosening of the hard bond of consequences in the service of a higher bond – that of human feeling. Ultimately Wordsworth's movement from nature to consciousness provides the model for George Eliot's similar movement from narrative "hardness" to a humanized or sympathetic form. The result, in *Adam Bede*, is a "higher" mode to complement Adam's "higher feeling" for Dinah.

We can isolate a place where the text of *Adam Bede* shifts modes in a surprising paragraph midway through the novel. In one of those great, unexplained influxes of emotion, which strike the reader as half accident, half genius, the author interrupts her story to speak of "an image of great agony" that she has seen in Europe, the cross. This image, erected by the roadside, disrupts the harmony of nature, much as George Eliot's digression disrupts the course of her story:

> . . . surely, if there came a traveller to this world who knew nothing of the story of man's life upon it, this image of agony would seem to him strangely out of place in the midst of this joyous nature. He would not know that hidden behind the apple-blossoms, or among the golden corn, or under the shrouding boughs of the wood, there might be a human heart beating heavily with anguish; perhaps a young blooming girl, not knowing where to turn for refuge from swift-advancing shame; understanding no more of this life of ours than a foolish lost lamb wandering farther and farther in the nightfall on the lonely heath; yet tasting the bitterest of life's bitterness. (2:112)

The passage has never been adequately explained. Although the "human heart beating heavily with anguish" obviously refers to Hetty, who is even now secretly with child, this fact does not account for the uniquely

symbolic mode of the digression. Nowhere else in the novel does the
story rise to this kind of intensity. In this short passage, the narrative
almost seems to internalize Hetty's anguish, take her pain into itself
through the symbol of the cross, much as Adam internalizes Hetty's
suffering. Like Adam, the story performs an act of sublimation, raising
the agony of a poor girl who understands "no more of this life of ours
than a foolish lost lamb" into the suffering of one who understands all,
Christ the Lamb. Christ's cross, so unexpectedly recalled by George
Eliot, is perhaps our culture's ultimate symbol of the act that we have
been calling, in different contexts, transcendence, sublimation, or compensation. It affirms that a single man attempted to take within himself
the sins and suffering of an entire world and raise them on high. George
Eliot's sudden memory attempts a similar miracle in miniature. Her
discourse opens itself to "an image of agony" greater than any of the
images animating the narrative alone. The novel takes on an "inward
suffering," which cannot be contained within the single line of consequences that the story traces. Like Adam, the discourse transcends itself,
crossing from one mode of existence to another.

THE VISIONARY POWER

> I know there's a deal in a man's inward life as you can't measure by the
> square, and say, "Do this and that'll follow," and, "Do that and this'll
> follow." There's things go on in the soul, and times when feelings come
> into you like a rushing mighty wind, as the Scripture says, and part
> your life in two a'most, so as you look back on yourself as if you was
> somebody else. (1:274)

For all its commonsensical language, Adam's speech represents one of
the most sophisticated accounts of transcendence that we have seen.
Feelings can come into one's soul, like the rushing mighty wind of the
pentecostal vision quoted in the Introduction, and "part your life in two
a'most." That part of one's inward life which cannot be measured by the
square creates a gap in the continuity of character, and by extension, in
the continuity of the story of one's life. After such an experience, the
whole question of what will "follow" becomes problematic. A character
can no longer count on traditional notions of causality that teach that if
one does this, that'll follow. Hence one looks back on the events of the
past and on one's old sense of self, "as if you was somebody else."
Adam's words capture all the violence of this change. More than
anything else, it is the discontinuity, the sense that his life has been split
into two parts, that reveals the power of an experience that he cannot
explain. "You can't make much out wi' talking about it," he continues,
"but you feel it" (1:274).

As we have seen, the visionary power makes its presence known to Wordsworth by a similar break in the continuity of his experience. The gap that the visionary power introduces in the story of one's life creates the need for a different mode of conceiving one's experience. Hence this power is important not for what it is, but for what it assists in coming to being. Wordsworth himself thinks of it as an attendant power (see P.5.595–7). It does not cause the shift to a new mode (of consciousness, of discourse) so much as attend at the transition. There is an attendant power in *Adam Bede* as well. Dinah Morris is almost always present at moments of spiritual crisis. (Her one absence, during Hetty's travail, is presented as a cruel trick of fate.) When sorrow has interrupted the course of daily life, Dinah helps restore a new order. "You're one as is allays welcome in trouble" (1:138), Dinah's aunt tells her, and for once Mrs. Poyser speaks for everyone in the novel.[11] Dinah attends Lisbeth Bede when her husband dies, the Methodist preacher at Hetton-Deeps, and many others; Dinah accompanies Hetty all the way to the gallows; Dinah is present at the Methodist meeting on the Hayslope green, making public witness there; and Dinah listens to the promptings of the Lord's "rushing mighty wind." Like the visionary power, Dinah helps illumine an invisible world. On the green, her preaching makes the villagers see Jesus in the flesh: "For Dinah had that belief in visible manifestations of Jesus, which is common among the Methodists, and she communicated it irresistibly to her hearers" (1:40). In moments of physical blindness, Dinah seems to see into the life of things: "[Dinah] closed her eyes, that she might feel more intensely the presence of a Love and Sympathy deeper and more tender than was breathed from the earth and sky" (1:235). In the character of Dinah, George Eliot attempts to represent the visionary power.

On the surface, such an attempt does not seem too difficult. As Richard Brantley has shown, many of Wordsworth's most cherished beliefs find an echo in Methodism.[12] Wordsworth's trust in the "spontaneous overflow of powerful feelings" anticipates Dinah's method of preaching: "[Dinah] was not preaching as she heard others preach, but speaking directly from her own emotions, and under the inspiration of her own simple faith" (1:37). Just as Wordsworth thinks the poet is "affected more than other men by absent things as if they were present" (*Prose* 1:138), so Dinah's faith gives her visions of her distant friends: "It's a strange thing – sometimes when I'm quite alone, sitting in my room with my eyes closed," she tells Hetty, "the people I've seen and known . . . are brought before me, and I hear their voices and see them look and move almost plainer than I ever did when they were really with me so as I could touch them" (1:211). Just as Wordsworth thinks the poet has a special sensibility to communicate to others, so Dinah's religion gives her a special awareness of the Lord: "I know what this great blessedness is," she says to the villagers on the green; "and because I know it, I want you to have it too" (1:43). Just as Wordsworth looks forward to the birth of a new age, so Dinah sees a time when "heaven is begun upon earth, because no cloud passes between the soul and God" (1:43). And just as Wordsworth's memory gives him a renovating link with culture, with the past, and with an infinite presence in nature, so Dinah and her fellow Methodists find a similar link in God: "A crowd of rough men and weary-hearted women drank in a faith which was a rudimentary culture, which linked their thoughts with the past, lifted their imagination above the sordid details of their own narrow lives, and suffused their souls with the sense of a pitying, loving, infinite Presence, sweet as summer to the houseless needy" (1:52).

But what happens to a character when it is used to embody a concept such as the visionary power? For one thing, Dinah becomes as indeterminate as Wordsworth's fleeting power. We have tremendous difficulty determining Dinah's status in the narrative. She is scarcely an agent of the action, although she "attends" many of its major events. In her greatest scene, the moment in the prison when she persuades Hetty to confess, Dinah does not cause Hetty's criminal conviction, the way Jeanie Deans causes Effie's conviction in *The Heart of Midlothian*. Dinah merely assists at a revelation that has no narrative consequences at all. If Hetty had been executed, her confession might at least have had the effect of saving her soul, but even that consequence is negated by Hetty's last-minute pardon.[13] More profoundly, Dinah's embodiment of the visionary power renders problematic the very concept of character. Dinah becomes not only a character in the represented world of the narrative but also the ghostly messenger from another, unrepresentable realm.[14] She is described as looking "almost like a lovely corpse into which the soul has returned charged with sublimer secrets and a sublimer love" (1:238). Lisbeth Bede comes closer than anyone in the novel to defining the special nature of Dinah's character: "Ye comed in so light, like the shadow on the wall, an' spoke i' my ear, as I thought ye might be a sperrit" (1:162). Later, Lisbeth tries to dispel her qualms about Dinah, simply by changing "ghost" to "angel": "I could be fast sure that pictur was drawed for her i' thy new Bible – th' angel a-sittin' on the big stone by the grave" (1:208). Even as an angel, however, Dinah is an attendant at the place where a disruption has occurred. The angel in the picture is guarding the tomb of Christ. The resurrection of Jesus interrupts the continuity of the natural world more violently than any other event in Christian history. As either angel or "sperrit," Dinah marks the place where the visible world ends.[15]

By now it must have become apparent that Dinah represents another example of a liminal figure. Her indeterminate status in the text results from her participation in both the narrative order and the "higher" mode of organization. By standing between these orders, she aids the other characters in the novel in making the difficult crossing. She brings to Adam, Hetty, and others not merely a moral but also a spiritual "rescue."[16] Like the visionary power, she comes between unthinking acts and their cruel consequences. For many readers, this intervention spoils the novel. Yet Dinah's position in the work has rarely been considered in the correct context.[17] She attends those places where the narrative breaks down, but her presence heralds the advent of a "higher" order.

HETTY, MARTHA RAY, AND THE UNCANNY

Before we discuss this "higher" order, we need to amplify our theory of repetition and narrative. The story of Hetty's suffering interrupts Adam's narrative. For two chapters we lose sight of Adam completely. During the course of this moving interruption, Hetty's story goes through a shift in levels as well. Yet everything concerning Hetty's case is more extreme. No set of consequences is as "hard" as the series of events that reduces Hetty to what Dorothy Van Ghent has described as "the chaos of animal fear, which, in the human being, is insanity" (179). In Chapters 36 and 37, which tell of Hetty's doomed attempt to find Arthur, events dominate her character so completely that they seem to eliminate all trace of human will. At the very climax of this sequence, however, the narrative of Hetty's suffering is itself interrupted. For seven long chapters the story is not resumed – not until Hetty's confession in the prison purges her animal fear, humanizing her once again. When Hetty opens her soul to Dinah, she concludes the story of her suffering on a "higher" level. Perhaps because of the resemblance between Hetty's story and Wordsworth's "The Thorn," the movement from the stern bond of consequences to the higher bond of human feeling is particularly visible.

Hetty's story is every bit as uncanny as the dark tale of Martha Ray. The two chapters – "Journey in Hope" and "Journey in Despair" – chart a circular course, whose bitter repetitions are only hinted at in their titles. The first chapter begins, "A long, lonely journey, with sadness in the heart; away from the familiar to the strange" (2:121). By the end of the second chapter, when Hetty has returned to each place that she visited before, going five days out of her way to Stratford-on-Avon simply because she had made the same mistake on the journey out, the strange will have become familiar through the tyranny of repetition. As we remember from Chapter 5, repetition or the involuntary return to a single spot is an identifying characteristic of the uncanny. The terrible repetition in Hetty's story reaches a climax when Hetty comes upon a hidden pool – the pool where she hopes to drown herself. She has never seen this pool before, yet it is familiar to her nonetheless. It is the uncanny repetition of another, the double of the pool in the Scantlands where she first dreamed of death. Dark, wintry waters hold some power over Hetty; she can picture no other way to die. Perhaps the low, dark pool evokes some memory within her, the memory of a birth that *her* child would not have. Whatever the fascination, it is the repetition of her journey back, not choice, that has brought Hetty to the edge of the water: "It was as if the thing were come in spite of herself, instead of being the object of her search" (2:146). The chapter ends with Hetty's escape from this fateful place but with no resolution of her dilemma. Under the guise of increasing the suspense, the narrative shifts away from the young woman, and we do not see Hetty again until her trial.

As we saw earlier, repetition holds the key to "The Thorn" as well. The tale of Martha Ray is dominated by a haunted ground, and the thorn that marks this fated spot stands beside a low, dark pool. We explained the unsettling power of Martha Ray's story by reference to Freud's concept of the "repetition-compulsion." This concept helped to explain what Wordsworth distrusts in the mode of narrative. But the idea that repetition plays a major role in stories seems to conflict with George Eliot's Law of Consequences, which dictates that one event leads inexorably to the next. Let us try adding the notion of repetition to what we have learned about narrative in this chapter. The "hardness" of narrative is its pressure to exist, the stubbornness of being. In "The Thorn," the narrator's endless repetitions exclude everything but his own obsession. The unnamed questioner in the poem can get no answers to the questions that interest both him and us. Narrative's usual burden of successiveness seems to have been displaced into a desire for success – the desire, that is, for the narrator's own obsession to triumph over all else. This is a retrograde movement, one that runs counter to the forward momentum of narrative, and even to the linear presentation of language itself. As Saussure puts it, words "are presented in succession; they form a chain" (70). Repetition, then, represents a conservative impulse, a turning back that seems contrary to the forward thrust of language as well as of narrative.

The fact that stories move forward, however, actually works in concert with the conservative effect of repetition. The movement of events can only lead to one end, the conclusion of the story itself. The aim of narrative, in a sense, is to reach a point where no further narrative is needed, where the tale is told, the story done. To the extent that narrative has the kind of independent "life" that we talked about in the Introduction, the aim of that life is "death." The author may have his or her own goals in writing; the novelist might yearn to prove a thesis or point a moral; but the narrative, qua narrative, can have only one aim, to reach its proper end. Freud's comments on the conflict between the life- and death-instincts might be helpful here. Both forces tend toward the same goal, according to Freud, but the latter strives to reach the final destination as quickly as possible while the former struggles to "prolong the journey" (*Beyond the Pleasure Principle* 35). Freud's conclusions about the function of the life-instincts are suggestive when applied to the "life" of narrative. Their chief purposes, he maintains, are "to assure that the organism shall follow its own path to death, and to ward off any possible ways of returning to inorganic existence other than those which are immanent in the organism itself" (33). As we well know, every story seeks to follow its own path to the end, to reach only that conclusion which is immanent in the narrative itself.

The compulsion to repeat, in narrative as in life, is ordinarily repressed, but it never ceases to strive toward satisfaction. The presence of such a force, however deeply buried in the text, is responsible for our ability to have expectations about a story and for our pleasure in the satisfaction of those expectations. We are able to anticipate developments only because we can discern a common pattern in events, an element that is repeated from one action to the next. This is a conservative pleasure, one that enjoys maintaining its own conception of the status quo, one that luxuriates in recurrence and continuity. Yet no story should be completely predictable. A good narrative must lead equally to surprise. Thus there is in narrative a "vacillating rhythm" (Freud's term) between the conservative pleasure of repetition and the adventurous hope that sequence will lead to discovery.

In *Adam Bede* the allure of repetition is deeply intertwined with the interest of the story's forward progress. In its benign form, this conservative presence enhances the sense of continuity we feel in George Eliot's fictional world: the steady repetition of days, the inevitable recurrence of seasons, the unchanging embrace of the community, within which even extraordinary disasters do no more than briefly disturb the diurnal round. In its darker manifestations this presence – like Freud's concept of the death-instinct – adds to our sense of a cruel "Nemesis" in the story, our feeling of something "remorseless and indifferent" in the very order of things, our awareness of a power bearing us downward, beyond pleasure, to an appointed end.

If repetition can have a benign as well as a sinister effect on narrative, what is it that makes some stories seem more uncanny than others? Wordsworth's ambivalence toward narrative, we recall, is most pronounced whenever the element of repetition in the mode is associated with certain topics – birth and death, or more especially, death at the moment of birth. Observe, for example, the poet's account of the crucial event in the story of Martha Ray:

> ["]For what became of this poor child
> No mortal ever knew;

Nay – if a child to her was born
No earthly tongue could ever tell;
And if 'twas born alive or dead,
Far less could this with proof be said.["]

(*Poetical Works* 2:245–6,lines 146–51)

The care these lines take to conceal the most important episode in Martha
Ray's life is remarkable. No mortal will ever know, no earthly tongue
will ever tell, no final proof will ever be found – the pressure to hide
something infects the Captain's tone with a near hysteria. This passage
brings to mind Schelling's definition of the uncanny, a definition Freud
quotes in italics: " '*Uncanny' is the name for everything that ought to have
remained . . . hidden and secret and has become visible*" (129, Freud's ellipsis).

In George Eliot's novel, the uncanniness of Hetty's story comes from
a similar desire to keep something hidden and secret. Hetty strives, up
until the very moment of her confession, to conceal that she ever gave
birth to a child. She does not bother to deny that she has killed her baby,
even though that is the crime for which she is being tried, but she seems
driven by a desire to hide her child's birth. The peculiar horror of Hetty's
crime – for the narrator as well as for Hetty – does not lie in the act of
murder. Rather, it comes from the crime's strange yoking of death and
birth. The "*unheimlich*," Freud tells us, unites the "unhomely" or strange
with the homely or familiar. The knowledge that life leads to death
seems homely enough, but such knowledge can become uncanny when
we find death in the very "home" of life, its birth.

Perhaps now we can understand why George Eliot interrupts Hetty's
story where she does. If we return to the end of "Journey in Despair," we
find that the author splits open the narrative at the very place where life
and death meet. When Hetty stands beside the dark pool, two forces
come into conflict within her: "She felt a strange contradictory wretchedness and exultation: wretchedness, that she did not dare to face death;
exultation, that she was still in life" (2:148). At the moment when this
conflict is most intense, the author intervenes. The exultation of a
movement forward into life, the wretchedness of a return to death are
split asunder. Moreover, it is the entire narrative – not just Hetty – that
has reached this uncanny point. For Wordsworth, such an uncanniness in
events immediately calls forth the visionary power. In fact, we have
defined Wordsworth's lyricism as the visionary disruption of narrative.
"The Thorn" is lyrical precisely because it continually resists the hard
"life" of narrative, a ballad because it is yet haunted by the ghost of that
life.

For George Eliot, too, the disruption of Hetty's story is a decisive
gesture of a visionary power – what the novelist calls "sympathy." The
narrator moves beyond Hetty's "pigeon-like stateliness" (1:230) to find

in her the "deep pathos" and "sublime mysteries" of human nature (1:277). By extending her sympathy to Hetty, the author extends her own self. This moving expansion of selfhood is a true act of transcendence – George Eliot rises above the limits of her old sympathy. The ultimate issue of the author's new sympathy for Hetty is the passage on the "agony of the Cross" that we have already examined. But in the current context George Eliot's sympathy produces the "saving" interruption of Hetty's story. Sympathy comes between the hard bond of consequences, splitting the story in two. The author turns her attention from the unpitying events of the narrative and addresses a question to an aspect of herself – to the sympathetic faculty that Wordsworth would call her "conscious soul":

> What will be the end? – the end of [Hetty's] objectless wandering, apart from all love, caring for human beings only through her pride, clinging to life only as the hunted wounded brute clings to it?
>   God preserve you and me from being the beginners of such misery! (2:153)

In the prison, seven chapters later, Hetty's story is resumed, but on a different level or in another mode. Repentance and salvation lie at the heart of this scene, not the fate of her child. The confession in the prison formed the genesis of George Eliot's novel. In her journals the author describes how her aunt, a Methodist preacher, "had visited a condemned criminal – a very ignorant girl, who had murdered her child and refused to confess; how she had stayed with her praying through the night, and how the poor creature at last broke out into tears and confessed her crime" (George Eliot, *Life* 2:48). Everything in the novel – Hayslope and Snowfield, Adam and Arthur, Mr. Irwine and the Poysers – grew from this single incident. Initially, George Eliot meant to end her novel here. Had she done so, Hetty's escape from the gallows would have constituted the novel's only real "rescue" – a mundane intervention indeed, closer to a trick ending than an exploration of the power of sympathy. Had George Eliot kept her original ending, her act of sympathy would have remained part of the safe, public sentimentality that we associate with the worst aspects of Victorianism, rather than going on to become the private, intensely spiritual virtue that we associate with the best aspects of Romanticism. But George Eliot proceeds to the last book of *Adam Bede*, uncovering a visionary power in her sympathy and altering the mode of her art.

THE "HIGHER" MODE

Earlier we saw how George Eliot's vision of the cross could briefly enlarge the narrative order, opening the story of Hetty's anguish to an image of agony greater than the narrative's own. By shifting modes, the

text succeeded, for one short moment, in humanizing the course of
events, in granting consequences the kind of "full consciousness" that
such a "remorseless and indifferent" force clearly does not possess. In
Book 6 we encounter an entire set of events that seems to have acquired
a humanized or sympathetic character. Adam's recovery, the growth of
his second love, Seth's selfless renunciation of Dinah, and Adam's union
with this "sperrit" or "angel" reveal a sympathy in the ordering of events
that George Eliot's iron Law of Consequences could not have led us to
expect. The unpitying rule of Nemesis seems to have been replaced by
the benevolent guidance of a "higher" principle.

We use the word "higher" in the technical sense derived from the
concept of sublimation, but George Eliot herself would probably have
felt that the evaluative connotation was appropriate. Just as she believes
that the "transformation of pain into sympathy" gives us "all our best
insight and our best love" (2:302), so she seems to think that the
transformation of a story of pain and suffering into the lyrical consola-
tions of feeling may be the highest end of art. The series of redemptive
acts that conclude the novel flow from a synthesizing, almost dialectical
process that is inherent in George Eliot's concept of sympathy,[18] rather
than from the linear conception of narrative that the first five books
establish as the norm. The inexorable form of causality that we witnessed
in Hetty's story has disappeared. In place of the uncanny energy that
seemed to have taken over her life, we find a new, entirely different
power: Adam "did not know that the power of loving was all the while
gaining new force within him; that the new sensibilities bought by a deep
experience were so many new fibres by which it was possible, nay,
necessary to him, that his nature should intertwine with another"
(2:303).

It is this new "power of loving" that moves the story forward now, a
Romantic principle that makes it "possible, nay, necessary" that his
nature should intertwine with another.[19] This is far removed indeed from
the kind of narrative "necessity" that we have been examining. The
"new fibres" of Adam's sensibility are trusted to tie events together now
that the old bond of consequences has been broken.

It might be objected that "sensibility" cannot order the course of
events in the real world. Such an objection rarely arises about a work in
the lyric mode, but novels, particularly realistic novels, generally rely on
the mode of narrative for their governing structure. George Eliot seems
to feel the force of such an objection, for she makes a number of attempts
to justify the different direction her work is taking. Here is one:

> It would be a poor result of all our anguish and our wrestling, if we won
> nothing but our old selves at the end of it – if we could return to the
> same blind loves. [But] it is at such periods that the sense of our lives

having visible and invisible relations beyond any of which either our present or prospective self is the centre, grows like a muscle that we are obliged to lean on and exert. (2:302)

Note George Eliot's version of the theme of the two kinds of connection that we saw earlier in Dickens: The "visible and invisible relations" Adam perceives are the kinds of connections that come from an "enlarged" sympathy. Adam's sensibility grows until he is *obliged* to exert it. The very existence of his new faculties requires their use. The way in which Adam "exerts" them is by responding to and participating in an altered vision of reality. We spoke earlier of a principle of compensation in Adam's love for Dinah. Adam's awareness of this principle is precisely the sense of invisible relations that he is now obliged to act upon. His new consciousness both enables him to perceive the "higher" necessity of a compensatory pattern and urges him to participate in it.

In truth, George Eliot is not able to demonstrate that a such a Romantic principle can order events with the rigor, the convincing realism, of a narrative of consequences. So instead she concentrates on defending the value of compensation itself. In support of Adam's second love, George Eliot composes an eloquent tribute to the value of all secondary experience, arguing even for its *superiority* to many primary or original modes of consciousness. She describes Adam as so filled with his love for Dinah that he can see nothing around him; his eyes are blind to brook, willows, fields, and sky:

> Again and again [Adam's] vision was interrupted by wonder at the strength of his own feeling, at the strength and sweetness of this new love – almost like the wonder a man feels at the added power he finds in himself for an art which he had laid aside for a space. How is it that the poets have said so many fine things about our first love, so few about our later love? Are their first poems their best? or are not those the best which come from their fuller thought, their larger experience, their deeper-rooted affections? The boy's flute-like voice has its own spring charm; but the man should yield a richer, deeper music. (2:326)

George Eliot's defense of "later love" amounts to a defense of the higher mode of the final book of her novel. This mode exalts a wider sympathy, a sophisticated philosophy of compensation, and a compelling role for the visionary aspirations of men and women – all laudable goals from one perspective, but to a carpenter whose chief ambition has been to leave behind him "a good solid bit o' work" (2:298), they might seem to have little practical advantage. When we read that the "growth of higher feeling within us is like the growth of faculty, bringing with it a sense of added strength" (2:365), we cannot help suspecting that George Eliot is thinking of herself more than of Adam. If so, then the real source of compensation is nothing other than the author's "growth of faculty." But George Eliot, unlike Wordsworth, cannot make her own "intellectual power, from stage to stage / Advancing" (*P*.11.43–4, 1805 version) the subject of her novel. Rather, she must depend upon her faith in the power of "sympathy" itself to convince us of the value of her higher art.

Readers have rarely been satisfied. By contrast with the earlier narrative, the principle that governs the final book seems to turn art into a "reckoning made twice over," as Adam would say, a chance to mend a wrong subtraction by doing your addition right. This sort of "figuring" is not realistic, even in the most popular sense of the word – hard-headed, practical, or fair. It substitutes a principle of desire – the hope that we can find some form of compensation for the sufferings of this world – for George Eliot's version of the reality principle, Nemesis. Yet there is a pathos in this substitution. *Are* the poems that come from fuller thought, larger experience, and deeper-rooted affections more moving than those that spring from the earliest passions of the soul? The question – and the doubt as well – is implicit in the assertions that end Wordsworth's "Intimations Ode." But we seem more willing to respond to the pathos of unrealistic desires in the mode of lyric. Perhaps it is the immense contrast of modes made necessary by the form of George Eliot's novel that prevents readers from sympathizing with the "richer, deeper music" of the last book of *Adam Bede*.

8

SHELLEY AND THE APOCALYPTIC CHARACTER

George Eliot's defense of compensation in the last book of *Adam Bede* presents the value of transcendence in purely personal terms. The chastened and subdued tones of "second love" make it possible for the individual to go on in spite of great loss. This power of personal consolation resembles the "soothing voice" that Arnold heard in Wordsworth's poetry, "Wordsworth's healing power" ("Memorial Verses," lines 35, 63); and it corresponds to the psychological mechanism of sublimation, which offsets the loss of early strength by the gain of a "higher" power.

As our discussion of Dickens made clear, however, the liminal moment has a social as well as a personal function. Considered strictly as liminal figures, Little Dorrit and Dinah Morris are not characters in their own right so much as attendant powers, who play a role in the transformation of others. As a psychological structure, transcendence may be reducible to a mechanism of defense; yet, on an interpersonal level, the process has a different value. George Eliot explores this larger, social role of transcendence in her later novels. In *Middlemarch*, for example, when Dorothea exchanges the youthful egotism of a "mind struggling towards an ideal life" (68) for the mature acceptance of a lesser lot, her act has an effect on others as well as on herself. We are told of Dorothea that "the effect of her being on those around her was incalculably diffusive" (896). Critics whose vision of Dorothea is circumscribed by the conventions of realistic character still fault the ending of this novel as a form of wish fulfillment. But, when one thinks of Dorothea as in part a liminal figure, the value of "her effect" on others may indeed be different from the value George Eliot attributes to her personal compromises. This is the burden of liminality: that it is a position in a process, not a state of being or an attribute of character. One may deny the psychological superiority of "second love" or of a "self-subduing act of fellowship" (*Middlemarch* 861) without negating the social function of liminality, its power to renew the social order.

Middlemarch might be said to carry the Wordsworthian model of transcendence as far as it can go. In exploring the social dimension of Dorothea's acts, George Eliot exposes both the value and the limit of any conception of transcendence that entails a compensatory exchange of strengths. *Daniel Deronda*, by contrast, might be seen as an attempt to go beyond the Wordsworthian model. The "apocalyptic" project of George Eliot's last novel has been read by at least two recent critics as deconstructive (Chase, Carpenter); and one of the things it deconstructs is the novelist's earlier faith that a determinate form of experience, such as transcendence, can possess a genuinely renovating power. Rather than privileging a particular structure of experience, *Daniel Deronda* forces the reader to look beyond anything that the text can claim as "a genuine fact or a genuine act" (Chase 223) for the source of the narrative's meaning and power.[1]

George Eliot's late attempt to move beyond transcendence provides an interesting parallel to the apocalyptic designs of Emily Brontë or of Shelley; and the new emphasis on union – both the romantic union of lovers and the mystical union of Mordecai's prophetic Zionism – resembles the apocalyptic themes of those authors as well.[2] In past chapters we have looked at this mode of vision as a critique of transcendence, but we have not yet considered apocalyptic vision in its own right. The attempt to consider such a problem requires us to think about the question of textuality. By what means can an apocalyptic vision be constituted as a text? Which structures (of the self, of language) are appropriate to a belief in the end of all structure? Is an apocalyptic character possible, either as a figure in a narrative or as a sign in a text?

DECONSTRUCTION AND APOCALYPTIC POETRY

Our earlier discussions of Emily Brontë and Shelley revealed that there was an important relation between apocalyptic vision and a deconstructive view of literary structure. We discovered, however, that what those nineteenth-century authors thought of this relation was fundamentally different from what twentieth-century theorists think of it. This difference is worth examining in more detail.

Although Shelley has a number of apocalyptic lyrics, perhaps we should begin by looking at a short poem by Emily Brontë, one that combines an apocalyptic theme with a deconstructive attitude toward structure, in order to demonstrate that the connection between the two is not a unique feature of Shelley's poetry. A poem by Emily Brontë that begins "Aye, there it is! It wakes tonight" attempts to dramatize a moment of self-annihilating union by deconstructing the very figures in which it represents that union.[3] Like Shelley's "Ode to the West Wind," Emily Brontë's lyric draws on the traditional figure of the wind as an image of apocalyptic revelation. This poem, which is not nearly so well known as Shelley's, bears reproducing in its entirety:

> Aye, there it is! It wakes to-night
> Sweet thoughts that will not die
> And feeling's fires flash all as bright
> As in the years gone by!
>
> And I can tell by thine altered cheek
> And by thy kindled gaze
> And by the words thou scarce dost speak,
> How wildly fancy plays.
>
> Yes, I could swear that glorious wind
> Has swept the world aside,
> Has dashed its memory from thy mind
> Like foam-bells from the tide –
>
> And thou art now a spirit pouring
> Thy presence into all –
> The essence of the Tempest's roaring
> And of the Tempest's fall –
>
> A universal influence
> From Thine own influence free;
> A principle of life, intense,
> Lost to mortality.
>
> Thus truly when that breast is cold
> Thy prisoned soul shall rise,
> The dungeon mingle with the mould –
> The captive with the skies.

The poem recounts an experience of complete union between a sleeping woman and the wind. It is a moving work, both intellectually and erotically. In essence, the entire poem is comprehended in the first sentence: "Aye, there it is!" As a pure orphic cry, it is enough; perhaps "Aye!" alone would have sufficed. Reading Emily Brontë's biography, one wonders how many potential lyrics got no farther. But this poem goes on, and as it progresses, an unmediated experience becomes increasingly entangled with the problem of textual mediation. In the first stanza the union is nearly perfect. There are no personal pronouns here. The point of view of this poem, which is one of the strangest things about the lyric, has not yet been indicated. There is no narrator mysteriously watching another person's ecstasy. Such individuation seems alien to the experience being described. The momentary indefiniteness of point of view makes for a productive uncertainty. "It wakes to-night" is nicely ambiguous. Is the verb transitive or intransitive? Do the thoughts wake, like some strange sweet creature that will not die, or does something else – "it," still not identified as the wind – rouse them? Like the cry with which the poem begins, this small protest against the coercion of syntax is a trace of the poem's larger struggle against the structures imposed by this world, including the structures of textuality.

By the second stanza two separate characters have emerged. Psychologically, this individuation seems appropriate. We have all read about or experienced the feeling of stepping out of ourselves during a moment of mystical possession. At such periods the visionary feels as if she is looking down on herself as though she were another person. But, if such a feeling is psychologically apt, it nevertheless represents a form of alienation. Within the experience of oneness, a splitting off has occurred. It is as if the intimate drama of relation between the woman and the wind has produced another, more distanced relation, the voyeuristic drama of observer and observed. This second relation is the perverse double, the visible counterpart of an invisible state. As such, it stands in relation to the actual union exactly as a text stands in relation to any unmediated experience. This secondary relation corrupts the primary experience, yet some such division is a precondition for representation. Emily Brontë simultaneously dramatizes an ecstatic experience and portrays the effect on ecstasy of her attempt to write about it.

The effect of this splitting off into two characters is a sudden need for interpretation. From outside, one cannot know for sure what another person is experiencing. Thus the "I" of the poem in the second stanza must begin to read the signs that are visible in the "other" woman's face, gestures, and words. The "altered cheek," the "kindled gaze," and "the words thou scarce dost speak" now become emblems of "how wildly fancy plays." But their status as signs inevitably introduces the possibility of their being misread. The risks of interpretation exist only in the world of texts. This new element of uncertainty is taken up in the next stanza, with its more insistent rhetoric. "Yes," the poem says, answering a doubt that has not before found expression, "Yes, I could swear" – swear to all manner of things. The poem is now willing to attest to the most apocalyptic of conclusions. In order to answer an uncertainty that the hermeneutic situation has itself created the poem rises to its strongest visions. The world is swept aside, even its memory disappears. The contraction of the vast globe to foam-bells on the tide conveys a sense of the violence involved and should be compared with Shelley's similar image in an apocalyptic chorus from *Hellas*.[4] We see now that the climactic visions of the next three stanzas are mobilized to quell doubts that the writing of the poem has raised. In short, the poem has deconstructed the conditions that produced its own visions.

We are not suggesting, however, that Emily Brontë's deconstruction of her vision vitiates it. For her, as for Shelley, the questions textuality introduces into experience can be viewed with either joy or despair. Although Emily Brontë acknowledges the uncertainty that interpretation creates, she also suggests a stance toward uncertainty that differs from that of post-structuralists. She challenges us to view the aporias of texts, the divisions that open in our experience, as occasions for a prophetic re-viewing of our position in the universe. The specific form this revision takes will involve us in another limiting text, but the strength to keep making such attempts testifies to a drive that is not reducible to any meaning – determinate or indeterminate – and hence is immune from the uncertainty that besets interpretation.

On some level, Emily Brontë's work acknowledges that all texts are indeterminate, all signification figurative, all interpretations undecidable. In this respect, she shares some of the basic assumptions underlying twentieth-century deconstruction. But she takes a different stance toward the fact of indeterminacy. We have called her stance prophetic, because Emily Brontë, like the Old Testament prophets, takes every proof of the unavailing nature of her language as a call to speak again. Modern deconstruction is often accused of being a form of nihilism, primarily because of *its* stance toward the indeterminacy of texts. Rather than taking the impasse of language as a call to action, deconstruction always seems to view it as an occasion for demystification. One must agree with J. Hillis Miller when he writes, "'Deconstruction' is neither nihilism nor metaphysics but simply interpretation as such" ("Critic as Host" 230); but when demystification becomes the only end of "interpretation as such," we become suspicious, for the process begins to look futile.

In the work of Shelley, a prophetic stance toward the indeterminacy of language is even more apparent than in Emily Brontë. Recently a number of critics have given us portraits of Shelley as a deconstructive poet whose true subject is language itself.[5] They have complicated the old image of Shelley's idealism as naive logocentrism by revealing the disjunctive presence in his poetry of a repressed countertext that challenges the claims of idealism. Rajan's account of Shelley is illuminating. She traces the "suppressed debate between his idealism and his skepticism" (*Dark Interpreter 83*) from "Alastor" to "The Triumph of Life," uncovering the different ways Shelley evades the ironies his poetry uncovers. What Rajan views as evasion, we have been calling "stance," but Rajan herself admits that different responses (or stances) toward the discoveries of skepticism are available. Drawing on German Romantic theorists, she identifies several possible stances: the sentimental, the tragic, and the ironic. "Skepticism is often the precursor of irony and negation, but in Shelley skepticism, on the contrary, involves a positive awareness of the possibility of both hope and despair" (*Dark Interpreter* 95). Irony and negation are the demystifying responses characteristic of contemporary deconstruction, whereas hope is the sentimental and despair the tragic pole of Shelley's vision.[6] It is important to realize, however, that none of these stances has any more intrinsic merit than the others, unless one adopts a dialectical and teleological view of history that deconstruction itself works to deny.

We might say that Shelley puts deconstruction at the service of prophecy. Characteristically, prophetic literature seeks a power that is not vitiated by the corrupt forms of our knowledge; hence, it often calls into question the structure of its own language. Just as Shelley deconstructs the false opposition between tyrant and slave in *Prometheus Unbound*, so he points to the futility of taking the oppositions of language as primary. To argue about whether a sign is the reflection of an ideal presence or only the trace of a trace is to be trapped within the same oppositional structure that a radical visionary works to undo. The self – with all its oppositions of inside and outside, presence and absence, the "I" and the other – is an illusion generated by the fallen conditions of existence, which include both our sensory apparatus and our language. Prophetic literature strives to effect a change, not to demonstrate a position, and it cares less about whether its words can reflect reality than about whether they will change their listeners. Shelley objects to the vulgar notion of a prophet as someone who knows the shape of the future, for the true prophet (or poet) cares little about knowledge per se.[7] Only that literature which will accept no answer offered by this world is prophetic. Rajan is uneasy with Act 4 of *Prometheus Unbound* because its "view of poetry as an activity that makes and validates images of beauty and truth" (*Dark Interpreter* 92) seems to return the poet to a naive idealism.[8] It does so, however, only if one thinks that the ultimate aim of Act 4 is to present a version (or vision) of the truth, rather than to effect a change. But a prophetic stance insists that the representations of literature are a form of action rather than a vehicle of knowledge, whether knowledge is conceived of in idealist or empiricist terms.[9]

Harold Bloom has captured the difference between a prophetic stance toward the problem of language and one concerned with an epistemo-logical debate by contrasting the Greek conception of the "word" as knowledge (*logos*) with the Hebrew conception of the "word" as power. This latter conception views "the word as a moral act, a true word that is at once an object or thing and a deed or act. . . . In contrast to this dynamic word, the *logos* is an intellectual concept, going back to a root meaning that involves gathering, arranging, putting-into-order" (*Map of Misreading* 42). From the biblical conception of the dynamic word, Bloom conceives his notion of poetic language as neither accurate representation nor empty traces, but as the measure of a drive or the will. "What is a trope?" Bloom asks. "It is one of two possibilities only – either the will translating itself into a verbal act . . . or else the will failing to translate itself and so abiding as a verbal desire" (*Poems of Our Climate* 393). Only by conceiving of language as a form of action is Shelley able to move beyond an idealist conception of the word as "logos" without becoming trapped in the ironic stance adopted by contemporary deconstruction.

IDENTITY AND APOCALYPTIC UNION

An apocalyptic vision requires that we think not only about the status of our words, but also about the structure of what we call character. Earlier, we saw that conceiving of a character as a liminal figure changed its status fundamentally. A similar alteration in our ideas about character is necessitated by the radically unstructured state implied by an apocalyptic vision. The question can be simply put. Who or what is the individual after he has been merged with another person or with the surrounding universe? D. H. Lawrence raises the issue in the speculative work he called *Apocalypse*: "To yield entirely to love would be to be absorbed, which is the death of the individual" (196). The critic René Girard phrases the dilemma in still darker terms: "The wish to be absorbed into the substance of the Other implies an insuperable revulsion for one's own substance" (54). This attitude is not entirely alien to Shelley. The poet's numerous references to "self-contempt"[10] and his unmistakable yearning for death at the end of "Adonais" reveal a loathing of the individual that sometimes accompanies his desire for union. Contempt for the ordinary or unrenovated self is a theme that runs throughout the writings of radical visionaries. Yet it is not the only issue that faces us when discussing an apocalyptic perspective on identity. In addition to the evils of the existing self, there are dangers created by the very quest for union.

These risks are dramatized most fully in Shelley's first major poem, "Alastor; or, The Spirit of Solitude." In the "Preface" to that poem Shelley tells of the "generous error" that compels the major character, an unnamed Poet, to undertake his doomed quest. A youth of genius, with pure feelings and a passionate imagination, "drinks deep of the fountains of knowledge, and is still insatiate" (69). He worships the beauty of the external world but can rest content with nothing that he sees. While his desire can operate in a realm that is capable of endless renewal, his insatiable hunger remains a source of joy, "but the period arrives when these objects cease to suffice" (69). As a result, he attempts to imagine what an object commensurate with his capacity for desire would be like. This object is a Being like himself rather than another aspect of inanimate

nature. The Poet's instincts so far are correct. The only object that will
suffice is another subject, a being who can meet his infinite desire with an
answering desire of its own. But something goes wrong after this
promising beginning. Instead of fulfillment, the Poet receives endless
frustration, for he can find no person in the external world equal to his
conception. "He seeks in vain for a prototype of his conception. Blasted
by his disappointment, he descends to an untimely grave" (69). The
failure that Shelley diagnoses in "Alastor" is a failure of the imagination,
and, as we shall see, it is one to which the apocalyptic imagination is
peculiarly susceptible.

The place where the Poet's imaginings go wrong can be located
precisely, both in the Preface and in the body of the poem. Let us look
first at the Preface. The Poet's awareness of the need for others occurs
only when he reaches a crisis in his own relation with the world. His
response to this need constitutes a clear act of the imagination: "He
images to himself the Being whom he loves" (69). He invests this image
with all the beauty and wisdom that he has ever encountered in the works
of philosophers and poets. As the Preface puts it, "The Poet is represented as uniting these requisitions, and attaching them to a single
image" (69). Thus this vision is ideal in more ways than one: it is not
only a fanciful dream but also an embodiment of the Poet's own highest
values.[11] Freud would call such a being an "ego-ideal," and his comments about the relation of this kind of fantasy to narcissism are clearly
relevant here. "That which he projects ahead of him as his ideal is merely
his substitute for the lost narcissism of his childhood" ("On Narcissism"
74). The narcissistic element in the Poet has not gone unnoticed. As
Thomas Weiskel observes, "The hero-Poet of 'Alastor; or, The Spirit of
Solitude' exhibits one of the clearest narcissistic careers in the whole
Romantic canon" (144).

If we turn to the poem, we can discover why the career of narcissism
proves so interesting to the apocalyptic imagination. The poem begins
with an introductory section by the narrator, a character who should
carefully be distinguished from both Shelley and the Poet.[12] This
explicitly Wordsworthian figure is a lover of nature who struggles to still
all his "obstinate questionings" ("Alastor" line 26). The only thing we
need to notice about the narrator here is that his faith in the natural
universe contrasts starkly with the belief in a prophetic form of revelation.[13] The actual story of the Poet's life begins with a lament for his
untimely death; then the poem moves back in time to record the details
of his childhood and early education. In youth, the Poet's thirst for
knowledge and delight has led him to explore the wonders of nature, the
ruins of ancient history, and finally the wastes of Arabia, Persia, and
India. But nothing has sufficed, not even the beautiful Arab maiden who

tended his needs but who dared not speak her love, "for deep awe" of him, as Shelley says, and also, we might add, for total lack of encouragement.

At length the Poet comes to the crisis that the Preface took such care to explain. Asleep one night, he has a visionary experience that will shape the remaining course of his life:

> A vision on his sleep
> There came, a dream of hopes that never yet
> Had flushed his cheek. He dreamed a veiled maid
> Sate near him, talking in low solemn tones.
> Her voice was like the voice of his own soul
> Heard in the calm of thought. . . . (lines 149–54)

In this passage we can see much more clearly than in the Preface the narcissistic character of the Poet's vision. Her voice is "like the voice of his own soul," and the subjects of her soft speech are soon revealed to be topics dear to the Poet's heart:

> Knowledge and truth and virtue were her theme,
> And lofty hopes of divine liberty,
> Thoughts the most dear to him, and poesy,
> Herself a poet. (lines 158–61)

Not only is she a poet, like our hero, but she seems to enjoy all the fabulous powers of expression that a more famous damsel with a dulcimer possessed. It is not hard to believe that the Poet in "Alastor," like the character of Coleridge in "Kubla Khan," might envy the talents of his own vision.[14]

There are several passages in Shelley's fragmentary essay "On Love" that emphasize the narcissistic element in the poet's conception of love. "We are born into the world," Shelley writes, "and there is something within us which from the instant that we live and move thirsts after its likeness" (473). Like Freud, Shelley locates the origin of this desire at a very early period in life; he says that it is one reason why "the infant drains milk from the bosom of its mother." More important, he too connects this thirst for our own likeness with the formation of an ego-ideal. Shelley explains this process with considerable grace; and one might even find the poet's phrase "a soul within our soul" as helpful as the Freudian term.

> We dimly see within our intellectual nature a miniature as it were of our entire self, yet deprived of all that we condemn or despise, the ideal prototype of every thing excellent or lovely that we are capable of conceiving as belonging to the nature of man. Not only the portrait of our external being, but an assemblage of the minutest particulars of which our nature is composed: a mirror whose surface reflects only the forms of purity and brightness: a soul within our soul that describes a

circle around its proper Paradise which pain and sorrow and evil dare
not overleap. (473–4)

The protection that such "a soul within our soul" gives us from the pain
and sorrow of the external world corresponds perfectly to the role that
Freud's ego-ideal plays in sheltering us from the disappointments and
failures that we encounter in life. Shelley and Freud also agree that this
ideal being is a precipitate of all the original elements in our first,
uninhibited sense of being, even those that we have been forced to give
up by the harsh agency of the reality principle. Thus they both see the
creation of this inner self as the individual's initial step toward the
establishment of a visionary conception of reality and toward the
preservation of that conception as one's personal myth. For Freud, of
course, this step is a necessary but lamentable stage in the child's
development of a proper ego, which is, as he says, "essentially the
representative of the external world, of reality" (*Ego and Id* 26). "Conflicts between the ego and the ideal," Freud continues, "will . . .
ultimately reflect the contrast between what is real and what is psychical,
between the external world and the internal world" (26). This is a
position which Shelley would have no difficulty endorsing: Only his
valuation of the terms would differ.

For Shelley, the soul within our soul is not a more or less serious
deviation in the development of the psyche, but a force that permanently
guides and shapes the creative power of the imagination. The inner being
looks around at all the universe, eager to make the "discovery of its
antitype." This is its highest hope; "this is the invisible and unattainable
point to which Love tends" (474). But, when love cannot find its
antitype in the external world, it creates at large the world in which such
a being could exist. In the words of Teresa Viviani that Shelley uses as an
epigraph for "Epipsychidion," "The loving soul launches beyond creation, and creates for itself in the infinite a world all its own, far different
from this dark and terrifying gulf" (trans. Reiman and Powers 373n1).
Thus Shelley connects the soul's search for its own likeness with an
apocalyptic capability. This seems at first a strange pairing.

In the opening chapter of *Civilization and Its Discontents*, Freud offers
some observations on what he calls the "oceanic feeling" that can help
clarify the relation between narcissism and the desire for union. Mystics
and lovers, Freud says, claim to experience a feeling "of being one with
the external world" (12). This sensation, which is quite rare, dissolves
the sharp lines of demarcation from the outside world that the self usually
maintains. "At the height of being in love the boundary between ego and
object threatens to melt away. Against all the evidence of his senses, a
man who is in love declares that 'I' and 'you' are one, and is prepared to
behave as if it were a fact" (13). Freud locates the origin of these feelings

in the primary narcissism of early childhood. "An infant at the breast," Freud writes, "does not as yet distinguish his ego from the external world as the source of the sensations flowing in upon him" (14). Interestingly, Shelley appears to believe the same thing. In another of his fragmentary essays, "On Life," Shelley traces his sense of union with the world back to an analogous feeling experienced by children. In childhood, "we less habitually distinguished all that we saw and felt from ourselves. They seemed as it were to constitute one mass" (477). For Shelley, our adult sense of separation from the world is a sad diminishment, and the ability to preserve the child's all-inclusive sense of self should be cherished:

> There are some persons who in this respect are always children. Those who are subject to the state called reverie feel as if their nature were dissolved into the surrounding universe, or as if the surrounding universe were absorbed into their being. They are conscious of no distinction. And these are states which precede or accompany or follow an unusually intense and vivid apprehension of life. (477)

Freud, naturally, regards such states as delusional, for they seek "something like the restoration of limitless narcissism" (19); but he does admit that our adult sense of self is a diminished thing: "Our present ego-feeling is, therefore, only a shrunken residue of a much more inclusive – indeed, an all-embracing – feeling which corresponded to a more intimate bond between the ego and the world about it" (15).

Our satisfaction in the large area of agreement between Shelley and Freud, however, can only be temporary. If we grant what Shelley and Freud in their very different ways both seem to maintain – that a thirst for our own likeness is an integral part of the desire for union – then why does the Poet's vision in "Alastor" lead only to alienation, suffering, and death? The fate of the doomed Poet in "Alastor" points to a difficulty inherent in the very structure of the apocalyptic imagination. The desire to merge with another being is threatened by the analogous but far different temptation to identify oneself with the other. The possibility of confusing these two experiences is the shadow that haunts all visions of union. Shelley, Emily Brontë, and, as we shall see, D. H. Lawrence all attempt to distinguish the two experiences, but the task is almost impossible – not only because, as Shelley says, "It is difficult to find terms adequately to express so subtle a conception" (478), but also because, in psychoanalytic terms, identification and union exhibit precisely the same structure. For a radical visionary, the problem with identification is that it does not abolish the limits of the old self in a union with the other; rather it sets up the other internally as the new limits of the self. In terms of any psychology we have, there is no way to separate this reinscription of the other from a genuine transformation of self and other in apocalyptic union.

Let us pause to discuss the difficulty further, for it will play an important part in our account of D. H. Lawrence. Freud defines identification as the "assimilation of one ego to another one, as a result of which the first ego behaves like the second in certain respects, imitates it and in a sense takes it up into itself" (*New Introductory Lectures* 63). When we identify with someone, we choose him or her as our model; we mold our self in the other's image. In developmental psychology, the process of identification plays a crucial role in the formation of the self. According to Freud, it is on the basis of our earliest identifications with others that we establish the boundaries of the ego. Jacques Lacan has extended this idea by postulating a phase in every child's life that he calls "the mirror stage," during which the child creates its self by identifying with an other, even if this "other" is only the child's own image in a mirror (*Ecrits* 1–7). This last point brings out an important characteristic of identification: Both Freud and Lacan emphasize that the process is initially a visual phenomenon. It is the *image* of the other that is crucial in the formation of the self. As a result, "the ego is first and foremost a bodily ego"; it is "a mental projection of the surface of the body" (*Ego and Id* 16). The role of the *image* in identification has two important consequences for visionary writers. First, it reinforces the conception of the self as limited by its visible outline, the body, thus contradicting the apocalyptic ideal of union. Second, it implicates all images, including those used in poetry, in a suspect structure of selfhood, thus further complicating the question of representation in language.[15] Freud indicates the contribution of identification to the process of representation when he says that one ego "imitates" another and then adds the footnote – "i.e. one ego coming to resemble another one" (*New Introductory Lectures* 63n1).

It is easy to discern Shelley's distrust of identification in poems other than "Alastor." It lies behind Prometheus's mistaken curse of Jupiter; in the bitterness of his defiance, Prometheus unknowingly comes to resemble his adversary. Numerous commentators have remarked the overt resemblance of the Phantasm of Jupiter to Prometheus when the former is forced to repeat the latter's curse. Wasserman writes, "It is necessary . . . to recognize this as the actual identification of the execrating Prometheus with Jupiter, the god he made in his image" (259–60; see also Milton Wilson 63–4). What seems to horrify Prometheus most is the visibility, the *image* of himself, in the features of his detested foe:

> I see the curse on gestures proud and cold,
> And looks of firm defiance, and calm hate,

And such despair as mocks itself with smiles,
Written as on a scroll. . . . (*Prometheus Unbound* 1.258–61)

We should not ignore, either, the connection of this visibility with writing. The authentic union that Prometheus will achieve with Asia is heralded by voice and music, not image and representation. As Demogorgon reveals, "the deep truth is imageless" (*Prometheus Unbound* 2.4.116).

In "Ode to the West Wind" Shelley finds that he must employ the vocabulary of identification because there is no other model available for the prophetic self. At the climax of the poem, the poet prays for union with the wind: "Be thou, Spirit fierce, / My spirit! Be thou me, impetuous one!" (lines 61–2). But how can this liberating and apocalyptic prayer be distinguished from a desire for the self to give up its freedom to an overpowering other? Shelley's only answer is a negative or deconstructive one. He would have spurned the imagery of identification, had any other figures of union been available:

If I were a dead leaf thou mightest bear;
If I were a swift cloud to fly with thee;
A wave to pant beneath thy power . . .

    . . . I would ne'er have striven

As thus with thee in prayer in my sore need.
Oh! lift me as a wave, a leaf, a cloud! (lines 43–53)

Shelley's concern with the threat of identification in prophecy is not idiosyncratic. It is a concern raised by many passages in the prophets of the Old Testament. The notion of divine dictation of human speech easily lends itself to the psychology of identification, particularly through the image of incorporation. Oral ingestion of the other person, Freud notes, is our first way of conceiving identification.[16] In Amos and Jeremiah, the idea of the Lord's words as something that the prophet takes inside himself is expressed in the actual imagery of eating: "When your words came, I devoured them" (Jr. 15:16; see also Amos 8:11). It is in Ezekiel, however, that this image achieves its apotheosis. During his second call to prophecy, Ezekiel is forced to consume a scroll covered with the Lord's words. This passage differs dramatically from his first call, the vision of the Chariot of the Lord, which so fascinated Shelley that he used it no less than four times in his poetry. The atmosphere of compulsion in Ezekiel's second vision clearly would have offended Shelley:

"Open your mouth and eat what I am about to give you." I looked. A hand was there, stretching out to me and holding a scroll. He unrolled it in front of me; it was written on back and front; on it was written "lamentations, wailings, moanings." . . . I opened my mouth; he gave me the scroll to eat and said, "Son of man, feed and be satisfied by the scroll I am giving you." I ate it, and it tasted sweet as honey." (Ezek. 2:8–3:3)

Biblical commentators often attempt to distinguish the structure of prophetic inspiration from ordinary psychological states, precisely because they fear that readers will interpret such passages as tyrannical. Abraham Heschel, for example, cautions that the "I" of the prophet is not overwhelmed by the "other" of God: "A specific aspect of prophetic religion or of the religious phenomenon in general, as opposed to the purely psychological, lies in the fact of a mutual inherence of the 'I' and the object of religious experience, for an intention of man toward God produces a counteracting intention of God toward man" (2:266). But Gerhard von Rad is more astute when he admits that the identification of self and other in prophecy can be considered liberating only through reference to a specifically religious paradox: "As the result of this divine call [the prophet] surrenders much of his freedom – occasionally he is completely overwhelmed by an external compulsion; but paradoxically, just because he has received this call he is able to enjoy an entirely new kind of freedom" (56). Only through a related form of paradox is Shelley able to become "the trumpet of a prophecy" at the end of "Ode to the West Wind."

To return to "Alastor," we can now see that the Poet betrays the apocalyptic potential of his imagination by transforming his vision into an occasion for identification.[17] The Poet seeks not to liberate himself from the forms of this world but to bind himself to a given conception of reality. In doing so, he exchanges the limitless potential for action contained in the totality of human desire for a single, obsessive quest – a quest, moreover, that is initiated, organized, and foredoomed by the constraints of a single psychological structure. The futility of the Poet's quest becomes most apparent in an important scene that takes place at a lovely well in the heart of a glen. Like Narcissus, the Poet gazes long into the mirror of the water, searching even his own image for a glimpse of the other with which he hopes to unite. Although his eyes behold only "their own wan light" (line 470), this well, like the well of myth, seems haunted by another spirit: not Echo's, of course, but a spirit like hers that invests the "undulating woods, and silent well, / And leaping rivulet, and evening gloom" (lines 484–5). The Poet looks up from the well, striving a last time to identify himself with this spirit, so that the two can form their own private world as one. The effort is in vain; the effort *is* what is vain about his quest for union. "A Spirit seemed / To stand beside him,"

> as if he and it
> Were all that was, – only . . . when his regard

> Was raised by intense pensiveness, . . . two eyes,
> Two starry eyes, hung in the gloom of thought,
> And seemed with their serene and azure smiles
> To beckon him. (lines 479–92, Shelley's ellipses)

We can end our discussion of identity and union here, for this moment from "Alastor" encapsulates the principal themes we have been exploring. The desire for one's own likeness produces a vision of the soul out of one's own soul, but this vision leads only to another failed attempt at identification, and so becomes a paradigm of imaginative frustration.

To answer the questions with which we began this chapter, no structure – of language or character – will adequately represent an apocalyptic union. Thus Romantic writers employed much of the archetypal imagery of the apocalypse, and then deconstructed those images. In the poem "Aye, there it is," Emily Brontë used the perverse relationship of observer/observed as an image of the "imageless" relationship of apocalyptic union, then called into question the figures of her poem. In "Alastor," Shelley explored the psychological structures of narcissism and identification, only to reveal their inadequacy. In *Wuthering Heights* and in "Adonais," each author proposed death as a figure for a union that knows no bar, but even that radical image was revealed to be inadequate. When we turn to Lawrence, we discover that the task of distinguishing an apocalyptic vision of union from the corrupt process of identification is even more problematic than it was for Shelley. In his apocalyptic lyric "New Heaven and Earth," Lawrence had to engage in the same critique of identification that we have been examining. Few lines communicate the shadow that haunts the dream of union as powerfully as these by Lawrence:

> I was a lover, I kissed the woman I loved,
> and God of horror, I was kissing also myself.
> I was a father and a begetter of children,
> and oh, oh horror, I was begetting and conceiving in my own body.
> ("New Heaven and Earth," Part 3)

9

WOMEN IN LOVE

D. H. Lawrence explores the question of transcendence with unceasing passion and an extravagant vocabulary. He takes seriously the possibility of transforming the human spirit, of working toward a liberating, even apocalyptic change. In his essays and letters Lawrence places these concerns in vital conjunction with formal questions about the nature of his art. What are the consequences for the novel of expanded modes of consciousness? How does a writer deal with the difficulty of representing the very forms of experience most essential to spiritual growth? A well-known letter to Edward Garnett shows Lawrence at his speculative best:

> You mustn't look in my novel for the old stable ego – of the character. There is another ego, according to whose action the individual is unrecognizable, and passes through, as it were, allotropic states which it needs a deeper sense than any we've been used to exercise, to discover are states of the same single radically-unchanged element. (*Letters* 2:183)

Passages such as this one outline a doctrine of states that closely approximates the Wordsworthian model of transcendence; and Lawrence understands how profoundly a concern with visionary experience will modify the form of the conventional novel.[1] But it is in Lawrence's fiction that such issues are most rigorously confronted. Lawrence's greatest novels – *The Rainbow* and *Women in Love* – reaffirm what the works of the greatest Romantic poets established, that the search for new forms of consciousness is inseparable from the struggle with literary form.

The character of Ursula in *Women in Love* is presented in terms that come directly from a Romantic conception of identity.[2] In the first pages of the novel Ursula feels herself on the verge of a new life. She seems about to transcend the limits of her old self, about to be born anew: "Her active living was suspended, but underneath, in the darkness, something was coming to pass. If only she could break through the last integuments!'' (3). By the end of the novel she thinks she has achieved the new life for which she had yearned. Like so many other figures who have experienced similar changes, Ursula feels as though she has no connection with her past self: "What had she to do with parents and antecedents?" (399–400).

If Ursula were the only important character in the novel, her story of crisis and renewal would be a perfect example of the liminal form of Romantic transcendence, the dialectical movement from a lower to a higher state of consciousness that we have identified with Wordsworth. But *Women in Love* is not solely, or even primarily, Ursula's story. Numerous elements work to put in question this attractively simple pattern. Not the least is Ursula's own skepticism. Her political and feminist critiques of Birkin's visionary theories serve to undercut the very principles upon which her new life rests. Hermione, too, stands as a vivid counterexample to Ursula's achievement, for Hermione demonstrates many of the dangers that beset any attempt to rise to a "higher" state of consciousness. Further, the stories of Gerald and Gudrun suggest disturbingly that self-fulfillment is meaningless so long as human nature remains unchanged. Like Shelley, Lawrence presents the movement from one state of consciousness to another as necessary and even desirable, only to deconstruct the very conditions that make it possible. Ursula's authentic yet limited form of transcendence must be seen in relation (or even in contrast) to the novel's larger apocalyptic vision.

Elsewhere in the letter to Edward Garnett, Lawrence writes that the "non-human, in humanity, is more interesting to me than the old-fashioned human element – which causes one to conceive a character in a certain moral scheme and make him consistent" (2:182). This is the position taken by Birkin, who claims to "loathe myself as a human being" (118) but to believe in a "real impersonal me," an unknown being that is "quite inhuman" (137–8). Compared to Birkin's austere program, Ursula's inner life remains unregenerately personal. At one point Lawrence refers to Ursula's "easy female transcendency" (255), by which he means her ability to find satisfaction in shared intimacy with her sister, to draw strength from such old-fashioned human sources as understanding and love. Her talk of severing connections with the past never quite hides her fundamental consistency of character. We have no trouble recognizing the woman at the end of the novel who asks Birkin, "Aren't I enough for you?" (472) as the same woman who at the beginning of the novel "wanted [Birkin] to herself" (121). Ursula's form of transcendence leaves the individual intact. She is the least "allotropic" of the four major characters in the book.

In an interesting essay titled "D. H. Lawrence and the Apocalyptic Types," Frank Kermode identifies Ursula as a force that opposes the book's apocalyptic impulses. "Ursula is repeatedly the voice of that skepticism which always, in history, attends apocalyptic prophecy" (134). Kermode's insight leads him to find a principle in this novel – and in the genre as a whole – that resists apocalyptic types. "The novel fights back at myth, and where myth says yes, the novel and Ursula often say no. The novel, as a kind, belongs to humanism, not to mystery religion" (135). Ursula, despite her own experience of transcendence, or perhaps because of it, because of her recognition of its "old-fashioned," humanistic nature, stands as the finite, human alternative to the "non-human" attractions of an apocalyptic vision.

This alternative introduces what is undoubtedly the largest question in Lawrence criticism. To what extent are the prophetic impulses in his novels incompatible with his artistic aims?[3] Lawrence himself stresses the novel's resistance to transcendent themes: "The novel is the highest form of human expression so far attained," he claims. "Why? Because it is so incapable of the absolute" (*Phoenix II* 416). But few novelists his equal have written so many visionary passages that seem false, spurious, or inauthentic. Scenes such as those that dramatize Birkin's belief in African mysteries "far beyond the phallic cult" (246) and the discovery of Birkin's immemorial Egyptian potency have received overwhelmingly negative comment from the majority of Lawrence's critics. So strong an advocate of his novels as F. R. Leavis sees in the Egyptian potency passage "an insistent and over-emphatic explicitness, running at times to something one can only call jargon" (*D. H. Lawrence: Novelist* 148). Other critics admit that "this is the kind of thing one wishes Lawrence would not do," note "the poor quality of the writing," and accuse it of being "willed, not imagined."[4] We should note, however that Birkin's revelations in those chapters are *not* what has made so many readers from E. M. Forster onward call this novel prophetic. In Lawrence the prophecy we can take to heart is rarely an explicit doctrine of how to live. What does take on a prophetic power in the work is its ability to bear witness, to speak out to others without suppressing or denying the great realities that seem to oppose its speech.

Martin Buber has written, "The task of the genuine prophet was not to predict but to confront man with the alternatives of decision" (177). This is the task Lawrence sets for himself in *Women in Love* when he says in the "Preface," "We are now in a period of crisis" (viii). Shelley, too, believed that literature always preceded or accompanied the great crises of history. "At such periods there is an accumulation of the power of communicating and receiving intense and impassioned conceptions respecting man and nature." Then, especially, poets become "the hierophants of an unapprehended inspiration, the mirrors of the gigantic shadows which futurity casts upon the present" (508). It is the "unapprehended inspiration" in Lawrence that bears the clearest stamp of the prophet.[5] Throughout most of the novel, Lawrence does confront his readers with genuine alternatives. Unlike much of the later fiction, *Women in Love* leaves undecided the question of which is more essential, the "non-human" values of an apocalyptic vision or the enduring human qualities of a novel.

CRITIQUE OF THE ROMANTIC WILL

Like Shelley and Emily Brontë, Lawrence is more successful at probing the boundaries of old forms of consciousness than in describing the shape of the new. The character of Hermione, for example, explores the limits of a pervasive cultural type. She represents the extreme edge, the fine, nervous culmination of a hundred years of Romantic internalization: "She was a *kulturträger*, a medium for the culture of ideas. With all that was highest, whether in society or in thought or in public action, or even in art, she was at one" (10). Her preoccupation with culture is an obvious form of compensation. "She knew she was accepted in the world of culture and of intellect. . . . So, she was invulnerable" (10). Her compensatory attainments display once again all the benefits, and the costs, of a gift for sublimation. In a delicately humorous moment during a conversation at her country house, Lawrence connects her love of the "highest" with the vertical expansion of transcendence, playing with the by now familiar link between sublimation and the sublime. "To me the pleasure of knowing is *so* great, so *Wonderful* – nothing has meant so much to me in all life, as certain knowledge," Hermione says. One of her guests asks what knowledge.

> Hermione lifted her face and rumbled –
> "M-m-m – I don't know. . . . But one thing was the stars, when I really understood something about the stars. One feels so *uplifted*, so *unbounded*. . . ." (78, Lawrence's italics and ellipses)

We have seen these same uplifting stars inspire Fanny Price at another estate, Mansfield Park. They gave Tess Durbeyfield such an unbounded feeling that she thought herself literally transported out of her body. With a little help from Gerald, however, Hermione's rapture is connected with English Romantic poetry. "It's like getting on top of the mountain and seeing the Pacific," Gerald suggests. And another guest, a bookish Italian woman, murmurs, "Silent upon a peak in Dariayn" (78).

The consequences of Hermione's late Romantic sensibility are vividly dramatized, often with satiric force, occasionally with a certain pathos. Her self-involvement verges on solipsism. Hermione speaks with a strange, drugged rhythm, as if the effort to communicate with the external world were a strain. When she moves, she appears to drift along as if scarcely conscious, "her long blanched face lifted up, not to see the world" (9). Birkin mockingly compares her to the Lady of Shalott, the woman in Tennyson's poem and Pre-Raphaelite paintings by Hunt, Waterhouse, and others who is shut off from the world forever, condemned to see what lies outside her tower only in a mirror.

Her extreme isolation from the external world coincides with an urgent desire to return to nature. These contradictory impulses may at first seem perplexing. Birkin clearly finds her inconsistency maddening. In the "Class-Room" chapter she attacks Birkin and Ursula for tearing things apart in order to know them. Speaking of the catkins that Ursula's class is studying, she asks, "Isn't it better that [the children] should see as a whole, without all this pulling to pieces, all this knowledge?" (33). Her argument echoes Wordsworth's organicist philosophy, which combines the worship of "natural piety," spontaneity, and childhood with the wish for wholeness and the fear of "murdering to dissect." Hermione continues, "Or is it better to leave them untouched, spontaneous. Hadn't they better be animals, simple animals, crude, violent, *anything*, rather than this self-consciousness, this incapacity to be spontaneous" (34). Understandably, Birkin grows furious hearing this argument from Hermione, the most intellectual, overconscious character in the book. Yet he should know that this particular inconsistency is an almost irresistible temptation to a Romantic temperament.[6] It is an appropriate irony that in Hermione's last appearance in the novel she is described by a phrase from one of Wordsworth's sonnets that indicts his century for its failure to connect with any authentic basis for faith: "She was a priestess without belief, without conviction, suckled in a creed outworn, and condemned to the reiteration of mysteries that were not divine to her" (284).

From Lawrence's perspective the most important consequence of Hermione's late Romantic sensibility is its manifestation as will. At every point, Hermione is described as a creature of "persistent, almost insane *will*" (80). She attempts to dominate and control everyone. Curiously, her most effective technique turns out to be a side effect of her solipsism. She focuses all her powers on one person or object at a time, shutting out everything else in the process, thus turning her narrow, solipsistic vision into a social advantage. "It was a peculiarity of Hermione's, that at every moment, she had one intimate, and turned all the rest of those present into onlookers. This raised her into a state of triumph" (128). Her strength of will is portrayed as demonic, an oppressive, stifling power, but with its own allure, a force like that which dwells in the demonic women Pre-Raphaelites so loved to paint. But for all its hypnotic strength Hermione's power of will is only compensatory, the last and somewhat desperate recompense for her greater inadequacies. Ursula ultimately comes to this conclusion: "Poor Hermione, it was her one possession, this aching certainty of hers, it was her only justification. She must be confident here, for God knows, she felt rejected and deficient enough elsewhere" (284). Even Hermione seems to understand this truth at times: "'If only we could learn how to use our will,' said Hermione, 'we could do anything. The will can cure anything, and put anything right'" (131). There is a pathos in this statement, a longing for health that recognizes its own divided state. But the pathos is quickly overwhelmed by a more brittle determination: "And in so many things, I have *made* myself well. I was a very queer and nervous girl. And by learning to use my will, simply by using my will, I *made* myself right" (131).

Birkin, Lawrence's chief representative in the novel, sees this use of the will as diseased, although he understands its attractions all too well. "'It is fatal to use the will like that,' cried Birkin harshly, 'disgusting. Such a will is an obscenity'" (131). He objects to it as a form of self-deception, believing that Hermione cannot possibly know the compensatory nature of her strength. "You have no sensuality. You have only your will and your conceit of consciousness, and your lust for power, to *know*" (35). This speech is usually read as advocating the physical, exhorting us to put our trust in what Lawrence often calls "blood-knowledge." There is, of course, a powerful attraction to the unconscious and the physical in Birkin, but this attraction forms part of *his* legacy from Romantic primitivism. There are other, equally important grounds in Lawrence for the rejection of the will, grounds that Lawrence shares with an entire tradition of radical visionaries.[7] For Birkin, as for Shelley, the individual will is the chief manifestation of an overweening desire for power. "'But your passion is a lie,' [Birkin] went on violently. 'It isn't passion at all, it is your *will*. It's your bullying will. You want to clutch things and have them in your power'" (35).

As a way of clutching people or objects and placing them under one's power, the will manages to transform all experience of the other into experience of the self. Hence the will is central to the ontological concerns raised by the novel.[8] For Hermione, nothing exists unless it has been mediated by a voluntary act of consciousness. The self becomes supreme; nothing else has any reality. Birkin describes Hermione's attitude this way: "You want to have everything in your own volition, your deliberate voluntary consciousness. You want it all in that loathsome little skull of yours" (36). Worse still, the dominion of will condemns Hermione to a secondary existence. The individual will, as conceived by Lawrence no less than by Shelley, is sadly derivative. Hermione can never experience anything in an original way, because all her desires are structured by received categories. "It all takes place in your head, under that skull of yours. Only you won't be conscious of

what *actually* is: you want the lie that will match the rest of your furniture" (35).

Since her self, even at its most egotistical, is still imitative, still a pallid
reflection of what others have seen and done and thought, no state of
consciousness Hermione can achieve will ever be anything other than
derivative. Her most exalted moment of understanding is condemned to
be an exhausted recapitulation of old epiphanies. The current of her
ecstasies inevitably follows the closed circuit of presence and absence,
leaving her trapped within the circle of her own emotions. Consequently, her passions are always completely reversible. "As high as we
have mounted in delight / In our dejection do we sink as low," wrote
Wordsworth (*Poetical Works* 2:236), who understood the dangers of this
kind of ecstasy as well as any Romantic poet except Coleridge. In
Hermione, the ecstasy she receives from knowledge can easily become
the ecstasy of doing violence. Such a reversal causes Hermione's mur-
derous attack on Birkin. When her hand closes on the heavy paper-
weight, she experiences a rapture that is indistinguishable from the bliss
of transcendence: "She was going to have her consummation of volup-
tuous ecstasy at last. It was coming! In utmost terror and agony, she
knew it was upon her now, in extremity of bliss" (98). The imagery is
sexual, but the moment is triumphantly epiphanic – the god is upon her.
She is filled with its presence as utterly as she will be emptied by its
absence when her attack has ended: "Then she staggered to the couch and
lay down, and went heavily to sleep" (99).

GUDRUN, GERALD, AND THE DANCE OF OPPOSITES

Women in Love rejects epiphanic or liminal modes of consciousness with
a fervor unusual among English novels. Birkin argues against them
persistently. Trying to explain to Ursula how one must lose the self to
achieve a new life, he insists: "I don't mean let yourself go in the
Dionysic ecstatic way. . . . I hate ecstasy, Dionysic or any other. It's like
going round in a squirrel cage" (243). As his nice image makes clear, it
is the closed round of the emotions that he finds objectionable. "It is a
tick-tack, tick-tack, a dance of opposites" (144) he tells Ursula in another
context; and he explains the same thing to Gerald: "It's the old
story – action and reaction, and nothing between" (88).

An even more telling critique of the "dance of opposites" emerges
from the unending battle of wills between Gudrun and Gerald. Gudrun's
vision of Gerald has an epiphanic character from the very outset. When
she first sees him, in the opening chapter of the novel, she is overwhelmed by his beauty: "His fair hair was a glisten like sunshine
refracted through crystals of ice. And he looked so new, unbroached,
pure as an arctic thing" (9). From the vantage of a low stone wall just

outside the churchyard, she watches him attend the wedding of his younger sister. It is eleven o'clock, on a bright spring morning, and there are a number of óther women gathered to watch the festivities. In the midst of this perfectly ordinary setting she has what amounts to a full-blown visionary experience: "And then she experienced a keen paroxysm, a transport, as if she had made some incredible discovery, known to nobody else on earth. A strange transport took possession of her, all her veins were in a paroxysm of violent sensation. 'Good God!' she exclaimed to herself, 'what is this?'" (9). The next time she sees Gerald, his appearance is just as startling, just as much a vision of power and beauty: He is the naked diver who launches in a white arc through the air and takes possession of a "whole otherworld," the "grey and visionary" lake (39). On the night when he comes to her house to consummate their relationship, he arrives completely without warning. He appears by her bed in the dark like an "apparition," a vision of the "young Hermes" (336). As he stands above her, "his face was strange and luminous. He was inevitable as a supernatural being" (335). Most striking of all is his appearance in the chapter "Water-Party." There the language describing him is literally epiphanic – "He was not like a man to her, he was an incarnation, a great phase of life" (173) – and his effect on Gudrun is one of pure, overwhelming presence or of equally pure but devastating absence. Gerald's sister has drowned, and he is diving into the dark waters in a vain attempt to rescue her. When he plunges into the lake, Gudrun is left alone in the boat: "She knew he was gone out of the world, there was merely the same world, and absence, his absence" (173). When he returns from the water, his beauty, his presence, almost destroys her: "Ah, this was too much for her, too final a vision" (173).

The terms, presence and absence, so easily translate into the more familiar sexual roles of dominance and submission that it is quite possible to miss the ontological and spiritual dimensions of the struggle between Gudrun and Gerald. But Lawrence himself never forgets them. Gudrun connects a sense of self-presence with her ability to dominate the other. At first she submits to Gerald, giving herself up to him as to a fate (341). Later, she tries to master him (403). Either way, her identity is bound up in the oppositional structure of their relationship: "Sometimes it was he who seemed strongest, whilst she was almost gone, creeping near the earth like a spent wind; sometimes it was the reverse. But always it was this eternal see-saw, one destroyed that the other might exist, one ratified because the other was nulled" (436).

Like the all-or-nothing structure of epiphany, power and submission are endlessly reversible terms. The dynamics of this "eternal see-saw" are boldly dramatized in the part of "Water-Party" where Gudrun forces

Gerald to confess his love. Gudrun has been dancing by herself, performing strange, palpitating movements before the horns of Gerald's cattle, "confident of some secret power in herself" (158) but wanting to put it to the test. Gerald comes up behind her unexpectedly and drives away the cattle. Gudrun rounds upon him, saying, "You think I'm afraid of you and your cattle, don't you?" With a smile described as "faint[ly] domineering," Gerald asks her why. She strikes his face with the back of her hand. "'That's why,' she said, mocking" (162). The contest for mastery in this early scene is unmistakable. The sign of Gudrun's fear is her need to strike him. But, far from giving her into his power, her ability to signify her fear transforms it into mastery. Self-expression is one of the most basic ways of confirming one's own sense of existence, and to make a blow a sign is a particularly striking form of signification. Only a deconstructive act that neither Gerald nor Gudrun is prepared to perform could reveal the self-presence conferred by such a sign to be illusory. For the moment, Gudrun has the upper hand. "Don't be angry with me," she asks, secure in her strength; to which Gerald replies, "I'm not angry with you. I'm in love with you" (163). Significantly, this declaration is accompanied by an almost total loss of self: "The terrible swooning burden on his mind, the awful swooning, the loss of all his control, was too much for him" (163). He is emptied out, destroyed that the other might exist. Yet, in only a few minutes, it is Gudrun who will find herself emptied out by the power of Gerald's beauty.

It hardly matters who is master and who slave in this relationship, because each role is only the mirror image of the other. This Shelleyan insight lies at the heart of Lawrence's vision of the couple. They are bound to one another by the very polarity of their roles. "He and she were separate, like opposite poles of one fierce energy" (389). Neither can fully exist without the other, because neither possesses an identity single in itself. Gudrun "suffer[ed] from a sense of her own negation" (157). Consequently, she looks to the other, to the very image of otherness, for the completion of her self: "She must always demand the other to be aware of her, to be in connection with her" (157). Gerald, too, "did not believe in his own single self" (330). Without Gudrun, he would not exist: "To have no claim upon her, he must stand by himself, in sheer nothingness" (436). Hence he also discovers that "he was given to his complement, the other, the unknown" (437). But oddly, the knowledge of his dependence upon the other gives him a kind of satisfaction: "This wound, this disclosure, this unfolding of his own covering, leaving him incomplete, limited, unfinished, like an open flower under the sky, this was his cruellest joy" (437). The pleasure comes from the knowledge that his very incompleteness bonds him to Gudrun, and more, that an identical incompleteness bonds her to him.

There is a passage late in the novel that displays the full interdependence of these two opposed beings. The passage is especially pertinent because it shows this interdependence in the context of an epiphanic moment. Gudrun and Gerald are asleep at the inn the morning after they have arrived in the Alps. Gudrun, waking some minutes before Gerald, watches him sleep. He is still beautiful to her, but she has come to doubt his power. This morning, however, like the morning when she first saw him at his sister's wedding, Gudrun is willing to try believing otherwise. As she watches him, she thinks, "There *are* perfect moments. Wake up, Gerald, wake up, convince me of the perfect moments" (409). Wonderfully, he does wake, and he sees her smiling down at him. It is a mocking, enigmatic smile, but he cannot help responding. "Over his face went the reflection of the smile, he smiled, too, purely unconsciously" (409). It fills her with delight; it thrills her to see this smile "reflected from her face. She remembered that was how a baby smiled" (409). This is the mirror stage in reverse – the perception of one's own image in the face of another, the reduction of the other to a "reflection" of the self. It should be apparent that such a reversal of the mirror stage is inherent in its very structure. If the self is only an internalization of the other, then, through the agency of repression, the other can be viewed as nothing more than an external version of the self.

Gerald's face had always represented for Gudrun the ultimate sign of his otherness. In their first lovemaking, she had traced his face with wondering care: "How perfect and foreign he was – ah, how dangerous! . . . This was the glistening, forbidden apple, this face of a man" (324). Now, her momentary power over his face gives her the full measure of gratification that their relationship can provide. Outside the window of the inn a man begins to sing a German song. Gudrun, hearing him in her happiness, thinks that she will always remember that song. "It marked one of her supreme moments, the supreme pangs of her nervous gratification. There it was, fixed in eternity for her" (410). This strange incident is almost a perfect epiphany, a moment out of James Joyce or Virginia Woolf, but with this difference: Lawrence, like Shelley before him, attempts to expose the mechanics of power that lie behind such "perfect moments." For Lawrence, Gudrun's pleasure is necessarily a "nervous gratification" rather than a deep, abiding form of satisfaction, because it springs from the very incompleteness of her identity. For this novelist, the compensatory character of all such moments vitiates them.

THE SOCIAL SELF

Throughout the novel Birkin's perspective remains radically apocalyptic. His uncompromising position arises from his conviction of our inability to change within the given terms of existence. He claims he would like everybody in the world destroyed. "I would die like a shot, to know that the earth would really be cleaned of all the people" (119–20). Man, as he is currently constituted, is "one of the mistakes of creation – like the ichthyosauri" (120). And Birkin has no faith in our ability to evolve. We are unable to change ourselves, because there is no room to develop within the limits of our current existence. The only course is to destroy the old life utterly. "We've got to bust it completely, or shrivel inside it, as in a tight skin. For it won't expand any more" (47).

Birkin's apocalyptic beliefs are accompanied by a vision of the new dispensation. If man were cleansed from the earth, then "unseen hosts" would be free to move about at will. His vision of the post-apocalyptic universe is as marvelous as anything in Act 3 of *Prometheus Unbound*, where spirits rejoice and where "toads, and snakes, and efts" put off their evil nature and are changed in shape and hue (*Prometheus Unbound* 3.4.74–7). Like Shelley's visions in that act, Birkin's idea of the new creation mixes idealized pastoral imagery with his own private collection of imaginary beings.

> Do you think that creation depends on *man*! It merely doesn't. . . .
> There is the grass, and hares and adders, and the unseen hosts, actual
> angels that go about freely when a dirty humanity doesn't interrupt
> them – and good pure-tissued demons: very nice. . . . If only [man]
> were gone again, think what lovely things would come out of the
> liberated days; – things straight out of the fire. (120)

Birkin's talk of "pure-tissued demons" is scattered and undeveloped, however, and Ursula is right to be skeptical. The heart of Birkin's apocalyptic vision lies not in his occasional remarks about angels and unseen hosts, but in his unrelenting deconstruction of old structures of existence.

Birkin's critique of the established order takes three principal forms. The first is a withering assault on the self. "We're all conceit, so conceited in our own papier-mâché realised selves. We'd rather die than give up our little self-righteous self-opinionated self-will" (37). Birkin repudiates the idea that the self, as generally constituted, has any substance or value. "Not many people are anything at all," Birkin says. "They jingle and giggle. It would be much better if they were just wiped out. Essentially, they don't exist, they aren't there" (19). They do not exist because they are only reflections of others. They are "simulacra of people" (119). They live according to an image of the way they are supposed to live, an image inevitably patterned on the way other people behave. In an essay that deals in part with psychoanalytic concepts of identification, Lawrence writes, "The moment man became aware of himself he made a picture of himself and began to live from the picture: that is, from without inwards. . . . All our education is but the elaborating of the picture. 'A good little girl' – 'a brave boy' – 'a noble woman' – 'a strong man' – 'a productive society' – 'a progressive humanity' – it is all the picture" (*Phoenix* 380). Here, as in Shelley, the critique of the self is equally an attack on imitation. What most people call their selves is only an attempt to imitate the behavior of others, to blend in with the mass of humanity. Birkin expresses his attitude toward this impulse succinctly: "I detest the spirit of emulation" (23).

Birkin's rejection of the self leads directly to his second criticism of the current order. If, in its lowest common denominator, the self is merely imitative, then the self's strivings for "higher" things are tainted as well. The shared aspirations of our entire civilization are no more than the false dreams of false selves. "Humanity is a huge aggregate lie, and a huge lie is less than a small truth" (118). Consequently, Birkin renounces the humanistic ideal – what he calls "the old ethic, of the human being, and of humanity" (101) – in order to be free from all encumbrances of received forms. "I don't believe in the humanity I pretend to be a part of, I don't care a straw for the social ideals I live by, I hate the dying organic form of social mankind" (124). At its best, civilization is just the self writ large. Even in its highest manifestations – in art, literature, or religion – civilization cannot escape its fallen origins. Birkin's attack on contemporary Christianity is as vitriolic as any of Shelley's animadversions on the church in *Queen Mab, The Revolt of Islam*, or Act 1 of *Prometheus Unbound*: "Look at all the millions of people who repeat every minute that love is the greatest, and charity is the greatest – and see what they are doing all the time. By their works ye shall know them, for dirty liars and cowards, who daren't stand by their own actions, much less by their own words" (119).

Early in the novel, Gerald attempts to argue this question with his friend; Birkin's answers delineate the central role that imitation plays in what he might term the corrupt drama of civilization. Gerald points to a typical instance of cultural sublimation. "Don't you think the collier's *pianoforte*," he asks, "is a symbol for something very real, a real desire for something higher, in the collier's life?" Birkin's reply sketches a neat theory of the imitative basis of all social desires:

> "Higher!" cried Birkin. "Yes. Amazing heights of upright grandeur. It makes him so much higher in his neighbouring collier's eyes. He sees himself reflected in the neighbouring opinion . . . and he is satisfied. He lives for the sake of that . . . reflection of himself in the human opinion. You do the same. If you are of high importance to humanity you are of high importance to yourself." (48)

According to this logic, no act of the individual, even the most idealistic, can truly have a reference to anything beyond the self. Liberal humanism – "the old ethic, of the human being, and of humanity" – is reduced to an elaborate form of narcissism. "'Can't you see,' said Birkin, 'that to help my neighbour to eat is no more than eating myself. "I eat, thou eatest, he eats, we eat, you eat, they eat" – and what then? Why should every man decline the whole verb. First person singular is enough for me'" (48). Birkin prefers his own defiant honesty to the arguments that even so dark a humanist as Sigmund Freud would advance to justify the sacrifices that the self must make to live in the world. In Birkin's eyes, "a huge lie is less than a small truth."

The third object of Birkin's critique requires close attention. In a number of passages Birkin turns from an analysis of the individual self and of the collective embodiment of that self to a denunciation of the very thing that Shelley offers as an antidote to the ills of this world, Romantic love. "I don't believe in love at all," he tells Ursula. "Love is one of the emotions like all the others – and so it is all right whilst you feel it. But I can't see how it becomes an absolute" (121). In what sounds like a deliberate repudiation of the Platonic tradition that lies behind Shelley, Birkin asks, "Why should we consider ourselves, men and women, as broken fragments of one whole?" (192). He shudders at the idea that a man is only the "broken half of a couple," a woman "the other broken half" (191).[9] Further, the kind of love that strives to merge man and woman into one being repels him. "Fusion, fusion, this horrible fusion of two beings, which every woman and most men insisted on, was it not nauseous and horrible anyhow, whether it was a fusion of the spirit or of the emotional body? . . . Why try to absorb, or melt, or merge?" (301). This "old way of love," as he calls it (191), seems no better to him than the solitary self. He tells Gerald that it is worse than "*Egoïsme à deux*" (344).

The old way of love, Birkin believes, springs solely from need. We require the other to fill a gap in ourselves. Because of our insufficiency, we become grasping, acquisitive; we hunger to *possess* the one we love. Ursula's feelings for Birkin owe something to these motives: "She wanted to have him, utterly, finally to have him as her own, oh, so unspeakably, in intimacy. To drink him down – ah, like a life-draught" (257). According to Freud, the desire to possess the loved one is a part of all our "object-choices." But, in a distinction that Lawrence would dispute, Freud tries to separate this urge to possess the other, in romantic love, from the process of identification:

> Identification has been not unsuitably compared with the oral, canni-balistic incorporation of the other person. It is a very important form of attachment to someone else, probably the very first, and not the same thing as the choice of an object. The difference between the two can be expressed in some such way as this. If a boy identifies himself with his father, he wants to *be like* his father; if he makes him the object of his

choice, he wants to *have* him, to possess him. (*New Introductory Lectures* 63)

In contrast to Freud's distinction, Ursula's love for Birkin involves both types of object relations. Her desire to "drink him down – ah, like a life-draught" has an obvious resemblance to the process of incorporation, while her desire to "have him as her own" is the kind of possessiveness that Freud associated with object-choice. Essentially, Lawrence is accusing the romantic choice of object that we call love of being nothing better than a disguised form of identification. One way of understanding Birkin's objections to the old way of love is to see them as a critique of the Freudian concept of desire.

Freud himself suggests several exceptions to his own distinction. The first is very young children (*The Ego and the Id* 19); the second, women. "It is however possible to identify oneself with someone whom, for instance, one has taken as a sexual object, and to alter one's ego on his model. It is said that the influencing of the ego by the sexual object occurs particularly often with women and is characteristic of femininity" (*New Introductory Lectures* 63). Here Lawrence and Freud would appear to be in perfect agreement. In a long meditation excoriating women in general and Ursula in particular, Birkin thinks, "She was only too ready to knock her head on the ground before a man. But this was only when she was so certain of her man, that she could worship him as a woman worships her own infant, with a worship of perfect possession" (192). Given Lawrence's attitude toward women, one is in danger of overlooking the fact that Lawrence believes that all selves – male or female – conflate romantic object-choice and identification.

For Lawrence, the self is always already a slave to the objects it has chosen to love. Ursula's contradictory tendencies toward possessiveness and self-abasement are produced not by her status as a woman but by the social basis of her self. If she bows down before the other, it is only because she has grown accustomed to setting up the other within her as part of the self. Hence Birkin is right in seeing her love, for all its humility, as "assertive *will*," as "frightened apprehensive self-insistence" (243). In this respect he thinks Ursula is no different from anyone else, man or woman. The conclusion of Ursula's thoughts about consuming Birkin illustrates the paradox of her feelings: "She believed that love was *everything*. Man must render himself up to her. He must be quaffed to the dregs by her. Let him be *her man* utterly, and she in return would be his humble slave – whether she wanted it or not" (258).

For Freud, the only occasion when a man might mistake object-choice for identification is after the loss of a loved one. Freud does not object to this confusion, for it is a crucial part of the healing process he calls mourning: "When it happens that a person has to give up a sexual object, there quite often ensues an alteration of his ego which can only be described as setting up of the object inside the ego, as it occurs in melancholia. . . . It may be that this identification is the sole condition under which the id can give up its objects" (*Ego and Id* 19). Lawrence's more radical perspective leads him to assert that every self is a product of what Freud would call melancholia or mourning. All our object relations, according to Lawrence, are governed by the paradoxical, destructive desire both to imitate and to possess. He sees only one answer: to throw off the self entirely. As Birkin tells Ursula, "There needs the pledge between us, that we will both cast off everything, cast off ourselves even, and cease to be, so that that which is perfectly ourselves can take place in us" (138). In this world, however, such an end seems remote. Hence Birkin finds himself wondering in despair, "Why bother about human relationships? Why take them seriously – male or female? Why form any serious connections at all?" (294).

THE REPRESENTATION OF UNION

Even in his periods of greatest dejection, however, Birkin does not reject the goal of a visionary union. He never ceases to believe in "the mystic conjunction, the ultimate unison between people – a bond" (143). When he objects to "fusion, fusion, this horrible fusion of two beings," he is criticizing the personal, merely "human" approach to Romantic union. "It isn't love I want. It is something much more impersonal and harder – and rarer," he tells Ursula. He remains unconvinced that any "emotional relationship" (137) can take one far enough beyond the limits of one's self and the constraints of one's world to achieve the apocalyptic bond that is necessary. The impersonal union he craves is *beyond* ordinary emotions, in the fully transcendent reference of the word "beyond." "There is a real impersonal me, that is beyond love, beyond any emotional relationship" (137).

The kind of union that Birkin seeks, the union that is beyond love, he calls "star-equilibrium" (311). "'What I want is a strange conjunction with you – ' he said quietly; ' – not meeting and mingling; – you are quite right: – but an equilibrium, a pure balance of two single beings: – as the stars balance each other'" (139). Through such an equilibrium, two beings can achieve the kind of union that was described by the passage quoted in the Introduction. Birkin and Ursula attain a perfect consummation, a new, superfine bliss that gives them a peace superseding knowledge and that creates an unrealized wonder, a new paradisal unit regained from duality.

This union is the last visionary experience we shall discuss in detail, and it is appropriate that the moment should be the most graphically described, fully dramatized episode that we have encountered. As is his wont, Lawrence raises the stakes in his art. He makes a deliberate attempt to represent a visionary union directly, as a physical meeting of two finite, very human characters, within the bounds of a dramatically structured narrative order. We need to examine this union's role as part of the narrative. Is it an adequate representation of an apocalyptic visionary experience?

Lawrence defines the issue with exemplary clarity. Months before the lovers find their "strange conjunction," Birkin tries to convince Ursula of the existence of such a bond. His arguments in the chapter "Mino" uniformly fail to persuade her, as perhaps all *arguments* should on such a question. Birkin struggles to explain the workings of a state that he has never experienced but only envisioned as necessary and therefore possible. His words do not represent this "strange conjunction" so much as analyze it, yet they become one of its most compelling presentations in the novel. The course of his analysis, however, identifies the main obstacles to any narrative representation of the ineffable:

> "There is," he said, in a voice of pure abstraction, "a final me which is stark and impersonal and beyond responsibility. So there is a final you. And it is there I would want to meet you – not in the emotional, loving plane – but there beyond, where there is no speech and no terms of agreement. There we are two stark, unknown beings, two utterly strange creatures, I would want to approach you, and you me. And there could be no obligation, because there is no standard for action there, because no understanding has been reaped from that plane. It is quite inhuman – so there can be no calling to book, in any form whatsoever – because one is outside the pale of all that is accepted, and nothing known applies." (137–8)

What kind of character would be stark, impersonal, an unknown being, an utterly strange creature, and quite inhuman? Shelley's Jupiter, Prometheus, or Demogorgon; Blake's "visionary forms dramatic"; Keats's Apollo, dying into life (though not the fallen Titans, for in defeat they have already become too human); even Wordsworth's "unknown modes of being" – these are recent English literature's most memorable representatives of the apocalyptic forms that Birkin is describing. What kind of narrative sequence would be appropriate to a plane where "there is no standard for action," where the concept of responsibility is irrelevant, and where nothing known applies? Even in an overtly visionary poem such as *Hyperion*, Keats finds this question too difficult to answer; after Apollo's birth, the attempted narrative comes to an abrupt end. What kind of discourse would make intelligible a realm where there is no speech and no terms of agreement, a realm from which no understanding has been reaped? A voice out of the whirlwind, a sound like the rush of a mighty wind, a poem of silence?

Speculating about such imponderables can be a particularly risky activity. If one tries to prove the impossibility of capturing the ineffable in words, one risks sounding as mystical as Birkin himself.[10] The limit of language, however, is not quite what we are attempting to explore here. The question of whether or not one can represent a visionary experience within the limits of a particular kind of literary form is a separate, and arguably more determinate, issue from the larger philosophical question. In *Women in Love* Lawrence attempts to represent the "strange conjunction" as a single, determinate event, within a sequence of other, causally connected, convincingly mimetic incidents. Yet, if Birkin is even partially accurate in his analysis of this state, the experience's status *as an event* must be questioned before anything else. An event is inadequate, because it exists only as a finite occurrence in a finite universe. If Lawrence is determined to capture an apocalyptic vision within the structure of a dramatic event, then the strategy of deconstruction, by means of which Shelley and Emily Brontë circumvented the limitations inherent in the structure of any finite experience, is not available.

The problems with Lawrence's bold decision become apparent in the chapter where the lovers' visionary union finally occurs. "Excurse" is perhaps the most frequently discussed chapter in all of Lawrence's novels. In it Birkin and Ursula consummate their mystic union by a specific sexual act, probably anal, then spend the remainder of the night under the trees of Sherwood Forest. The critics who object to this chapter adduce many reasons for its failure, ranging from dislike of the sexual practice, through criticism of the scene's overblown rhetoric and heavy-handed symbolism, to impatience with Lawrence's overt expounding of his metaphysical ideas.[11] More important, many readers object to the political implications of an act that seems to cast the woman first in a worshipful, then in a submissive posture. There is, however, another reason for criticizing this section that has not been explored. The scene fails to live up to the requirements of Lawrence's own prophetic vision; that is, it violates some of the very principles that the novel as a whole, and this chapter in particular, seem to validate. "Excurse" asserts its vision as authoritative, an apocalyptic revelation that is final and complete. In claiming the actual presence and reality of this union, it inadvertently reestablishes the authority of an epiphanic state, and with it, the very structure of presence and absence that the rest of the novel has resisted:

> He stood before her, glimmering, so awfully real, that her heart almost stopped beating. He stood there in his strange, whole body, that had its marvelous fountains, like the bodies of the sons of God who were in the beginning. There were strange fountains of his body, more mysterious and potent than any she had imagined or known, more satisfying, ah,

finally, mystically-physically satisfying. She had thought there was no source deeper than the phallic source. And now, behold, from the smitten rock of the man's body, from the strange marvellous flanks and thighs, deeper, further in mystery than the phallic source, came the floods of ineffable darkness and ineffable riches. (306)

Lovers, like poets, may give their visions a "local habitation and a name," but perhaps such an exact location should be avoided. Coleridge, too, saw a "mighty fountain" as an image of power, but in his poem the seething waters flow through the measureless caverns of Xanadu. Shelley's fountains in "Epipsychidion" – a more immediate precursor of Lawrence's text – spring from within his lovers' bodies, but the moment of consummation is still to come, in a wished-for future, on a distant "Elysian isle." Although Shelley's imagery is quite as sexual as Lawrence's, it conveys the aspiring reach of the poet's desire rather than the assured grasp of satisfaction:

> Our breath shall intermix, our bosoms bound,
> And our veins beat together . . .
>   . . . the wells
> Which boil under our being's most inmost cells,
> The fountains of our deepest life, shall be
> Confused in passion's golden purity,
> As mountain-springs under the morning Sun. (lines 568–72)

Lawrence's image of fountains flooding "from the smitten rock of the man's body" encourages a reductive literalness even as it invokes this entire figurative tradition.[12] The passage is one of physical discovery, not spiritual recognition – the Romantic internalized quest brought back out to the external world. Far from revealing a force that can find articulation only in the delirious leaps of poetic language, the images strain to add power to an event that is conspicuously lacking in power. The lovers' satisfaction might remind us that fulfillment – completion – is a value of epiphanic experience, not prophetic faith. It is Gerald, after all, who craves "a great experience, something final" (431). The sense of triumphant accomplishment in this passage tends to demystify the event, not to restore a sense of its primal mystery. The author's repeated assertions of presence, of discoveries made *here*, of sources pinned down and defined, once and for all, bind the imagination. As a result, the passage puts Lawrence in a position of dominance over the reader. Unlike an act of the prophetic imagination, which enlarges the reader's own capacity for imagination, this moment shrinks the realm of visionary possibility to a single portal of the human body and a specific act "beyond the phallic mysteries." A truly prophetic quest for power should elicit an answering quest in the reader. But we, like Ursula, are left to choose between submission and defiance.

Fortunately, the novel does not culminate in this passage. On the next page Birkin and Ursula begin a dialogue that will shape the course of the remaining eight chapters. Over dinner, the lovers plan how they will spend the rest of their lives. Their first action, Birkin decides, must be to drop their existing responsibilities so that they will be free to wander and explore. Ursula is not as eager as he to shed all the trappings of their old life – she particularly likes the romantic cottage at the mill – but she is willing to acquiesce in what she thinks of as her lover's whimsy. She does not understand how deep Birkin's desire for this new life runs. Birkin craves a freedom, with Ursula, and with a "few other people." More than any sexual union, this "freedom together," as he calls it, among a man and a woman and a few others, constitutes the heart of his apocalyptic program.[13]

The lovers' disagreement on this subject is critical, for it restores the novel to its most authentic strength, the struggle between Birkin's prophetic hopes and Ursula's more human grasp of ordinary realities:

> "You see, my love," she said, "I'm so afraid that while we are only people, we've got to take the world that's given – because there isn't any other."
> "Yes, there is," he said. "There's somewhere where we can be free – somewhere where one needn't wear much clothes – none even – where one meets a few people who have gone through enough, and can take things for granted – where you be yourself, without bothering. There is somewhere – there are one or two people – "
> ....
> "Yes," she said wistfully. Those "few other people" depressed her.
> (307–8)

Birkin's eager insistence that there *is* such a place returns us to the realm of speculation. The poverty of his description – "somewhere where one needn't wear much clothes" – is touching. We can feel the strength of desire that motivates this attempt to dream such a post-apocalyptic world into existence. Even his qualifications – that it is not a physical place but a perfected relation – acknowledge the fragility of his hopes.

Their wandering takes them to the celebrated chapter "Continental" and the novel's ending in the deathly snows of the Alps. Increasingly, Ursula comes to realize that "no new earth had come to pass" (382), and her doubts serve to put in question the moment of union that she and Birkin had shared. After Gerald's death Birkin too begins to despair of finding a new world for himself. His failure to find in Gerald a friend who could be one of the "few others" works with Ursula's doubts to undermine further the apocalyptic character of what he thought he had achieved.

In their very struggle with doubt, however, the final pages of the novel have a prophetic power far beyond anything in "Excurse." Birkin's last restatement of his vision displays the courage of a prophet who prolongs his witness even in the midst of defeat. His words are prophetic in the way that the Suffering Servant in Isaiah and much of Job are prophetic: They record a refusal to submit in the face of seemingly impossible conditions. In the Bible this refusal to submit is set against the history of a world that opposes faith. In a sense history *is* what opposes the prophet's vision. But, in another sense, history is what allows the knowledge of this vision to endure. The history of Birkin, Ursula, Gerald, and Gudrun ends in defeat, a defeat reflected in Ursula's last words to Birkin:

> "You can't have two kinds of love. Why should you!"
> "It seems as if I can't," he said. "Yet I wanted it."
> "You can't have it, because it's false, impossible," she said.

To which, a prophetic vision has only one answer: "I don't believe that" (473).

NOTES

1 In the "Phaedrus" Plato discusses that "inspired madness" which is "a divine release of the soul from the yoke of custom and convention" (1:450). He says that there are four types of madness that must be regarded not as forms of human infirmity but as "divine gift[s]": prophetic, Dionysiac, poetic, and erotic.

2 Jonathan Culler has suggested a way of considering the subject close to the one presented here: "The novel is conventionally tied to the world in a way that poetry is not. . . . In poetry deviations from the *vraisemblable* are easily recuperated as metaphors which should be translated or as moments of a visionary or prophetic stance; but in the novel conventional expectations make such deviations more troubling and therefore potentially more powerful" (189–90).

3 Bruce Kawin's study of reflexive fiction and the ineffable proceeds from a similar assumption. Kawin writes, "A substantial percentage of literature's attempts to confront or describe the ineffable – any ineffable – at some point generate (as a function of the frustration of those attempts) a sense of their own limits as texts" (*The Mind of the Novel* 21).

4 There have been no general studies of Romantic vision in the novel, and with the exception of studies of *Wuthering Heights* very few considerations of Romantic vision in individual novels. In part, this stems from the inadequate notion of Romanticism that informs those attempts that have been made to relate the novel to Romantic poetry. Several years ago Stuart Curran remarked that "Victorian scholars talk of Romanticism and Romantic poets with a looseness that would be offensive to specialists in the earlier period, who in turn lose all depth when they cross 1832. Although the last years have seen repeated professions about the unities of nineteenth-century literature, many critics, especially those whose focus is a single author, reflect an unhealthy isolation" (638). Donald Stone's work has gone some way toward remedying this isolation; but his restriction of the Wordsworthian strain (one of two strains of influence he identifies, the other being the Byronic) to "quietude" makes any consideration of the visionary aspect of Wordsworth

out of the question. Moreover, Stone's neglect of formal or generic problems makes his work of more interest to a reader tracing common themes or attitudes than to a reader concerned with theoretical questions about the relation of poetry and the novel.

5 Reiman and Powers have established the most reliable texts for the poems and the prose that they include in their *Shelley's Poetry and Prose*. Unless otherwise noted, all quotations from Shelley will be from their edition.

6 M. H. Abrams has emphasized how closely accounts of Romantic transcendence follow the pattern of biblical conversion experiences (*Natural Supernaturalism* 32–70).

7 Chatman states the obvious assumptions that lie behind our understanding of character in narratives: "Narrative existents [i.e., characters] must remain the same from one event to the next. If they do not, some explanation (covert or overt) must occur. If we have a story like 'Peter fell ill. Peter died. Peter was buried,' we assume that it is the same Peter in each case" (30).

8 Since A. C. Bradley drew renewed attention to the visionary Wordsworth in 1909, the theme of transcendence has been an increasingly important topic in Romantic studies. The authors of this critical revision who have had the most influence on this study include G. Wilson Knight (1941), Northrop Frye (1947), Geoffrey Hartman (1954), David Ferry (1959), Harold Bloom (1961), M. H. Abrams (1971), Thomas Weiskel (1976), and Thomas McFarland (1981).

9 It used to be common to refer to Blake, Wordsworth, and Shelley as "mystics." Today, those literary critics who go into the matter at any length usually distinguish the visionary experience of Romantic poets from mysticism. For the controversy regarding Blake, see Frye (*Fearful Symmetry* 25–6). For a reasoned counter-view of the issue of Blake's mysticism, see Damrosch (47–51). On the difference between Wordsworth's poetry and mysticism, see Hirsch (16–17 and passim). In discussions of Shelley the debate generally centers on his relation to neo-Platonic ideas of the One. See, for example, Grabo (179–80) and Pulos (75–7).

10 Bloom, *Ringers in the Tower* 13–35. A recent study by Patricia A. Parker, *Inescapable Romance*, interestingly develops Bloom's insight in the course of considering the elements of romance in the lyrics of Keats.

11 All quotations from *The Prelude* are from the 1850 version, unless otherwise noted, and are identified by the abbreviation *P*, followed by the book and line number.

12 The fully achieved visions of Blake, for example, have had little influence on the course of the novel. Those Victorian novelists who knew Blake's work often thought him virtually insane. See Donald Stone (320–1). According to Stone, the Romantic poets most English novelists knew best were Wordsworth, Byron, Scott, and to a lesser extent Shelley.

13 Compare Wordsworth's lines about divine madness that directly precede his discussion of the incommunicability of visionary experience:

> Some called it madness – so indeed it was,
>
> . . . .
>
> If prophecy be madness; if things viewed

By poets in old time, and higher up
By the first men, earth's first inhabitants,
May in these tutored days no more be seen
With undisordered sight. (*P*.3.150–4)]

For an excellent account of the sources of Erasmus's concept of ecstasy and its later influence, see Michael Screech's *Erasmus and Ecstasy*.

14 The question of the modern epiphany's relation to Romanticism has been opened once again by Robert Langbaum's recent essay "The Epiphanic Mode in Wordsworth and Modern Literature." In 1956, Hugh Kenner had claimed that the epiphany is not Romantic because it is objective rather than subjective. Morris Beja answered him by relating the epiphany to Romanticism in both its incongruity and its incommensurability with any perceived cause. Langbaum agrees with Beja, adding four further ways in which the Romantic moment looks forward to the epiphany. For our purposes, the modern epiphany might best be considered a variant of the Wordsworthian spot of time, one that emphasizes the sensible world more than the vision that usurps it.

15 Rudolf Otto locates the "numinous" in our sense of the *mysterium tremendum*, "that which is quite beyond the sphere of the usual, the intelligible, and the familiar, which therefore falls quite outside the limits of the 'canny,' and is contrasted with it, filling the mind with blank wonder and astonishment" (26).

16 This conception of liminality is derived from the work of Victor Turner. Literary critics have increasingly emphasized the role of a threshold experience in transcendence. See Angus Fletcher, "'Positive Negation': Threshold, Sequence, and Personification in Coleridge"; Thomas Weiskel, "The Liminal Sublime," in *The Romantic Sublime*; and Harold Bloom, "Coda: Poetic Crossing," in *Poems of Our Climate*.

17 Compare Sharon Cameron's point about transcendence in Emily Dickinson's poetry: "Since the immortal world cannot be seen, it must be specified in lieu of any concrete form, discerned in the shape of a formal absence" (5).

18 Robert Scholes, following Saussure, has written that even the sign has a narrative structure: "The sign, then, as well as the sentence and all larger units of discourse, is primarily narrative" (17).

19 The word "narrative," unless defined otherwise, has become a broadly inclusive term covering such specific categories as story, plot, *récit, sujet,* and *fabula*. "Story" or "*fabula*" is the raw material of narrative, the events in their temporal sequence; "plot" or "*sujet*" is the order in which the events are actually presented by an author. Here, by the word "narrative" we mean simply the sequence of events, whether in the form of story or plot. Narratives always have a sequence. No matter how events are arranged (temporally, causally) or rearranged (through flashback, digression, ellipsis, iteration), one thing must happen after another.

20 Kermode describes the elements of a narrative that are beyond authorial determination this way: "It sounds good to say that the novelist is free; that, like the young man who asked Sartre whether he should join the Resistance or

stay with his mother, he can be told 'You are free, therefore choose; that is to say, invent.' . . . But the novelist is not like that; he is more Thomist than Sartrean, and every choice will limit the next. He has to collaborate with his novel" (*Sense of an Ending* 141).

21 Recently, *Critical Inquiry* (7 [1980]) devoted a special issue to the question of whether or not "the illusion of sequence" is an unavoidable aspect of all narratives. Although the contributions by Kermode ("Secrets and Narrative Sequence"), Ricoeur ("Narrative Time"), and Derrida ("The Law of Genre") challenged the notion that sequentiality is an inherent part of narrative, the *illusion* of sequence – announced in their title – emerged unscathed as something that narrative always generates.

22 Earlier in *S/Z*, Barthes implies that sequence is conservative because it reduces what he calls the "plural" nature of the text, the ability of a text to "establish permutable, reversible connections, outside the constraint of time" (30). "[T]here is the same constraint in the gradual order of melody and in the equally gradual order of the narrative sequence. *Now, it is precisely this constraint which reduces the plural of the classic text*" (30, Barthes's italics). This theme is taken up in Hayden White's contribution to the *Critical Inquiry* symposium. He suggests that the sequential aspect of narrative imposes a reassuring but politically conservative order on all material, whether historical or fictional ("The Value of Narrativity in the Representation of Reality," 5–28).

23 Robbe-Grillet contrasts the otherness of narrative with our tendency to humanize objects: "At every moment, a continuous fringe of culture (psychology, ethics, metaphysics, etc.) is added to things, giving them a less alien aspect, one that is more comprehensible, more reassuring" (18).

24 In *S/Z* Barthes provides one example of how the life of the narrative can determine the life of a character. Balzac's character Sarrasine has been warned not to pursue his love for the Italian singer La Zambinella. Barthes writes, "[On the one hand] Sarrasine is free to heed or to reject the unknown man's warning. . . . No less structurally, however, Sarrasine is not free to reject the Italian's warning; if he were to heed it and to refrain from pursuing his adventure, there would be no story. In other words, *Sarrasine is forced by the discourse* to keep his rendezvous with La Zambinella: the character's freedom is dominated by the discourse's instinct for preservation" (135, Barthes's italics).

25 This pattern is not unique to Wordsworth. Cameron finds the disruption of narrative to be Emily Dickinson's chief method of representing a visionary experience.

26 These two models correspond to the common division of religious experiences into opposed types. W. T. Stace defines the two kinds of mysticism as the "introvertive" (pure consciousness) and the "extrovertive" (a unifying vision of oneness) (131–2). Ninian Smart, despite his objections to Stace, also divides all religious experiences into two types: the numinous (which, significantly, he finds in the poetry of Wordsworth) and the mystical (contemplative sense of oneness) (Katz 10–21).

27 The reading presented here has been influenced most by Hartman's chapter "The Via Naturaliter Negativa" in *Wordsworth's Poetry* (31–69) and by Weiskel (167–204).

28 George Levine's discussion of landscape in the Victorian novel may help explain why it is appropriate to take a passage prompted by the Alps as a model for the way Romantic vision disrupts narrative. Levine writes, "On the whole, Victorian fiction breathes only at low altitudes. Air is thin among the huge and terrifying reaches of Shelley's Mont Blanc. . . . Wordsworth believed that the mind and nature could marry, even at the heights. . . . In novels, the heights are not for marriage, but for dreams or disasters. . . . From the beginning of 'Mont Blanc' to the end of D. H. Lawrence's *Women in Love,* the heights are wild and seductive and incompatible with ordinary life" (*Realistic Imagination* 207–8).

29 The phenomenological account of how representation reduces the otherness of objects can help us understand Wordsworth's practice. Georges Poulet writes that in literature objects become "subjectified objects. In short, since everything has become part of my mind thanks to the intervention of language, the opposition between the subject and its objects has been considerably attenuated" (58). We shall have more to say about Wordsworth and phenomenology in Chapter 5.

30 The use of "humanism," here and elsewhere, draws on Knoepflmacher's exploration of *Religious Humanism in the Victorian Novel,* although it expands Knoepflmacher's definition to include earlier (Romantic) attempts to "infuse poetry into an otherwise drab and prosaic age by lifting it 'above the humdrum of life'" (20).

1. CLARISSA

1 *Les crimes de l'amour, Oeuvres completes,* vol. 3 (Paris, 1961), 26–8; quoted and translated by Eaves and Kimpel, 603.n49.

2 The same can be said of Richardson's influence in Germany and Holland. For an account of Richardson's reputation in all four countries, see McKillop, *Samuel Richardson: Printer and Novelist* (226–83).

3 For the relation between Richardson and Sade, Rousseau, and Laclos, see Praz (95–107).

4 Like the creations of Fancy, Lovelace's tricks might be said to have "no other counters to play with but fixities and definites"; they seem to be "no other than a mode of Memory emancipated from the order of time and space"; and they are certainly "blended with, and modified by that empirical phenomenon of the will, which we express by the word CHOICE" (*Biographia Literaria* 1:305).

5 Margaret Anne Doody also sees the novel as a struggle between contrasting modes of imagination. In general, Doody's emphasis on consciousness and imagination anticipates the view of *Clarissa* presented here, although she is not concerned with relating this view to the emergence of Romanticism. She writes, "Both Clarissa and Lovelace might be said to live in the imagination. There is something more real for each than the 'reality' which the world sees. [For Clarissa, this is the love of God.] Lovelace also lives on the evidence of the unseen. His allegiance is to the invisible power of his own will, which is the way in which he has chosen to recognize his consciousness" (104–5).

6 Her belief in her autonomy, like her rhetoric, is unsupported by any of the social, economic, or physical instruments of authority. Braudy, Warner, and Castle have treated the struggle for power – in the psychological, linguistic, and social realms, respectively – as the central drama of Clarissa's character.

7 Anna Barbauld writes, "There is something in virgin purity, to which the imagination willingly pays homage. In all ages, something saintly has been attached to the idea of unblemished chastity. . . . It was reserved for Richardson to overcome all circumstances of dishonour and disgrace, and to throw a splendour round the *violated virgin*, more radiant than she possessed in her first bloom" ("Life of Samuel Richardson" xcv–xcvi). Anna Seward compares the perfection of Clarissa's virtue to the "transcendent sculptor" of the Venus de Medicis or the Apollo Belvidere (in Ioan Williams 360). Such comments are part of what Marilyn Butler calls a conservative backlash in the Romantic movement that occurred in the last five years of the eighteenth century and the first decade of the nineteenth. Jane Austen's conservative fiction and Wordsworth's turn from radicalism to become the poet of *The Excursion* are two of the more familiar manifestations of this development; but the popularity of such "uplifting" authors as Hannah More and the interruption of the vogue for violent Gothic novels between *The Monk* (1795), say, and *Frankenstein* (1818) are equally part of this movement (see Butler, *Romantics* 94–109, 155–62). To anticipate some of the concerns of the next chapter, we might note the resemblance between mid-eighteenth century theories of "purity" in poetry and the early nineteenth-century conception of the sublimity of virtue. Although Warton's notion of pure poetry was intended to be radical vis-à-vis the kind of verse written by Pope, it appealed to archaic models, encouraged an antiquarian's delight in folklore, and attempted to separate the domain of true poetry from any practically available sphere of action. To the extent that Clarissa's virtue becomes an object of contemplation, a thing of beauty and a joy forever, it participates in this conservative tendency to separate aesthetic effects from ordinary experience.

8 "Sensibility" is another complex term. Hagstrum's lucid book *Sex and Sensibility* offers the most complete account of the changing meanings of this term. In brief, Hagstrum traces an evolution in the use of this word from its early eighteenth-century meaning of intellect, with special reference to moral intelligence, to its later denotation of emotional and amorous sensitivity. Richardson is undoubtedly a pivotal figure in this change. For Clarissa, the word retains its rational and moral component. Eaves and Kimpel have even argued that her idea of the heart is "closer to the Christian conscience, to Milton's Holy Spirit, than to the urgings of passion" (608; see also Brissenden, *Virtue in Distress* 98–100). But the concept contains an emotional dimension for Clarissa as well. Hagstrum's more comprehensive list of qualities that Richardson included in the word seems correct: "It embraces death, romantic love, response to external nature, benevolence, forgiveness, Christian virtue, Protestant piety" (199). For a recent view that complements Hagstrum's, see Bell (15–39).

9 Hagstrum notices an erotic element in their bond (202), and Eagleton thinks that Anna comes close to arguing for militant feminist separatism (78). See also Janet Todd (9–68).

10 Garber compares the seclusion of the lady's closet where Clarissa retires to write letters to the motif of "paradisal enclosure" in Milton and other Puritan writers (*Autonomy of the Self* 6–7). This is part of an interesting treatment of Clarissa's struggle for "contextual autonomy" – the desire to be self-sufficient within the context of a social order – that Garber relates to emerging Romanticism (3–17).

11 Castle argues that even with Anna, Clarissa's correspondence is not free from coercive interpretations, aggressive "constructions" (76–8). Perhaps useful as a corrective, the "construction" Castle puts on their correspondence goes too far in stressing the limiting character of Anna's response. Castle pays little attention to the *need* for an interpreter, both to constitute the self as a subject and to liberate that self from the isolation of subjectivity.

12 This thesis restates in formal terms some of Christopher Hill's conclusions about Clarissa's incompatibility with eighteenth-century social values. Hill writes: "It is Richardson's greatness, it seems to me, that his respect for Clarissa's integrity led him to push the Puritan code forward to the point at which its flaw was completely revealed, at which it broke down as a standard of conduct for this world" (334–5).

13 See also Arthur Lindley, who contends that Lovelace is "the active embodiment of the author's narrative imagination" (203).

14 Anthony Winner develops the implications of this interpretation in one of the best readings of Lovelace's character.

15 For a discussion of the resemblances between *Caleb Williams* and Richardson's last two novels, see Rothstein (*Systems of Order and Inquiry* 211–12).

16 *Sanditon* continues: "If she could not be won by affection, he must carry her off. He knew his Business. – Already had he had many Musings on the Subject. If he *were* constrained so to act, he must naturally wish to strike out something new, to exceed those who had gone before him – and he felt a strong curiosity to ascertain whether the Neighbourhood of Tombuctoo might not afford some solitary House adapted for Clara's reception; – but the Expence alas! of Measures in that masterly style was ill-suited to his Purse, & Prudence obliged him to prefer the quietest sort of ruin & disgrace for the object of his Affections, to the more renowned – " (6:405–6).

17 Traugott, for example, writes, "Lovelace is a talented comic writer, but he is fatally driven to confuse art and life" (179). Doederlein charts the history of critical attempts to exonerate Lovelace and to shift the blame for the rape onto other characters, including Mrs. Sinclair, Mrs. Harlowe, Mr. Harlowe, the other males of the Harlowe family, and, of course, Clarissa herself.

18 See Traugott (178). Morris Golden's treatment of the episode is a significant exception to the general practice. In the first chapter of his study, Golden regards Lovelace's fantasies of rape as evidence of the sadistic element in his constitution.

19 This notion of aggressivity is taken from Lacan. Lovelace's desire, with its heavy emphasis on mastery and possession, is trapped within the stage that

Lacan calls the "Imaginary." As this term suggests, one way to characterize Lovelace's mode of imagination is to look at its origin in aggressive impulses. By contrast, Clarissa experiences everything in the register of what Lacan calls the "Symbolic." For more on the connection between aggression and the Imaginary, see Chapter 4 of this volume.

20 The different erotic positions assumed by the characters in *A Man with a Maid* could be read as an expansion upon a few hints contained in Lovelace's two letters. The protagonist of the Victorian novel subdues not a paragon of purity like Clarissa, but a defiant and spirited woman like Anna Howe. Later in the book, his depredations enlarge to include the lady's maidservant, and then a mother and her daughter. The man's pleasure in watching women humbled together, and humbling one another, elaborates motifs that are clearly present in Lovelace's imagination, not only in his employment of female assistants to help in his ruin of Clarissa, but also in the fantasies he develops around Anna. At one point in the transcript of Anna's letters, one of Lovelace's female aides adds this note: "For the Lord's sake, dear Mr. Lovelace, get this fury to London!"; to which Lovelace responds, "Her fate, I can tell thee, Jack, if we had her among us, should not be so long deciding as her friend's. What a gantlope would she run, when I had done with her, among a dozen of her own pitiless sex, whom my charmer shall never see!" (2:365).

21 In a discussion of *Great Expectations*, Peter Brooks comments, "The nineteenth-century novel in general – and especially that highly symptomatic development, the detective story – regularly conceives plot as a condition of deviance and abnormality, the product of cities and social depths, of a world where *récit* is *complot*, where all stories are the result of plotting, and plotting is very much machination" (138–9).

22 For representative comments on the possibility of poetry existing in works of prose, see Wordsworth (*Prose* 125), Coleridge (*Biographia Literaria* 2:14), Shelley (484–6), and Hazlitt (5:13–14).

23 Some had already become standard. Anna Seward, writing in 1787, praises the "transcendent sublimity" of the pen-knife scene (Ioan Williams 362). Observe, also, her comment on the death of Clarissa: "Cold to the sense of devotion, dead to hope, and trust of a blessed immortality, must be the heart, which does not triumph, and delight (however the eyes may overflow) in the death of Clarissa, in the everlasting rest of a broken heart, in the emancipation of an oppressed, an injured, and angelic spirit, soaring over all its cruel persecutors, to unfading light, and ever-during felicity" (361). In another essay, "An Inquiry into those Kinds of Distress which Excite Agreeable Sensations," Anna Barbauld returns to the same group of scenes to discuss the "charm" around Clarissa "which prevents her receiving a stain from any thing which happens" (*Works* 2:223–4).

24 This attitude is most prevalent in those critics who view *Clarissa* primarily as a novel about the self's place in society. Thus Stephen Cox writes, "There is little question, however, that in reserving the novel's climax for Clarissa's protracted dying and the sympathy that pours in upon her, Richardson greatly reduced the artistic value of his novel. . . . The basic problem is that Richardson neglects the complex issues of personal integrity and motivation

that he has pursued throughout the rest of the novel and focuses instead on the starkly simple issue of Clarissa's death" (80). Cynthia Griffin Wolff, whose more complex reading has many useful things to say about the Puritan background and religious function of Clarissa's withdrawal from the social world of the novel, nevertheless concludes, "Yet in remaining true to his heroine, Richardson has failed at least partially to solve the problems with which he begins the novel. Thus as a novel of character, an example of psychological realism, the work is superb; as a novel which attempts the further task of placing character into a coherent moral or social framework, the narrative leaves us not completely satisfied" (165).

25 Thus Kinkead-Weekes sees the three parts in which Richardson published the novel as a way of dividing the book into sections focusing on social, moral, and religious issues respectively. Even so, he has some trouble with Clarissa's death: "At the end of *Clarissa*, indeed, Richardson seems to realise that his deepest moral convictions run clean counter to the drama that gives his fiction its most vivid life. He makes drama die before his heroine does, by deliberately de-dramatising her as she reaches towards her apotheosis" (453).

26 Konigsberg demonstrates that Richardson consciously followed tragic models (74–94). William Park sees the novel as a struggle between Clarissa's tragic vision of events and Lovelace's comic view, with the former winning out in the end. Near the conclusion of his essay he mentions, in passing, another conflict: "The tension between a bourgeois vision and a tragic one is in part a tension between the genre of the novel and the plot of tragedy" (469). Warner also thinks of the text as torn between the tragic and comic perspectives of the two main characters, although he regards the struggle of genres as inherently irresolvable (77–87). On the other side of the question, Mary Poovey ("Journeys from this World to the Next") makes the best case for regarding the novel as a divine comedy, in which Clarissa's transfiguration completes a Providential pattern. Alan Wendt also takes this position, although he does not explicitly frame his argument in terms of genre. Michael Bell develops a variation on the conflict-of-genres theory, this time between Lovelace's comedy and Clarissa's religious allegory (34–5).

27 The addition of some of Clarissa's moral sentiments and the account of the hours of a typical day, both taken from the time of her life when she was engaged in ordinary, worldly activities, are efforts to reemphasize the exemplary aspects of her character after her transfiguration has distanced her from the ethical sphere of the narrative.

2. PURE POETRY/IMPURE FICTION

1 The discussion of this period draws on the ground-breaking work of Monk, Abrams's *Mirror and the Lamp*, and Maclean, as well as the more recent history of eighteenth-century poetry by Rothstein.

2 Exceptions to this generalization include Frye's essay "Towards Defining an Age of Sensibility" (*Fables of Identity* 130–7) and a new study by John Sitter.

3 See Freedman, Joseph Frank, and Edel. But also see Reuben Brower, who objects to the metaphor of the "novel as poem." For discussions of European

Romantic theory of the novel as a "mixed" genre, see Gasché, Mellor (19–22), and Marshall Brown (199–214).

4 For the distinctive role of crisis in the Romantic lyric, see Abrams, "Structure and Style in the Greater Romantic Lyric."

5 The phrase is from Robert Potter's reply in 1783 to Samuel Johnson, who had censured the odes of Gray. Potter's reasons for preferring lyric poetry to all narrative genres, including epic, emphasize the former's special capacity to treat visionary subjects: "Hence it appears that this composition not only allowed, but even required sudden and bold transitions, and the highest flights of imagination to which even the Epic Muse dared not aspire: [the Epic Muse] prescribed laws to herself, which confined her to one great action . . . but the Lyric is a Muse of fire that rises on the wings of Extasy, and follows her Hero or her God from one glorious action to another, from earth to heaven" (14).

6 This is the design behind the essays collected in the volume *The Gothic Imagination: Essays in Dark Romanticism*; see especially the "Introduction" by G. R. Thompson. Kiely, too, wants to view the narrative experiments of the Gothic novels as akin to Romantic lyric poetry (7). Elizabeth MacAndrew's distinction between Romanticism and the Gothic provides a good starting point for an examination of the differences between visionary poetry and novels of horror: "Although related to Romanticism, Gothic works differ from those of the Romantic mainstream in their concern with human psychology in this world, as opposed to Romanticism's primary interest in a transcendental, mystic view of Nature and mankind's yearnings for things not of this world" (252). Like MacAndrew, Robert Hume also emphasizes that the Gothic writers "have no faith in the ability of man to transcend" (289).

7 See the reviews of *The Mysteries of Udolpho* collected in Ioan Williams (389–95). A typical description of the virtues of this genre stresses its narrative strengths, such as its skill at arousing and sustaining suspense: "Curiosity is kept upon the stretch from page to page, and from volume to volume, and the secret, which the reader thinks himself every instant on the point of penetrating, flies like a phantom before him, and eludes his eagerness till the very last moment of protracted expectation" (389).

8 Despite the attention that the topic of pure poetry has received from recent scholars who want to challenge a theory that would deny Donne, Dryden, and Pope the status of poets, the theoretical connection between purity and vision has not been explored. The seminal piece in this discussion, Robert Penn Warren's "Pure and Impure Poetry," is concerned with defining poetry in such a way as to include discursive reasoning as well as imagery and feeling. See also Pottle (89–107) and T. S. Eliot. The most interesting recent discussion of the subject is an analysis of the role that purification plays in the language of modern American poetry by Hartman (*Criticism in the Wilderness* 115–32).

9 Garber makes a similar point: "The central form of Gothic is a confrontation, led to and symbolized by the meeting of modes, one element of which has just suddenly, rudely emerged" ("Meaning and Mode" 157).

10 This premise underlies the work of those critics who find in the Gothic novel

a "quest for the numinouse" (Varma 209, 211–12). See also Varnado and Porte. Morris is persuasive when he argues that this interpretation "ignores how far Gothic supernaturalism is an artificial, aesthetic creation which can command terror without necessarily commanding belief" (318).

11 In an important article on "The Gothic Sublime," Morris remarks that "the Gothic novel pursues a version of the sublime utterly without transcendence. It is a vertiginous and plunging – not a soaring – sublime, which takes us deep within rather than far beyond the human sphere" (306).

12 Lowry Nelson points out that the Gothic novel itself evolved away from a dependence on the "supernatural" and toward what he calls the "subnatural," the "impulse to evil" that exists within rather than beyond nature (249).

13 Valéry's account of the rigorous purification to which a poet's language must be submitted before it can attain the status of music is a notable modern instance (see his essay on "Pure Poetry," 184–92).

14 Even today, when we encounter difficulty in a novel, we regard it not as a sign of an author's sacred mission but rather as evidence of the author's "experimental" bias – a bias whose connections with empiricism and the scientific method provide an accurate guide to the genre's habitual orientation toward the natural world.

15 The danger of madness was frequently associated with Shakespeare's lines about the lunatic, lover, and poet quoted on the first page of this study. Tasso was the figure most often cited in the late eighteenth century, but in the early nineteenth century several sensibility poets, particularly Collins and Smart, began to run him a close race (see, for example, Nathan Drake's "On the Government of the Imagination; on the Frenzy of Tasso and Collins," 29–44). Anna Barbauld has an interesting poem, written in 1797, that warns Coleridge of the dangers of madness that come from writing too much "metaphysical" poetry. Loss of sight was almost always associated with Milton, while early death was generally connected with Chatterton.

16 By "ethics" we mean a broader spectrum of human activity than is generally associated with the word today. Ethics, for Aristotle, encompassed virtually every aspect of public and private life that was not concerned with metaphysics, including notably intellectual, scientific, and physical excellence, as well as the traditional moral virtues. For more on the connection between ethical concerns and narrative genres, see the discussion of Jane Austen in Chapter 3.

17 See, for instance, Warton (*Essay on Pope* x). Bowles likewise writes, "I must here observe that when I speak of passions as poetical, I speak of those which are most elevated or pathetic" (8).

18 Anna Barbauld, for example, goes into raptures over the novels of "the seductive, the passionate Rousseau," as long as she can view them as a species of poetry: "He has hardly any thing of story; he has but few figures upon his canvass; he wants them not; his characters are drawn more from a creative imagination than from real life, and we wonder that what has so little to do with nature, should have so much to do with the heart" (3:120). Then she spends the remainder of her discussion of Rousseau expressing her moral repugnance at the manners and conduct that his narrative recounts.

19 For the part Aristotle's writing played in the opposition between mimetic and expressive views of art, see Abrams, *The Mirror and the Lamp* pp. 9–12, and, with particular reference to music, p. 91.

20 There are many indications that within "music" Aristotle meant to include poetry as well as wordless songs. His translator explains that he has employed the word "music" to render "the skill presided over by the muses." He continues: "Aristotle uses it chiefly in a fairly restricted sense, to describe performances which make their primary appeal to the ear, and which are given on musical instruments, with or without sung words. *'Mousike'* covered also performances which included dancing, and it could be used in the even wider sense of 'the arts' in general" (*Politics* 461). Writers in the late eighteenth and early nineteenth century were very interested in the parallel between music and pure poetry, often regarding the former as the model or the ideal of the latter.

21 This word translates *catharsis*. The translator uses the phrase "working off the emotions" here, but elsewhere he uses "purifying," and he explains in his notes that he uses the different English renderings interchangeably for the sake of variation (*Politics* 473 n.3).

3. MANSFIELD PARK

1 For Charlotte Brontë's comments and G. H. Lewes's reply, see note 23 of this chapter. It is worth noting that in *Jane Eyre* Charlotte Brontë chooses to celebrate as "one of those genuine productions so often vouchsafed to the fortunate public of those days – the golden age of modern literature" (375) no other poem than *Marmion*. She alludes as well to *The Lay of the Last Minstrel, The Bride of Abydos,* and *The Corsair.*

2 Avrom Fleishman argues that Austen is a Romantic because she participated in a conservative, traditionalist, and nationalist turn within the movement itself. Sulloway and Auerbach think she is Romantic for just the opposite reason, because her feminism is "subversive" of traditional values. McGann effectively disputes this latter position when he observes, "Many subversive ideas (even in the Romantic Period) are not at all Romantic ideas, and many Romantic ideas are by no means subversive" (30). To add to the confusion, a new book by Margaret Kirkham develops still a different position, that Austen is not a Romantic, that she is "anti-Romantic," and that it is her opposition to Romanticism that is subversive: "Austen's anti-Romanticism . . . is an aspect of her feminism" (Kirkham 31).

3 Thus those critics who see this scene as evidence of Austen's affinity with Burke are also correct (Duckworth 49). Fanny's excessive expectations of the past can be reproved at the same time that a Burkean attitude toward tradition is endorsed. See Murrah, who compares Fanny's desire for Gothic atmosphere in the chapel with the attitudes of Catherine Morland in *Northanger Abbey.*

4 A recent treatment of this scene links the "Sotherton garden sequence" with the "discussion of the efficacy of the sermon to inculcate moral behavior" (Gillis 118), although the author views Fanny, too uncritically, as Austen's

surrogate (124). For other discussions of the trip to Sotherton, see Duffy (83–6) and Banfield (4–14).

5 Lionel Trilling introduced this commonplace to the literature on the novel. In his essay on *Mansfield Park*, he writes, "Most troubling of all is [the novel's] preference for rest over motion" (185). Tony Tanner picked up the idea next, writing in his "Introduction" to the novel that "it is the story of a girl who triumphs by doing nothing. She sits, she waits, she endures; and when she is finally promoted, through marriage, into an unexpectedly high social position, it seems to be a reward, not so much for her vitality, as for her extraordinary immobility" (8). Leo Bersani is thus following accepted wisdom when he maintains that the novel "proposes an ethic of stillness" and that Austen's sympathy for "the tremblingly still Fanny Price corresponds to her sense of the social dangers of movement" (75).

6 Kirkham establishes this point with numerous examples (104–5). See also Tave (*Some Words* 174–5) and Morgan (154–5).

7 An exception is Yeazell's recent essay (146–7). Yeazell interestingly relates the novel's emphasis on space and boundaries to the question of "purity." In light of our earlier argument about the different uses poetry and the novel make of the division between pure and impure, it is significant that Fanny "establishes her purity not by an outward, symbolic transformation but by an inner response, the experience of revulsion" (Yeazell 142). Once again, we see a novel in which the issue of purity is treated in terms of conduct, rather than of "salvation or final ends" (Yeazell 147).

8 We should think particularly of her difference from the kind of characters that Todorov has called "narrative-men," figures whose beings are almost entirely constituted by their effect on the course of events. See the Introduction above.

9 For the theory of the *locus amoenus*, see Curtius (192–201). For Spenser's "dialectical treatment" of this tradition, see Nohrnberg (502–7).

10 For an account of the episodes that occur in this room, see Schneider.

11 Moler sees this speech, as well as the one about the beauties of evergreens that follows it and the rhapsody about the harmony of the stars, as couched in the vocabulary of Hannah More (Moler 124–5, 146–9). His assumption that Fanny is being mocked for these stilted speeches does not make them less Romantic. Bradbrook's sources in Romantic fiction seem just as relevant. Bodenheimer has argued persuasively that Fanny's attention to nature develops in sophistication during the course of the novel and that the change makes "a strong argument for the complication and deepening of Fanny's emotional and imaginative life" (613).

12 Gene W. Ruoff compares Fanny's feelings for her brother to those of Wordsworth for Dorothy, and he has a useful discussion of the relation of *Mansfield Park*'s plot of "endogamy" to Romantic narrative. Ruoff considers, then rejects as a matter of lesser importance, R. F. Brissenden's suggestion in "*Mansfield Park*: Freedom and Family" that Fanny's feelings for William, and by extension for Edmund, are incestuous. Julia Brown, however, states the case for incest in even stronger terms, and she relates Fanny's "incestuous" impulse to Romanticism: "The attraction between 'like' personalities has its

source in Romanticism: the other is loved because of his or her share in the self or his representation as a higher self" (Brown 98).

13 See Alan D. McKillop, "Local Attachment and Cosmopolitanism." This discussion is indebted to McKillop for an understanding of the importance of nostalgia to the writers of the late eighteenth and early nineteenth centuries.

14 Julia Brown discusses Fanny's melancholy and suggests that it may explain the popularity of *Mansfield Park* among Victorian readers (86–7).

15 We shall have more to say in Chapter 5 about the function of recognition and reversal in narrative.

16 See the comments by Whately (97–8), Macaulay (122), Lewes (125, 130, 153–4), and Simpson (249–50) in Southam's *Critical Heritage* volume. See also Rachel Trickett's helpful discussion of these articles. In more recent years, Edwin Muir has praised Jane Austen as the pioneer of the "dramatic novel" and discussed her ability to lose herself dramatically in her characters (42–8, 51–9). Litz, also, returns to the Shakespearean analogy in the course of discussing Austen's dramatic conception of character (Litz, "'A Development of Self': Character and Personality in Jane Austen's Fiction").

17 The same can be said of Sir John Everett Millais's study in Romantic melancholy *Autumn Leaves*. This painting, which Ruskin called the "most poetical work the artist has yet conceived," shows the attraction that this mood held for later Victorians.

18 D. A. Miller has given the best treatment of the problem of closure in Austen. He points to the conflict between the moral "settlements" necessary to bring an Austen novel to a close and the instability of character and situation that initiate the narrative, and he correctly emphasizes that this conflict is a dilemma inherent in all narrative discourse: "Closure can *never* include, then, the narratable in its essential dimension: all suspense and indecision" (98). He also has noticed the importance of the word "cure" in Austen. Henry's problem, Miller remarks, is that an "incurable (and hence interminable) narratability traverses him" (24–5).

19 For a discussion of a related topic, see the connection Juliet McMaster finds between "love" and "pedagogy." See also the earlier treatment of education in *Mansfield Park* by Joseph Wiesenfarth (*Errand of Form* 86–108).

20 Despite the difference in vocabulary, Bakhtin's animadversions on the "autotelic" language of poetry should be compared to Austen's worries that poetry fosters a tendency to dwell in a world of its own and thus block out all that is "real and unabsurd" in our feelings. Bakhtin writes: "The [poetic] word plunges into the inexhaustible wealth and contradictory multiplicity of the object itself, with its 'virginal,' still 'unuttered' nature; therefore it presumes nothing beyond the borders of its own context (except, of course, what can be found in the treasure-house of language itself)" (278).

21 This account of Jane Austen's Aristotelianism is indebted to the work of the philosopher Alasdair MacIntyre (222–6). For a further discussion of his work, see Chapter 5.

22 Perhaps the best account of the "ideological contradictions" that Austen's art attempts to reconcile is in Mary Poovey's book *The Proper Lady and the Woman Writer*; see especially 179–82, 203–7 (on the opposed ideological

perspectives implied by the drama and the irony), and 208–24 (on *Mansfield Park*).

23 The contrast is made at the expense of the work of Charlotte Brontë, the writer who had most vehemently denounced Austen's lack of poetry. In a letter to Lewes, she had written, "Can there be a great artist without poetry? What I call – what I will bend to, as a great artist, then – cannot be destitute of the divine gift. . . . Miss Austen being, as you say, without 'sentiment,' without *poetry*, maybe *is* sensible, real (more *real* than *true*), but she cannot be great" (*Critical Heritage* 127). Lewes's essay makes this reply: "If, as probably few will dispute, the art of the novelist must be the representation of human life by means of a story; and if the *truest* representation, effected by the *least expenditure* of means, constitutes the highest claim of art, then we say that Miss Austen has carried the art to a point of excellence surpassing that reached by any of her rivals" ("The Novels of Jane Austen" 152). One modern critic has advanced the notion that Jane Austen should be called a "poet." Significantly, his claim is based on Austen's exceptionally dramatic conduct of the action. Invoking Aristotle, George Whalley finds "poetry" in the "disposition of forces within the whole universe of a novel, particularly that mutual definition of plot and character the product of which Aristotle called *drama*, the thing done, or what I may elsewhere – to distinguish it from the 'action' that is sheer motion – also call 'pure action' " (108).

24 Woolf's sense that poetry could not be included in a novel without damaging the form is a major theme in her literary criticism, a theme that is largely ignored by contemporary critics who use her fiction as an example of the way lyric and the novel can be fused. A more sophisticated account of the twentieth-century "lyrical novel" would have to be aware of the ways in which the poetic impulse in Woolf's fiction produces a deformation of structure. For other comments on the incompatibility of poetry and the novel, see Woolf's collection of essays *Granite and Rainbow* (22, 137).

25 A small sampling of the writers who have called this novel an example of poetic fiction includes Swinburne (763), Woolf (*Granite and Rainbow* 136), Cecil (189–93), Klingopulos (passim), Kettle (205), Ewbank (154–5), Allen (227), Freedman (30), Kiely (7), Hardy ("The Lyricism of Emily Brontë" 95), Loxterman (passim), and Anderson (passim).

4. WUTHERING HEIGHTS

1 Scholars have been unable to prove that Emily Brontë knew the work of Shelley, but so many resemblances can be detected in her poems that a number of commentators have argued for a direct influence. Bradby thinks that Shelley is the Romantic poet who most influenced her. Gerin also points out many similarities between the two authors (153–4). Chitham gives the best account of the circumstantial evidence that is available favoring a direct influence.

2 J. Hillis Miller first made this point in *The Disappearance of God* (170–9).

3 Parker follows the same general line of reasoning in her article. Kermode's chapter on the novel in *The Classic* also emphasizes the element of indeterminacy in the novel (128–30).

4 The importance that Miller attributes to this question is certainly borne out by the number of critics who have attempted to answer it. Critics who argue for a transcendent (and, generally, Romantic) reading of the novel include Cecil (161–2), Buchen, Davies, Patterson, Widdowson, Grudin, Reed (85–119), Apter, and Anne Williams. Two critics who dispute a supernatural reading of the novel are Q. D. Leavis and Eagleton (*Myths of Power* 98–122).

5 *Les écrits techniques de Freud*, vol. 1 of *Le séminaire* (Paris: Seuil, 1975), 178; quoted in Jameson, "Imaginary and Symbolic in Lacan" 362.

6 Gilbert and Gubar make a similar point for different reasons in their reading of the patriarchal elements in the novel. See especially 280.

7 The extent to which Lacan's way of treating such a rebellion might be viewed as politically conservative rather than radical and apocalyptic has been assessed by Fredric Jameson: "Insofar as the Lacanian version generates a rhetoric of its own which celebrates submission to the Law, and indeed, the subordination of the subject to the Symbolic Order, conservative overtones and indeed the possibility of a conservative misappropriation of this clearly anti-Utopian scheme are unavoidable. On the other hand, if we recall that for Lacan 'submission to the Law' designates, not repression, but rather something quite different, namely alienation – in the ambiguous sense in which Hegel, as opposed to Marx, conceives of this phenomenon – then the more tragic character of Lacan's thought, and the dialectical possibilities inherent in it, become evident" ("Imaginary and Symbolic in Lacan" 373).

8 Donald Pease describes a structure in Blake's prophecies that aims at the same end, overcoming the finitude of any single representation: "Thus the imagination overcomes every attempt to limit it to a single representation: as a relation *between two* terms, the imagination must always appear on the other side of any attempt to grasp it singly. . . . Limiting the imagination to a single representation is a dissimulation of Satan, who memorizes, or fixes, the movement of imagination and pretends that he is *either* the creator *or* the outward form of creation" (73).

9 Dorothy Van Ghent suggestively treats the relation of windows to the whole question of identity and otherness in her chapter on *Wuthering Heights* in *The English Novel* (153–70).

10 Lacan locates the mirror stage very early in childhood, from six to eighteen months, but Anthony Wilden gives us ample reason for metaphorically extending the period in which it can occur. "What seems fairly clear is that the *stade du miroir* never 'occurs' at all – any more than the genesis of the ego does. . . . It is evident that the *stade du miroir* is a purely structural or relational concept" (Wilden 174).

11 We shall discuss Shelley's objections to the imitative bases of the self in Chapter 8.

12 Leo Bersani also stresses the way in which Emily Brontë's novel breaks down "coherent, individuated, intelligible structures of personality" (189–90).

13 Angel Medina, criticizing the indiscriminate use of Lacan's notion of the mirror stage, notes that the concept applies to *psychotic* personages, not to the *neurotic* symptoms that are found in most characters. In psychoanalytic terms, Catherine's visions clearly constitute a psychotic episode. She regresses to a

period when there are no boundaries between self and other. Medina's comment brings out the different relation to transcendence that we are trying to uncover in *Wuthering Heights*: "The psychotic cannot perceive the boundaries of meaning of his biography (birth/death, love/struggle, sacrifice/ suffering, redemption/guilt); he cannot pass from one set of boundaries over to another; hence he has no reflective personality that would be born of this transcendence. The neurotic is capable of transcending at least one set of boundaries, usually that of birth/death" (570).

14 Georges Bataille, for example, writes: "In my opinion these lines from *The Prisoner* are the most powerful example of that feeling which underlies Emily Brontë's poetry. . . . Finally it matters little whether Emily Brontë really had what we call a mystical experience, for she appears to have reached the very essence of such an experience" (15). See also Blondel (192–218), Willy, Dobson, Lane, and Miles.

15 A typical reading along these lines is Denis Donoghue's: "Catherine and Heathcliff meet in death, souls united. Death becomes that 'existence of yours beyond you' to which Catherine referred in Chapter 9. . . . This death is a *liebestod*, sexual union transfigured, the soul's inward gaze seeing nothing but itself and its shared identity" (130–1).

16 Homans's essay "Repression and Sublimation of Nature in *Wuthering Heights*" leads us to add Nature to the list of prominent figures for transcendence that the novel itself calls into question.

17 "Deconstruction is not a dismantling of the structure of a text but a demonstration that it has already dismantled itself" ("Stevens' Rock" 341).

5. WORDSWORTH AND THE CONFLICT OF MODES

1 By the word "mode," we refer to what Aristotle called the "modes of imitation," the three basic forms of presentation – lyric, narrative, and drama. Wellek and Warren caution us that "these three more-or-less ultimate categories" are not to be confused with specific historical genres (227). These modes are fundamental to every form of literature, no matter what its genre. They are the "building blocks" (Fowler 236) of literature, not the archetypes from which later historical forms are derived. Hence they cannot be used to define the genre of an individual poem because more than one mode is frequently present in the same work (Hernadi 163); and it has been suggested that every work of literature contains all three modes in differing proportions (Guillén 115). We shall see that the different genres of the poems Wordsworth called "lyrical ballads" were determined by the particular nature of the *conflict between modes* within each poem.

2 Don Bialostosky, who insists that Wordsworth's thinking about genre was influenced by a Platonic rather than an Aristotelian model, believes that the emphasis on the internal-external dichotomy has more to do with Coleridge's reinterpretation of Wordsworth's poetics than it does with Wordsworth's actual theory of genres. Nevertheless, the influence of this way of viewing the issue has been pervasive.

3 The text for "The Ruined Cottage" is from the Ms.D. version edited by James Butler in the new Cornell edition of Wordsworth.

4 Wordsworth's attitude toward stories has been increasingly recognized as an important topic. Langbaum (*Poetry of Experience* 56) emphasizes the "subjectivity" of Wordsworth's lyrical ballads, whereas Kroeber (*Romantic Narrative Art* 42–3) stresses the opposite quality, the "impersonality" that the ballad form gives to the poet's personal musings. Jacobus (159, 166, 248–9), Ryskamp (358), and Sheats (184–5) all follow the line of discussion marked out by Langbaum and Kroeber in commenting on the mixture of lyrical and narrative elements in Wordsworth's early poems. A third position is indicated by Parrish (Chaps. 3–4), who maintains that the unique quality of Wordsworth's lyrical ballads lies in their "dramatic" nature. Danby (36–7) and Jordan (166, 176) both grant the importance of drama in the poems but deny that it is the significant element in determining their form. In addition to these critics, see Jonathan Wordsworth's discussion of the genre of "The Ruined Cottage" in *The Music of Humanity* (66–86) and James Averill on the same work and on the Lucy poems (199–200, 207–10). One of the best estimates of Wordsworth's position can be found in Andrew Griffin's article on "Simon Lee": "Can the surface *business* of any narrative (characters, causes, events, consequences) adequately express or even coexist with the deep, still truths of the imagination? Wordsworth's answer is, I think, that it cannot; that the imagination cannot spin a tale, that it never really moves at all but stands still, pointing and praising, contemplating things to which the narrative and natural eye is blind" (393). All of these critics, however, stay within the essentially phenomenological terms that Wordsworth provides.

5 For evidence of this idea's resemblance to phenomenology, compare it with Gaston Bachelard's contrast of the "poetic image," which is a manifestation of pure being, and the "fabricated image," which is a form "without deep, true, genuine roots" (75; see also xi–xxxi).

6 See, respectively, *The Fate of Reading* (124–46, 147–78) and *Beyond Formalism* (283–97). The distance of these projects from genre study can be gauged by comparing them with a traditionally historical account of the development of a genre, his essay "Wordsworth, Inscription, and Romantic Nature Poetry" (*Beyond Formalism* 206–30).

7 Of the many discussions of Wordsworth's dialectical way of thinking, see Abrams (*Natural Supernaturalism* 21–32) and Bloom (*Visionary Company* 127), both of whom concentrate on the image of "marriage"; Jones (54–110), who concentrates on the interchange between solitude and relationship; and Garber, who discusses the dialectic at work in Wordsworth's "poetry of encounter."

8 John Beer discusses the positive effect of connection in a chapter titled "A Link of Life?" (44–78).

9 It does not matter whether the observer supplies this sentiment of Being or whether the objects of nature actually possess feelings of their own. Jonathan Wordsworth is good on the irrelevance of such questions to the poet's thinking: "At this stage in his thought only the One Life matters, and how it is perceived is relatively unimportant" (*Music of Humanity* 212).

10 R. D. Havens describes Wordsworth's "deep-seated" belief in "animism" as a "reversion to primitive ways of thinking" (79; 68–87 passim). Hartman relates the concept to the poet's sensitivity to the spirit of place.

11 Ferguson examines the function of repetition in "The Thorn" in terms of its relation to Wordsworth's theory of language (13–16). Several general treatments of repetition in narrative have been useful for this discussion. See J. Hillis Miller's essay "Ariadne's Thread" and his book *Fiction and Repetition*, as well as John Irwin's *Doubling and Incest/Repetition and Revenge* and Peter Brooks's *Reading for the Plot*. According to Brooks, attention to the problem of repetition brings out the dynamic nature of narrative, which most structuralist accounts have ignored. "I think we do well to recognize the existence of textual force, and that we can use such a concept to move beyond the static models of much formalism, toward a dynamics of reading and writing" (Brooks 47). Brooks's interest in "the dynamic of the narrative text as pure motor force" (46) is very close to the concerns of this chapter and the succeeding one; his concept of the "narrative motor" (45), a force independent of the values that authors attribute to their stories, is what we have been calling the "life" of narrative.

12 Owen, in his edition of *Lyrical Ballads*, reads "permanently" as "prominently" (Owen 139).

13 Compare Kawin's discussion of repetition: "Repetition is fundamental to human experience. It can lock us into the compulsive insatiability of neurosis, or free us into the spontaneity of the present tense; it can strengthen an impression, create a rhythm, flash us back, or start us over; it can take us out of time completely" (*Telling* 5).

14 Jonathan Wordsworth emphasizes the role that extreme passivity plays in creating this effect. As important as the quality of motionlessness is, it is not the sole way in which figures become associated with liminality in Wordsworth. Any character that seems to bring life and death into close proximity can excite the poet's imagination in this way.

15 See the comment by the poet that Crabb Robinson records in his *Diary* on September 11, 1816. Wordsworth points out that he "represents the child as observing the day-moon, which no town or village girl would ever notice" (*Lyrical Ballads* 301).

6. LITTLE DORRIT

1 The novel's glorification of childhood innocence, as well as its contrast between nature and the city, has made it a prime example of the Wordsworthian strain in Dickens. Guerard's chapter in *The Triumph of the Novel* reads the novel in light of Wordsworth's "The White Doe of Rylstone" (79–87); Sanders notices the similarity to "We Are Seven" (85–6); Donald Stone reads the novel as combining "Wordsworthian quiescence" and "Byronic energy" (271–6), the two forces that he sees as composing "the romantic impulse in Victorian fiction." According to Philip Collins (16), Dickens knew the poetry of Wordsworth and especially admired "We Are Seven."

2 Considered from the point of view of genre, such moments have led one critic to suggest that Dickens's fiction should be considered a development of the

"fairy tale" (Harry Stone 30–2), another to maintain that it is a species of "romantic realism" (Fanger 65–100). Robert Newsom argues that the "Romantic" and the "familiar" in Dickens do not simply merge "into some new synthesis," but rather remain in tension (7). Lawrence Frank's recent psychoanalytic study of the Romantic self in Dickens does not discuss *Little Dorrit*. Perhaps the best attempt to account for Dickens's combination of Romantic and realistic motifs in generic terms has been made by Edwin Eigner. He argues that the "combination of positivist and visionary strains" (7) in Dickens results in an entirely new form of literature, a genre that he names "the metaphysical novel." As indicated in the previous chapter, we shall not be looking at Dickens's novels from the perspective of genre. Rather, this chapter follows Garrett Stewart's lead in considering Dickens's Romanticism on a more local scale. The balance struck at individual points in the text between realistic and Romantic elements can be significant, without being form-determining (that is, generically determinative) for the work as a whole.

3 Some critics have taken the connection between innocence and death in Dickens's work as a sign of the novelist's distance from Romantic attitudes. See Coveney (139–40) and Qualls (98–9). One need only think of all the innocents in Wordsworth's poetry who die young – the boy of Winander, Lucy Gray, Matthew's daughter, the infants in "The Thorn," "The Mad Mother," and "We Are Seven," Ellen in "The Childless Father," and above all, Lucy in "She dwelt among the untrodden ways" and the other Lucy poems – to dismiss this notion as mistaken. Donald Stone, on the other hand, sees Dickens's view of death as one of his most Romantic attributes (260).

4 Peter Garrett discusses this episode as "a movement toward escape or transcendence" (41), relating it to other instances of "elevated transcendence" such as the passage in *Our Mutual Friend* where Jenny Wren says that the peace and joy of sitting on the roof of Riah's house is so great "you feel as if you were dead" (334). Sitting on her perch, Jenny calls to her friend Riah to come up to her and join the dead: "As he mounted, the call or song began to sound in his ears again, and, looking above, he saw the face of the little creature looking down out of a Glory of her long bright radiant hair, and musically repeating to him, like a vision: 'Come up and be dead! Come up and be dead!' " (335).

5 Stewart discusses the "transcendental visions of Jenny Wren" (207) throughout his chapter on *Our Mutual Friend*. He also distinguishes the nature and function of Jenny's visions from "Little Nell's actual death-wishes" (214). Robert Baker emphasizes the power of Jenny's "dreams" and "fictions" to "transcend the spiritual and imaginative inarticulateness" of her world (70–1).

6 Alexander Welsh draws attention to Amy Dorrit's ministering function (176–7). He also notes the aura of danger that this sacred role gives to several of Dickens's heroines (182, 205, 207–10).

7 The opening paragraphs of the novel have justly attracted praise. Lucas responds to the strangeness, the nonhuman aura in the passage (248); Showalter notes the "abrupt and precise divisions, the visible line of demarcation" (26).

8 Hartog draws out many of the parallels between Amy and Wordsworth's children in the course of discussing the political differences between the novelist and the poet. He also comments usefully on Clennam's Wordsworthian characteristics.

9 D. W. Jefferson, who calls her Dickens's "greatest and most sustained tribute to human goodness," thinks that such an ideal figure must be recognized as "poetic" (309). For yet another idealized portrait of Amy Dorrit, see Fleishman, "Master and Servant" (580–1).

10 An interesting variant of Garis's position is Philip Weinstein's idea that Amy has sexual desires that are repressed (54–6).

11 Butt and Tillotson quote a passage that may have inspired Flora's musings from a journalist who is speculating, before the publication of the book, about the possible meaning of the title *Little Dorrit* (Butt 233). They also discuss the peripheral illustrations on the monthly cover but have little to say about the center picture.

12 This view of Dickens is in substantial agreement with that of Robert Caserio. Caserio's insistence on the importance of "recognition" and "reversal" in Dickens's plots has influenced the conception of narrative presented in this chapter as a whole.

13 George Ford points out that Dickens's prefaces were often written as defenses against the charge that his characters and plots were not "probable" (*Dickens and His Readers* 129–55), so this comment on the pattern of the novel is as much a defense of the narrative as of such non-narrative features as imagery, analogy, and symbol.

14 Note, for example, Arthur's excuse for his curiosity about Mr. Meagles's family group. He speaks because he "may never in this labyrinth of a world exchange a quiet word with you again" (18). J. Hillis Miller's reading of the novel relates the image of wandering within a maze to the static image of the prison (*Charles Dickens* 232–5). The labyrinth and the prison in Dickens can be seen as a dark version of the labyrinth and temple imagery that we discussed in Chapter 3.

15 Stewart describes the lyrical power of figures such as Amy in his sixth chapter, "Escape Artists." His discussion of "fire-gazers" is particularly suggestive (160–70), as is his comment on the "lyric inwardness of style" associated with such figures (238–40).

16 Thus wholly optimistic readings of this passage such as those by Beaty (234), Librach (546, 548), and Kelly (49) neglect the willed, fictive nature of these soothing songs. Duckworth's treatment more accurately indicates this passage's problematic status: "What after all is this sovereign value, Nature, that saves and restores Clennam? It is the 'echo' of a 'whisper,' heard in the 'tone' of a 'voice' when a written text (Wordsworth's?) is read by a Mother (Little Dorrit) who substitutes for Arthur's 'real mother,' who never knew her child" ("*Little Dorrit* and the Question of Closure" 127). We might notice that Dickens, like Wordsworth, seems to believe that one can only be taught to hear the "soothing songs" of this voice at the knees of one's Mother, whether she be real or imaginary (cf. "Blest the infant Babe" in *The Prelude* [2.232–65]).

7. ADAM BEDE

1 Some years ago, Thomas Pinney complained that there had been no full treatment of Wordsworth's influence on George Eliot ("George Eliot's Reading of Wordsworth"). Since that time, a number of critics have begun to remedy that situation. Most discussions of this subject emphasize the importance either of Wordsworth's view of nature (Squires 41–52; Auster, *Local Habitations* 45–7; Witemeyer 137–42; Knoepflmacher, "Mutations of the Wordsworthian Child of Nature" 415–21) or of his conception of memory (Pinney, "The Authority of the Past"; Knoepflmacher, *George Eliot's Early Novels* 22–3). Few treat the influence on the novelist of Wordsworth's more disruptive, visionary aspirations, although an article by Karen Mann reaches interesting conclusions about the visionary "power of sound" in George Eliot's fiction. The limited conception of Wordsworth that has hurt most examinations of this topic is still apparent in Donald Stone's work: "The extent of [George Eliot's] unWordsworthian Romantic will to power needs to be assessed lest we allow her to be turned into a figure too good to be true or to be read" (Stone 174). As has become clear, there is nothing "unWordsworthian" about a Romantic will to power. Wordsworth's visionary passages, which celebrate the mind's dominion over outward sense, represent a far more radical example for later novelists than has been recognized.

2 The term "narratable" is taken from D. A. Miller's discussion of Jane Austen and George Eliot. For an explanation of how Miller uses this term, see Chapter 3 above.

3 Elsewhere in the novel, George Eliot articulates her own theory of the unconscious: "Was there a motive at work under this strange reluctance of Arthur's which had a sort of backstairs influence, not admitted to himself? Our mental business is carried on much in the same way as the business of the State: a great deal of hard work is done by agents who are not acknowledged" (1:259).

4 As Levine points out, George Eliot explains the willow wand episode only by reference to the superstitions of country people. Levine helpfully relates this to Scott's tendency to justify the "marvelous" in his novels by grafting them "'upon some circumstance of popular tradition or belief which sometimes can give even to the improbable an air of something like probability'" (Levine, *Realistic Imagination* 109–10).

5 Harold Bloom's description of such visionary "crossings" notes three characteristics: (1) a movement of the senses from sight to sound, (2) an increase in internalization or self-consciousness, no matter how inward the starting point, and (3) an oscillation between mimetic and expressive theories of representation (*Poems of Our Climate* 404). In Adam's early visionary experience, we find all three of these characteristics. He reflects on the superiority of ear to eye, grows self-conscious about his own attitude toward his father, and even debates the comparative value of a mimetic and an expressive theory of representation. His decision to ignore the portent is based on his feeling that the former way of seeing the world is superior to the latter: "For my part, I think it's better to see when your perpendicular's true, than to see a ghost" (1:72).

6 Compare with Reva Stump's point that Adam's insight is "one of the steps in the process by which he learns the art of vision" (13). Stump distinguishes between the act of having visions, which are often "destructive daydreams," and the process of developing "moral vision," which she defines as an ability to see life "in realistic terms and in relation to a broader referent than self" (4). Her use of the word "vision" thus differs from the way it has been used in this study, for the visionary capability hinted at in this scene and explored in depth elsewhere in the novel is more than a propensity for daydreaming, and it leads to the development of a moral vision that cannot always comfortably be described in realistic terms.

7 Newton recognizes the importance of sublimation in George Eliot's thinking and relates it to her "Romantic humanism." Newton, however, views sublimation as a way of containing and disciplining "Byronic egotism" (39–40); Newton does not deal with sublimation as part of a Wordsworthian structure of internalization. To view sublimation solely as a positive way of channeling egotistic emotions misses the morally ambiguous characteristics of the psychological structure itself.

8 For George Eliot's attitude toward the theory of compensation, see Bonaparte, *Will and Destiny* (29–30). Bonaparte is right in stressing George Eliot's resistance to compensation when it appears as an attempt to alter the harsh course of events and consequences, but as we shall show, George Eliot believes compensation has a different value when it operates on the level of spiritual renewal. Whether or not it is valid to separate these two levels is part of the question we are considering.

9 Knoepflmacher notes the relation between Adam's "conversion" and Coleridge's poem (*Religious Humanism* 37).

10 Harvey connects the theme of consequences with George Eliot's narrative technique in a way that anticipates some of the conclusions of this section (117–21). He writes, "The theme of the novel, with its strong sense of nemesis, its emphasis on consequences rather than motives, clearly demands the heavy stress on temporal evolution that is reflected in the precision of the narrative chronology. . . . The art of narrative, at its lowest, implies a simple sequential interest; this happened and then that and then that" (117).

11 Compare Dinah's loving attendance on others with the "ministering" function that we traced in Dickens's liminal figures.

12 On Dinah's resemblance to John Wesley and the basis for this similarity in George Eliot's reading, see Eliot, *A Writer's Notebook* (xxi–xxii, 24–7).

13 This point is taken from Robert Liddell's discussion of the novel (70–2).

14 In a negative treatment of Dinah, Christopher Herbert notes her "otherworldliness," commenting that "Her eyes are fixed on Heaven, on escape from the natural world" (419).

15 Thus Creeger was right when he said that Dinah's Methodism suggested an alternative world to the "pastoral realism" of Hayslope.

16 The theme of moral rescue is central to Barbara Hardy's interpretation of George Eliot in *The Novels of George Eliot*.

17 Here, and throughout this chapter, we are finding evidence of the truth of Felicia Bonaparte's remark: "Most of what we have taken to be the failures of

Eliot's realism are, in fact, the triumphs of her poetry. . . . And it is because we have not recognized the relationship between realism and poetry in Eliot's work that we have divided her fiction into two very distinct halves, admiring the one, regretting the other" (*Triptych and Cross* 5).

18 Henry Auster uses the phrase "synthesizing, dialectical, creative work" (93) to describe the Romantic element in George Eliot's imagination. See his suggestive essay, "George Eliot and the Modern Temper."

19 For a complementary account of this new kind of bond, see Wiesenfarth, *George Eliot's Mythmaking* (89). He discusses the "gradual emphasis on a new law – the law of Love" in terms of a shift from tragedy to comedy.

8. SHELLEY AND THE APOCALYPTIC CHARACTER

1 Carpenter sees this deconstructive strategy as an essential element in George Eliot's "prophetic vision" (Carpenter 67), rather than as an "acknowledgment of the limited possibilities of language" (Chase 223). The disagreement between Carpenter and Chase is not one of interpretation; they agree about the nature of the aporia in the text. Rather, it concerns what to make of this problematic moment. Carpenter sees the moment as part of an apocalyptic strategy to reach beyond the limits of textuality, whereas Chase reads it as challenging "fundamental tenets of belief about the structure and validity of language" (226n4).

2 In the final book of *Daniel Deronda* Mordecai explains his concept of union in terms of an apocalyptic teleology: "Human life is tending toward the image of the Supreme Unity: for as our life becomes more spiritual by capacity of thought, and joy therein, possession tends to become more universal, being independent of gross material contact; so that in a brief day the soul of a man may know in fuller volume the good which has been and is, nay, is to come, than all he could possess in a whole life where he had to follow the creeping paths of the senses" (802). Note the critique of merely personal "possession," which is dependent upon the finite structures of the self, and the prophecy of a "universal" form of possession, which escapes those boundaries.

3 This poem comes from the non-Gondal notebook, so it does not form a part of Emily Brontë's mythical sequence about the kingdom of Gondal. Hatfield numbers this lyric A9, indicating that it is the ninth poem of the 31 pieces in the book. In Hatfield's chronological ordering of Emily Brontë's poems, this work is number 148.

4 "Worlds on worlds are rolling ever / From creation to decay, / Like the bubbles on a river / Sparkling, bursting, borne away" (*Hellas*, lines 197–200).

5 The most influential of these is Paul de Man, whose essay "Shelley Disfigured" views "The Triumph of Life" as the exemplary text in Shelley's canon, because its repetitive erasures of its own figures force us to confront contradictory properties of language that we tend to conflate: language's ability to posit and language's ability to mean. In "The Critic as Host," J. Hillis Miller sees Shelley as deconstructive because of "the co-presence . . . of idealism and scepticism, of referentiality which only proleptically refers, in

figure, therefore does not refer at all, and of performatives which do not perform" (252). Tilottama Rajan thinks that the "coexistence of Shelley's skepticism with his idealism" seems "to invite deconstruction," but she recognizes that "the alternation between skepticism and idealism is symptomatic of a certain resistance to deconstruction" (*Dark Interpreter* 83).

6 The comic has been replaced by Schiller's sentimental; what Schiller called the naïve is no longer available, although structurally it resembles what Cassirer calls "mythical thought." Yet another possible stance, the prophetic, is mentioned by Rajan but only in passing (*Dark Interpreter* 94).

7 "Not that I assert poets to be prophets in the gross sense of the word, or that they can foretell the form as surely as they foreknow the spirit of events: such is the pretence of superstition which would make poetry an attribute of prophecy, rather than prophecy an attribute of poetry" (Shelley 483). Such a conception of prophecy is faithful to the biblical view of the prophet's role. Martin Buber writes, "The task of the genuine prophet was not to predict but to confront man with the alternatives of decision" (177).

8 Rajan's most recent treatment of *Prometheus Unbound* sees the prophetic poetry of Act 4 in a way much more congenial to our interpretation. She locates two conflicting scenes of reading in the poem, one of which would lead toward a deconstructive view of the work, the other of which suggests that the reader perform what Rajan calls a "reconstructive" act. "Thus we can see emerging from this scene the outlines of a Shelleyan hermeneutic designed to reverse the deconstructive potential within a text that fails to confirm itself by meeting the classical criteria for unity" ("Deconstruction or Reconstruction" 325). This is an important insight. By linking Shelley's procedure with other theories of Romantic hermeneutics, Rajan convincingly demonstrates that indeterminate features of the poet's text may call forth "a reading based on sympathy rather than doubt" (326). Rajan writes, "The presence of the reader similarly complicates a deconstructive interpretation, because the explicit reader may, after all, elect not to deconstruct, following a range of reconstructive options from sympathetic understanding to demythologization" (333).

9 Much criticism of Shelley has revolved around the question of whether his epistemology is idealist or empiricist. C. E. Pulos makes a case for the latter, as does Jean Hall. Wasserman traces Shelley's evolution from one position to the other, "a skeptical empiricism that will evolve ultimately into the idealism that he was to call the 'intellectual philosophy'" (7). The view of prophetic poetry presented here would obviate the need for much of this debate.

10 Milton Wilson draws attention to Shelley's frequent use of this term, as well as "self-mistrust" and "self-despising" (145–50).

11 Carlos Baker finds the source of Shelley's ideal image in Plato's theory of the epipsyche (53). Rajan's reading of "Alastor" (*Dark Interpreter* 73–83) usefully complicates the concept of epipsyche by relating it to Sartre's perception of the negativity of the imagination: "Because the need to imagine an ideal arises only from the fact that this ideal is not possessed, because the imagination thereby posits its object as absent or even nonexistent, the imagination must enter its own nothingness to disclose the very reality that it seeks to transform" (78).

12 Most recent critics have seen the narrator as separate from the Poet. Thurston, in the most complete treatment of this subject, maintains that there are three positions that must be distinguished in the poem, those taken by the Preface, by the narrator, and by the Poet.

13 This reading of the narrator's character is supported by the interpretations of Thurston, Wasserman (15–21), and Bloom (*Visionary Company* 285–90).

14 G. Wilson Knight points to the numerous parallels between "Alastor" and "Kubla Khan," reading the former as in part "a commentary on the composition" of the latter (186).

15 Paul Fry likewise suggests that Shelley's ideas about the nature of identity are integrally related to his thinking about language. "Shelley's 'faculty psychology,' then, is in many ways consistent with the linguistic psychoanalysis of our own day, especially with that of Lacan" (192).

16 See *New Introductory Lectures* (63) and "Mourning and Melancholia" (171), where he compares the desire to incorporate the other to cannibalism.

17 At least one critic has anticipated us in viewing the major portion of the Poet's story as dramatizing the dangers of identification. Leslie Brisman discusses the "crossing of identification by which the Poet can turn to something outside, something he comes upon, and say 'that I am he.' . . . Among the repeated efforts to identify himself with the forms of external nature are the beautiful swan passage (lines 272–95) and the verse paragraph beginning with the word *as* and exploring the very nature of the metaphorical 'as if' (lines 326–51)" (145).

9. WOMEN IN LOVE

1 Critics have been quick to point out Lawrence's affinity with the visionary project of the English Romantic poets. Despite Colin Clarke's comment that "virtually nothing has been written on Lawrence's debt to the English Romantic poets" (xiv), a great deal has been written on the subject over the last fifty years. See Huxley (xi), Leavis (*Revaluation* 165–6), Vivian de Sola Pinto (17–18), Hough (4–5), Goodheart (40), Lindenberger (326–41), Clarke (passim), Hochman (xii, 10), Abrams (*Natural Supernaturalism* 323–4), Langbaum (*Mysteries of Identity* 251–353), Murfin (*Swinburne, Hardy, Lawrence* and *The Poetry of D. H. Lawrence*), and Price (270–1).

2 Langbaum views Lawrence's theories of identity as lineally descended from Wordsworth.

3 The list of critics who have addressed this question largely overlaps with those who discuss his Romanticism. Eugene Goodheart phrases the problem in a way that parallels the concerns of this book: "Lawrence's difficulty is to reconcile his impulse toward transcendence . . . with the obligation of every artist to present reality which has already been enacted and is recognizable" (88). See also Forster (143–4); Spilka (*Love Ethic of D. H. Lawrence* 3, 8–31); Kermode (*D. H. Lawrence* 1, 21–31, 56–60); and Bersani (157, 182–5).

4 Hough (81), Daleski (178), and Goodheart (34), respectively. For a counter view, see Colin Clarke.

5 Lawrence himself taught us: "Never trust the artist. Trust the tale" (*Studies in Classic American Literature* 2).

6 Geoffrey Hartman has described the strong current of "anti-selfconsciousness" that ran even through the most self-conscious of the Romantic poets (*Beyond Formalism* 298–310).

7 There is a tendency for readers of Lawrence to overestimate the importance of Birkin's belief in sensuality, the dark involuntary being. He *is* a spokesman for some of Lawrence's theories about sexuality; but, in all of his speeches, there are other, less idiosyncratic strands of argument. The discussion with Hermione and Ursula in the "Class-Room" chapter is a good example. A close reading of the relevant pages (33–38) reveals coherent reasons for endorsing Birkin's position that have nothing to do with any special pleading for Lawrentian sexual mysteries. Eugene Goodheart has traced the similarity of these ideas to positions held by Blake, Nietzsche, Dostoyevsky, and Rilke, a group of radical thinkers he calls "tablet-breakers" (Goodheart 4–37).

8 Michael Cooke usefully notes that the Romantic (and Lawrentian) notion of consciousness is contained within in the larger (and less philosophically idiosyncratic) topic of the will. See *The Romantic Will* (xi–xii). His suggestion that we consider the Romantic dialectic of self and nature as one of self and system has also been helpful in thinking about Birkin's resistance to both.

9 Here, as at numerous other places, Lawrence's ideas foreshadow those of other visionary social critics such as Norman O. Brown. Compare Birkin's arguments with Brown's objections to Platonic Eros: "The Platonic Eros is the child of defect or want. Its direction is away from the insufficient self; its aim is to possess the object which completes it (there is a Platonic residue in Freud's inadequate notion of object-choice)" (49).

10 The question of whether or not mystical experiences can be put in words has received much serious debate in recent years. See the essays collected in Katz (ed.), *Mysticism and Philosophical Analysis,* especially Katz, "Language, Epistemology, and Mysticism," and Streng, "Language and Mystical Awareness." Kawin addresses this issue with learning and wit (*Mind of the Novel* 22–8, 97–115, 213–32).

11 The chief participants in the critical controversy include Knight ("Lawrence, Joyce and Powys"), Ford (*Double Measure*), Daleski (174–80), Kinkead-Weeks ("The Marble and the Statue"), Clarke (ix–xiv, 148–52), Spilka ("Lawrence Up-Tight"), Ford et al. ("Critical Exchange" 54–70), Kermode (*D. H. Lawrence* 140–3), and Bersani (162–3, 169–74).

12 The literalism of the debate over what act is being performed illustrates the magnitude of the problem.

13 We should note the similarity to Shelley's impossible hope at the end of "Epipsychidion" that Emily, Mary, and Claire would live together with him in perfect happiness.

WORKS CITED

Abrams, M. H. *The Mirror and the Lamp: Romantic Theory and the Critical Tradition*. New York: Oxford University Press, 1953. Rpt. New York: Norton, 1958.

"Structure and Style in the Greater Romantic Lyric." In *From Sensibility to Romanticism: Essays Presented to Frederick A. Pottle*. Eds. Hilles and Bloom. New York: Oxford University Press, 1965; rpt. 1970, 527–60.

Natural Supernaturalism: Tradition and Revolution in Romantic Literature. New York: Norton, 1971.

Allen, Walter. *The English Novel: A Short Critical History*. New York: Dutton, 1954.

Anderson, W. E. "Lyrical Form in *Wuthering Heights*." *University of Toronto Quarterly* 47 (1977): 112–34.

Apter, T. E. "Romanticism and Romantic Love in *Wuthering Heights*." In *The Art of Emily Brontë*. Ed. Anne Smith. London: Vision, 1976, 205–22.

Aristotle. *The Poetics*. Trans. S. H. Butcher. 4th ed. London: Macmillan, 1920.

The Ethics of Aristotle: The Nicomachean Ethics. Trans. J. A. K. Thomson. Rev. by Hugh Tredennick. Harmondsworth: Penguin Books, 1976.

The Politics. Trans. T. A. Sinclair. Rev. by Trevor J. Saunders. Harmondsworth: Penguin Books, 1982.

Arnold, Matthew. *Poetry and Criticism of Matthew Arnold*. Ed. A. Dwight Culler. Boston: Houghton Mifflin, 1961.

Auerbach, Nina. "Jane Austen and Romantic Imprisonment." In *Jane Austen in a Social Context*. Ed. David Monaghan. London: Macmillan, 1981, 9–27.

Austen, Jane. *The Novels of Jane Austen*. Ed. R. W. Chapman. 3rd ed. 5 vols. Oxford: Oxford University Press, 1933.

The Works of Jane Austen. Ed. R. W. Chapman. Rev. by B. C. Southam. Vol. 6 in *The Novels of Jane Austen*. Oxford: Oxford University Press, 1954; rpt. 1969.

Auster, Henry. *Local Habitations: Regionalism in the Early Novels of George Eliot*. Cambridge, Mass.: Harvard University Press, 1970.

"George Eliot and the Modern Temper." In *The Worlds of Victorian Fiction*. Ed. Jerome H. Buckley. Cambridge, Mass.: Harvard University Press, 1975, 75–101.

Averill, James H. *Wordsworth and the Poetry of Human Suffering*. Ithaca: Cornell University Press, 1980.

Bachelard, Gaston. *The Poetics of Space*. Trans. Maria Jolas. Boston: Beacon Press, 1969.

Baker, Carlos. *Shelley's Major Poetry: The Fabric of a Vision*. Princeton: Princeton University Press, 1948; rpt. 1966.

Baker, Jeffrey. *Time and Mind in Wordsworth's Poetry*. Detroit: Wayne State University Press, 1980.

Baker, Robert S. "Imagination and Literacy in Dickens' *Our Mutual Friend*." *Criticism* 18 (1976): 57–72.

Bakhtin, Mikhail. *The Dialogic Imagination: Four Essays*. Ed. Michael Holquist. Trans. Caryl Emerson and Michael Holquist. Austin: University of Texas Press, 1981.

Banfield, Ann. "The Moral Landscape of *Mansfield Park*." *Nineteenth-Century Fiction* 26 (1971): 1–24.

Barbauld, Anna Laetitia. "On the Poetical Works of Mr. William Collins." In *The Poetical Works of William Collins with a Prefatory Essay by Mrs. Barbauld*. London: T. Cadell, Jun. & W. Davies, 1802.

"Life of Samuel Richardson, with Remarks on His Writings." In *The Correspondence of Samuel Richardson*. Ed. Barbauld. 6 vols. London: Richard Phillips, 1804, 1:vii–ccxii.

The Works of Anna Laetitia Barbauld with a Memoir by Lucy Aikin. 3 vols. Boston: David Reed, 1826.

Barthes, Roland. "Introduction to the Structural Analysis of Narratives." In *Image-Music-Text*. Trans. Stephen Heath. New York: Hill & Wang, 1977, 79–124.

S/Z. Trans. Richard Miller. New York: Hill & Wang, 1974.

Bataille, George. *Literature and Evil*. Trans. Alastair Hamilton. New York: Urizen Books, 1973.

Beaty, Jerome. "The 'Soothing Songs' of *Little Dorrit*: New Light on Dickens's Darkness." In *Nineteenth-Century Literary Perspectives*. Ed. Clyde de L. Ryals. Durham, N.C.: Duke University Press, 1974, 219–36.

Beer, John. *Wordsworth and the Human Heart*. New York: Columbia University Press, 1978.

Beja, Morris. *Epiphany in the Modern Novel*. London: Peter Owen, 1971.

Bell, Michael. *The Sentiment of Reality: Truth of Feeling in the European Novel*. London: George Allen & Unwin, 1983.

Bersani, Leo. *A Future for Astyanax: Character and Desire in Literature*. Boston: Little, Brown, 1976.

Bialostosky, Don H. *Making Tales: The Poetics of Wordsworth's Narrative Experiments*. Chicago: University of Chicago Press, 1984.

Bible, The Jerusalem: Reader's Edition. Ed. Alexander Jones. Garden City, N.Y.: Doubleday, 1968.

Blondel, Jacques. *Emily Brontë: expérience spirituelle et création poétique*. Paris: Presses Universitaires de France, 1955.

Bloom, Harold. *The Visionary Company: A Reading of English Romantic Poetry*. 2nd ed. Ithaca: Cornell University Press, 1971.

The Ringers in the Tower: Studies in Romantic Tradition. Chicago: University of Chicago Press, 1971.

A Map of Misreading. New York: Oxford University Press, 1975.

Poetry and Repression: Revisionism from Blake to Stevens. New Haven: Yale University Press, 1976.

Wallace Stevens: The Poems of Our Climate. Ithaca: Cornell University Press, 1977.

Bodenheimer, Rosemarie. "Looking at the Landscape in Jane Austen." *Studies in English Literature* 21 (1981): 605–623.

Bonaparte, Felicia. *Will and Destiny: Morality and Tragedy in George Eliot's Novels.* New York: New York University Press, 1975.

The Triptych and the Cross: The Central Myths of George Eliot's Poetic Imagination. New York: New York University Press, 1979.

Bowles, William Lisle. *Letters to Lord Byron on a Question of Poetical Criticism.* 3rd ed. with corrections. *To Which Are Now First Added, the Letter to Mr. Cambell As Far as Regards Poetical Criticism; and the Answer to the Writer in the Quarterly Review, as Far as they Relate to the Same Subject.* 2nd ed. London: Hurst, Robinson, 1822.

Bradbrook, Frank W. "Sources of Jane Austen's Ideas about Nature in *Mansfield Park.*" *Notes & Queries* 206 (1961): 222–4.

Bradbury, Malcolm. "An Approach through Structure." In *Towards a Poetics of Fiction.* Ed. Mark Spilka. Bloomington: Indiana University Press, 1977, 3–10.

Bradby, Godfrey Fox. *The Brontës and Other Essays.* London: Oxford University Press, 1937.

Bradley, A. C. "Wordsworth." In *Oxford Lectures on Poetry.* London: Macmillan, 1950.

Brantley, Richard. *Wordsworth's "Natural Methodism."* New Haven: Yale University Press, 1975.

Braudy, Leo. "Penetration and Impenetrability in *Clarissa.*" In *New Approaches to Eighteenth-Century Literature.* Ed. Phillip Harth. New York: Columbia University Press, 1974, 177–206.

Brisman, Leslie. *Romantic Origins.* Ithaca: Cornell University Press, 1978.

Brissenden, R. F. *Virtue in Distress: Studies in the Novel of Sentiment from Richardson to Sade.* New York: Macmillan, 1974.

"Mansfield Park: Freedom and the Family." In *Jane Austen: Bicentenary Essays.* Ed. John Halperin. Cambridge: Cambridge University Press, 1975.

Brontë, Charlotte. *Jane Eyre.* Ed. Margaret Smith. London: Oxford University Press, 1975; rpt. 1980.

[Extracts from letters on Jane Austen.] In *Jane Austen: The Critical Heritage.* Ed. B. C. Southam. London: Routledge & Kegan Paul, 1968, 126–7.

Brontë, Emily. *Wuthering Heights.* Ed. Hilda Marsden & Ian Jack. Oxford: Clarendon Press, 1976.

The Complete Poems of Emily Jane Brontë. Ed. C. W. Hatfield. New York: Columbia University Press, 1941.

Brooks, Peter. *Reading for the Plot: Design and Intention in Narrative.* New York: Knopf, 1984.

Brower, Reuben A. "The Novel as Poem: Virginia Woolf." In *The Interpretation of Narrative: Theory and Practice*. Ed. Morton W. Bloomfield. Cambridge, Mass.: Harvard University Press, 1970, 229–47.

Brown, Julia Prewitt. *Jane Austen's Novels: Social Change and Literary Form*. Cambridge, Mass.: Harvard University Press, 1979.

Brown, Marshall. *The Shape of German Romanticism*. Ithaca: Cornell University Press, 1979.

―――. "'Errours Endlesse Traine': On Turning Points and the Dialectical Imagination." *PMLA* 99 (1984): 9–25.

Brown, Norman O. *Life Against Death: The Psychoanalytical Meaning of History*. Wesleyan, Conn.: Wesleyan University Press, 1959. Rpt. New York: Vintage Books, n.d.

Buber, Martin. "Prophecy, Apocalyptic, and the Historical Hour." In *On the Bible: Eighteen Studies*. New York: Schocken Books, 1968, 172–87.

Buchen, Irving H. "Emily Brontë and the Metaphysics of Childhood and Love." *Nineteenth-Century Fiction* 22 (1967): 63–70.

Burke, Edmund. *A Philosophical Enquiry into the Origin of Our Ideas of the Sublime and Beautiful*. Ed. James T. Boulton. Notre Dame: University of Notre Dame Press, 1968.

Butler, Marilyn. *Jane Austen and the War of Ideas*. Oxford: Clarendon Press, 1975.

―――. *Romantics, Rebels, and Reactionaries: English Literature and Its Background 1760–1830*. New York: Oxford University Press, 1982.

Butt, John and Kathleen Tillotson. *Dickens at Work*. London: Methuen, 1957.

Cameron, Sharon. *Lyric Time: Dickinson and the Limits of Genre*. Baltimore: The Johns Hopkins University Press, 1979.

Carlisle, Janice. "*Little Dorrit*: Necessary Fictions." *Studies in the Novel* 7 (1975): 195–214.

Carpenter, Mary Wilson. "The Apocalypse of the Old Testament: *Daniel Deronda* and the Interpretation of Interpretation." *PMLA* 99 (1984): 56–71.

Carroll, John. "Lovelace as Tragic Hero." *University of Toronto Quarterly* 42 (1972): 14–25.

Caserio, Robert L. *Plot, Story, and the Novel: From Dickens and Poe to the Modern Period*. Princeton: Princeton University Press, 1979.

Cassirer, Ernst. *Mythical Thought*. Trans. Ralph Manheim. Vol. 2 of *The Philosophy of Symbolic Forms*. New Haven: Yale University Press, 1955.

Castle, Terry. *Clarissa's Ciphers: Meaning and Disruption in Richardson's "Clarissa."* Ithaca: Cornell University Press, 1982.

Cecil, David. *Early Victorian Novelists: Essays in Revaluation*. New York: Bobbs-Merrill, 1935.

Chase, Cynthia. "The Decomposition of the Elephants: Double-Reading *Daniel Deronda*." *PMLA* 93 (1978): 215–27.

Chatman, Seymour. *Story and Discourse: Narrative Structure in Fiction and Film*. Ithaca: Cornell University Press, 1978; rpt. 1980.

Chitham, Edward. "Emily Brontë and Shelley." *Brontë Society Transactions* 17 (1978): 189–96.

Clarke, Colin. *River of Dissolution: D. H. Lawrence and English Romanticism*. New York: Barnes & Noble, 1969.

Coleridge, Samuel Taylor. *The Complete Poetical Works*. Ed. Ernest Hartley Coleridge. 2 vols. Oxford: Clarendon Press, 1912.

    Biographia Literaria or Biographical Sketches of My Literary Life and Opinions. Eds. James Engell and W. Jackson Bate. 2 vols. In *The Collected Works of Samuel Taylor Coleridge*. Princeton: Princeton University Press, 1983.

    Collected Letters of Samuel Taylor Coleridge. Ed. E. L. Griggs. 2 vols. Oxford: Oxford University Press, 1956.

Collins, Philip. *Dickens and Education*. London: Macmillan, 1963.

Collins, William. *The Works of William Collins*. Eds. Richard Wendorf and Charles Ryskamp. Oxford: Clarendon Press, 1979.

Cooke, Michael G. *The Romantic Will*. New Haven: Yale University Press, 1976.

Coveney, Peter. *The Image of Childhood: The Individual and Society: A Study of the Theme in English Literature*. Harmondsworth: Penquin Books, 1967.

Cox, Stephen D. *"The Stranger Within Thee": Concepts of the Self in Late-Eighteenth-Century Literature*. Pittsburgh: University of Pittsburgh Press, 1980.

Creeger, George R. "An Interpretation of *Adam Bede*." *ELH* 23 (1956): 218–38.

Culler, Jonathan. *Structuralist Poetics: Structuralism, Linguistics, and the Study of Literature*. Ithaca: Cornell University Press, 1975.

Curran, Stuart. "Recent Studies in the Nineteenth Century." *Studies in English Literature* 14 (1974): 637–68.

Curtius, Ernst Robert. *European Literature and the Latin Middle Ages*. Trans. Willard R. Trask. New York: Pantheon Books, 1953. Rpt. New York: Harper & Row, 1963.

Daleski, H. M. *The Forked Flame: A Study of D. H. Lawrence*. London: Faber & Faber, 1965.

Damrosch, Leopold Jr. *Symbol and Truth in Blake's Myth*. Princeton: Princeton University Press, 1980.

Danby, John. *The Simple Wordsworth: Studies in the Poems 1797–1807*. London: Routledge & Kegan Paul, 1960.

Davies, Cecil W. "A Reading of *Wuthering Heights*." *Essays in Criticism* 19 (1969): 254–72.

De Man, Paul. "Shelley Disfigured." In *Deconstruction and Criticism*. New York: Seabury Press, 1979, 39–74.

    "Dialogue and Dialogism." *Poetics Today* 4 (1983): 99–107.

De Saussure, Ferdinand. *Course in General Linguistics*. Ed. Charles Bally et al. Trans. Wade Baskin. New York: McGraw Hill, 1966.

De Sola Pinto, Vivian. "D. H. Lawrence: Prophet of the Midlands." *A Public Lecture given in the Great Hall of the University of Nottingham, 26 Oct. 1951*. Pamphlet, n.d.

Derrida, Jacques. *Of Grammatology*. Trans. Gayatri Spivak. Baltimore: The Johns Hopkins University Press, 1976.

    "The Law of Genre." *Critical Inquiry* 7 (1980): 55–82.

Dickens, Charles. *The Old Curiosity Shop*. Ed. Angus Easson. Harmondsworth: Penquin Books, 1972.

    Dombey and Son. Ed. Alan Horsman. Oxford: Clarendon Press, 1974.

    Little Dorrit. Ed. Harvey Peter Sucksmith. Oxford: Clarendon Press, 1979.

Great Expectations. Ed. Angus Calder. Harmondsworth: Penquin Books, 1965.

Our Mutual Friend. Ed. Stephen Gill. Harmondsworth: Penquin Books, 1971.

The Letters of Charles Dickens. Ed. Walter Dexter. 3 vols. Bloomsbury: The Nonesuch Press, 1938.

Diekhoff, John S. "The Happy Ending of *Adam Bede*." *ELH* 3 (1963): 221–27.

Dobson, Mildred A. "Was Emily Brontë a Mystic?" *Brontë Society Transactions* 11 (1948): 166–75.

Doederlein, Sue Warrick. "Clarissa in the Hands of the Critics." *Eighteenth-Century Studies* 16 (1983): 401–14.

Donoghue, Denis. "Emily Brontë: On the Latitude of Interpretation." In *The Interpretation of Narrative: Theory and Practice.* Ed. Morton W. Bloomfield. Cambridge, Mass.: Harvard University Press, 1970, 105–34.

Doody, Margaret Anne. *A Natural Passion: A Study of the Novels of Samuel Richardson.* Oxford: Clarendon Press, 1974.

Dostoyevsky, Fyodor. *The Possessed.* Trans. Andrew R. MacAndrew. New York: New American Library, 1962.

Douglas, Mary. *Purity and Danger: An Analysis of Concepts of Pollution and Taboo.* London: Routledge & Kegan Paul, 1966; rpt. 1978.

Drake, Nathan. "On the Government of the Imagination; on the Frenzy of Tasso and Collins." In *Literary Hours, or Sketches Critical and Narrative.* London: Burritt, 1798, 29–44.

"On Lyric Poetry." In *Literary Hours, or Sketches Critical and Narrative.* London: Burritt, 1798, 377–404.

Duckworth, Alistair M. *The Improvement of the Estate: A Study of Jane Austen's Novels.* Baltimore: The Johns Hopkins University Press, 1971.

"*Little Dorrit* and the Question of Closure." *Nineteenth-Century Fiction* 33 (1978): 110–30.

Duffy, Joseph M. "Moral Integrity and Moral Anarchy in *Mansfield Park*." *ELH* 23 (1956): 71–91.

Eagleton, Terry. *Myths of Power: A Marxist Study of the Brontës.* London: Macmillan, 1975.

The Rape of Clarissa: Writing, Sexuality and Class Struggle in Samuel Richardson. Minneapolis: University of Minnesota Press, 1982.

Eaves, T. Duncan and Ben D. Kimpel. *Samuel Richardson: A Biography.* Oxford: Clarendon Press, 1971.

Edel, Leon. *The Modern Psychological Novel.* Rev. ed. New York: Grosset & Dunlap, 1964.

Eigner, Edwin M. *The Metaphysical Novel in England and America: Dickens, Bulwer, Melville, and Hawthorne.* Berkeley: University of California Press, 1978.

Eliot, George. *Adam Bede.* 2 vols. In *The Works of George Eliot.* Cabinet Edition. Edinburgh: Blackwood & Sons, 1888.

The Mill on the Floss. Ed. Gordon S. Haight. Oxford: Clarendon Press, 1980.

Middlemarch. Ed. W. J. Harvey. Harmondsworth: Penguin Books, 1965.

Daniel Deronda. Ed. Barbara Hardy. Harmondsworth: Penguin Books, 1967.

George Eliot's Life as Related in Her Letters and Journals. Ed. J. W. Cross. 3 vols. New York: Harper & Brothers, 1885.

Essays of George Eliot. Ed. Thomas Pinney. London: Routledge & Kegan Paul, 1963.

A Writer's Notebook 1854–1879, and Uncollected Writings. Ed. Joseph Wiesenfarth. Charlottesville: University Press of Virginia, 1981.

Eliot, T. S. "Introduction." In Valéry, *The Art of Poetry.* Trans. Denise Folliot. New York: Bollingen, 1958. Rpt. New York: Vintage Books, 1961, vii–xxiv.

Erasmus, Desiderius. *The Praise of Folly.* Trans. Clarence H. Miller. New Haven: Yale University Press, 1979.

Ewbank, Inga-Stina. *Their Proper Sphere: A Study of the Brontë Sisters as Early-Victorian Female Novelists.* Cambridge, Mass.: Harvard University Press, 1966.

Fanger, Donald. *Dostoevsky and Romantic Realism: A Study of Dostoevsky in Relation to Balzac, Dickens, and Gogol.* Chicago: University of Chicago Press, 1965; rpt. 1967.

Ferguson, Frances. *Wordsworth: Language as Counter-Spirit.* New Haven: Yale University Press, 1977.

Ferry, David. *The Limits of Mortality: An Essay on Wordsworth's Major Poems.* Middletown, Conn.: Wesleyan University Press, 1959.

Fleishman, Avrom. *A Reading of Mansfield Park: An Essay in Critical Synthesis.* Minneapolis: University of Minnesota Press, 1967.

"Master and Servant in *Little Dorrit.*" *Studies in English Literature* 14 (1974): 575–86.

Fletcher, Angus. *The Prophetic Moment: An Essay on Spenser.* Chicago: University of Chicago Press, 1971.

"'Positive Negation': Threshold, Sequence, and Personification in Coleridge." In *New Perspectives on Coleridge and Wordsworth.* Ed. Geoffrey Hartman. New York: Columbia University Press, 1972.

Ford, George H. *Dickens and His Readers: Aspects of Novel-Criticism Since 1836.* Princeton: Princeton University Press, 1955. Rpt. New York: Gordian Press, 1974.

Double Measure: A Study of the Novels and Stories of D. H. Lawrence. New York: Norton, 1965.

Ford, George H., Frank Kermode, Colin Clarke, and Mark Spilka. "Critical Exchange." *Novel* 5 (1971): 54–70.

Forster, E. M. *Aspects of the Novel.* New York: Harcourt, 1972.

Foucault, Michel. *Language, Counter-Memory, Practice: Selected Essays and Interviews.* Trans. Donald F. Bouchard and Sherry Simon. Ithaca: Cornell University Press, 1977; rpt. 1980.

Fowler, Alastair. *Kinds of Literature: An Introduction to the Theory of Genres and Modes.* Cambridge, Mass.: Harvard University Press, 1982.

Frank, Joseph. "Spatial Form in Modern Literature." In *The Widening Gyre: Crisis and Mastery in Modern Literature.* Bloomington: Indiana University Press, 1968.

Frank, Lawrence. *Charles Dickens and the Romantic Self.* Lincoln: University of Nebraska Press, 1984.

Freedman, Ralph. *The Lyrical Novel: Studies in Hermann Hesse, Andre Gide, and Virginia Woolf.* Princeton: Princeton University Press, 1963.

Freud, Sigmund. *Totem and Taboo: Resemblances between the Psychic Lives of Savages and Neurotics*. Trans. A. A. Brill. New York: Random House, 1946.

"On Narcissism: An Introduction." In *General Psychological Theory: Papers on Metapsychology*. Ed. Philip Rieff. Trans. Cecil M. Baines. New York: Macmillan, 1963, 56–82.

"Mourning and Melancholia." In *General Psychological Theory: Papers on Metapsychology*. Ed. Philip Rieff. Trans. Joan Riviere. New York: Macmillan, 1963, 164–79.

"The 'Uncanny.'" Trans. Alix Strachey. In *On Creativity and the Unconscious: Papers on the Psychology of Art, Literature, Love, Religion*. New York: Harper & Row, 1958, 122–61.

Beyond the Pleasure Principle. Trans. James Strachey. New York: Liveright, 1950; rev. 1961.

The Ego and the Id. Trans. Joan Riviere. Rev. and ed. James Strachey. New York: Norton, 1960.

Civilization and Its Discontents. Trans. James Strachey. New York: Norton, 1962.

New Introductory Lectures on Psychoanalysis. Trans. James Strachey. New York: Norton, 1965.

Fry, Paul. *The Poet's Calling in the English Ode*. New Haven: Yale University Press, 1980.

Frye, Northrop. *Fearful Symmetry: A Study of William Blake*. Princeton: Princeton University Press, 1947; rpt. 1969.

Anatomy of Criticism: Four Essays. Princeton: Princeton University Pres, 1957. Rpt. New York: Atheneum, 1965.

Fables of Identity: Studies in Poetic Mythology. New York: Harcourt, Brace & World, 1963.

A Study of English Romanticism. New York: Random House, 1968. Rpt. Chicago: University of Chicago Press, 1982.

The Secular Scripture: A Study of the Structure of Romance. Cambridge, Mass.: Harvard University Press, 1976.

The Great Code: The Bible and Literature. New York: Harcourt Brace Jovanovich, 1981.

Garber, Frederick. *Wordsworth and the Poetry of Encounter*. Urbana: University of Illinois Press, 1971.

"Meaning and Mode in Gothic Fiction." In *Studies in Eighteenth-Century Culture*. Ed. Harold E. Pagliaro. Vol. 3. Cleveland, Ohio: The Press of Case Western Reserve University, 1973, 155–69.

The Autonomy of the Self from Richardson to Huysmans. Princeton: Princeton University Press, 1982.

Garis, Robert. *The Dickens Theatre: A Reassessment of the Novels*. Oxford: Clarendon Press, 1965.

Garrett, Peter K. *The Victorian Multiplot Novel: Studies in Dialogical Form*. New Haven: Yale University Press, 1980.

Gasché, Rudolphe. "The Mixture of Genres, the Mixture of Styles, and Figural Interpretation: *Sylvie*, by Gerard Nerval." *Glyph* 7 (1980): 102–30.

Gerard, Albert S. "Emblems of Misery: Wordsworth's *The Thorn.*" In *English Romantic Poetry: Ethos, Structure, and Symbol in Coleridge, Wordsworth, Shelley, and Keats.* Berkeley: University of California Press, 1968, 64–88.

Gerin, Winifred. *Emily Brontë: A Biography.* Oxford: Oxford University Press, 1971; rpt. 1978.

Gilbert, Sandra M. and Susan Gubar. *The Madwoman in the Attic: The Woman Writer and the Nineteenth-Century Literary Imagination.* New Haven: Yale University Press, 1979.

Gillis, Christina Marsden. "Garden Sermon, and Novel in *Mansfield Park*: Exercises in Legibility." *Novel* 18 (1985): 117–25.

Girard, René. *Deceit, Desire, and the Novel: Self and Other in Literary Structure.* Trans. Yvonne Freccero. Baltimore: The Johns Hopkins University Press, 1965; rpt. 1976.

Golden, Morris. *Richardson's Characters.* Ann Arbor: University of Michigan Press, 1963.

Goodheart, Eugene. *The Utopian Vision of D. H. Lawrence.* Chicago: University of Chicago Press, 1963.

Grabo, Carl. *The Magic Plant: The Growth of Shelley's Thought.* Chapel Hill: University of North Carolina Press, 1936.

Gray, Thomas. *The Complete Poems of Thomas Gray: English, Latin and Greek.* Eds. H. W. Starr and J. R. Hendrickson. Oxford: Clarendon Press, 1966.

Gregor, Ian and Brian Nicholas. *The Moral and the Story.* London: Faber and Faber, 1962.

Griffin, Andrew L. "Wordsworth and the Problem of Imaginative Story: The Case of 'Simon Lee.'" *PMLA* 92 (1977): 392–409.

Grudin, Peter D. "*Wuthering Heights*: The Question of Unquiet Slumbers." *Studies in the Novel* 6 (1974): 389–407.

Guerard, Albert J. *The Triumph of the Novel: Dickens, Dostoevsky, Faulkner.* New York: Oxford University Press, 1976.

Guillén, Claudio. *Literature as System: Essays toward the Theory of Literary History.* Princeton: Princeton University Press, 1971.

Hagstrum, Jean H. *Sex and Sensibility: Ideal and Erotic Love from Milton to Mozart.* Chicago: University of Chicago Press, 1980.

Hall, Jean. *The Transforming Image: A Study of Shelley's Major Poetry.* Urbana: University of Illinois Press, 1980.

Halperin, John. *The Life of Jane Austen.* Brighton: Harvester Press, 1984.

Hardy, Barbara. *The Novels of George Eliot: A Study in Form.* 1959; rpt. with corrections. New York: Oxford University Press, 1967.

"The Lyricism of Emily Brontë." In *The Art of Emily Brontë.* Ed. Anne Smith. London: Vision, 1976, 94–118.

"An Approach through Narrative." In *Towards a Poetics of Fiction.* Ed. Mark Spilka. Bloomington: Indiana University Press, 1977, 31–40.

Hardy, Thomas. *Tess of the d'Urbervilles.* Eds. Juliet Grindle and Simon Gatrell. Oxford: Clarendon Press, 1983.

Jude the Obscure. Ed. Norman Page. New York: Norton, 1978.

Hartman, Geoffrey H. *The Unmediated Vision: An Interpretation of Wordsworth,*

Hopkins, Rilke, and Valéry. New Haven: Yale University Press, 1954. Rpt. New York: Harcourt, 1966.

Wordsworth's Poetry 1787–1814. 2nd ed. New Haven: Yale University Press, 1971.

Beyond Formalism: Literary Essays 1958–1970. New Haven: Yale University Press, 1970.

The Fate of Reading and Other Essays. Chicago: University of Chicago Press, 1975.

Criticism in the Wilderness: The Study of Literature Today. New Haven: Yale University Press, 1980.

Hartog, Dirk Den. "*Little Dorrit*: Dickens' Dialogue with Wordsworth." *Critical Review* (Australia) 23 (1981): 3–19.

Harvey, W. J. *The Art of George Eliot.* London: Chatto & Windus, 1961.

Hassan, Ihab. *The Right Promethean Fire: Imagination, Science and Cultural Change.* Urbana: University of Illinois Press, 1980.

Havens, Raymond D. *The Mind of a Poet: A Study of Wordsworth's Thought with Particular Reference to "The Prelude."* Baltimore: The Johns Hopkins University Press, 1941.

Hazlitt, William. *The Complete Works.* Ed. P. P. Howe. Centenary Edition. 21 vols. London: J. M. Dent, 1930.

Herbert, Christopher. "Preachers and the Schemes of Nature in *Adam Bede.*" *Nineteenth-Century Fiction* 29 (1975): 412–27.

Hernadi, Paul. *Beyond Genre: New Directions in Literary Classification.* Ithaca: Cornell University Press, 1972.

Heschel, Abraham J. *The Prophets.* 2 vols. New York: Harper & Row, 1962; rpt. 1969.

Hill, Christopher. "Clarissa Harlowe and Her Times." *Essays in Criticism* 5 (1955): 315–40.

Hirsch, E. D. *Wordsworth and Schelling: A Typological Study of Romanticism.* New Haven: Yale University Press, 1960.

Hochman, Baruch. *Another Ego: The Changing View of Self and Society in the Work of D. H. Lawrence.* Columbia, S.C.: University of South Carolina Press, 1970.

Holloway, John. "Introduction." In *Little Dorrit.* Ed. Holloway. Harmondsworth: Penguin Books, 1967, 13–29.

Homans, Margaret. "Repression and Sublimation of Nature in *Wuthering Heights.*" *PMLA* 93 (1978): 9–19.

Women Writers and Poetic Identity: Dorothy Wordsworth, Emily Brontë, and Emily Dickinson. Princeton: Princeton University Press, 1980.

Hough, Graham. *The Dark Sun: A Study of D. H. Lawrence.* New York: Macmillan, 1957.

Hume, Robert D. "Gothic versus Romantic: A Revaluation of the Gothic Novel." *PMLA* 84 (1969): 282–90.

Huxley, Aldous. "Introduction." In *The Letters of D. H. Lawrence.* Ed. A. Huxley, 1932.

Irwin, John T. *Doubling and Incest/Repetition and Revenge: A Speculative Reading of Faulkner.* Baltimore: The Johns Hopkins University Press, 1975.

Jacobus, Mary. *Tradition and Experiment in Wordsworth's "Lyrical Ballads" (1798).* Oxford: Clarendon Press, 1976.

Jakobson, Roman and Morris Halle. *Fundamentals of Language.* The Hague: Mouton, 1956.

James, Henry. *Literary Criticism.* Ed. Leon Edel. 2 vols. New York: The Library of America, 1984.

Jameson, Fredric. "Imaginary and Symbolic in Lacan: Marxism, Psychoanalytic Criticism, and the Problem of the Subject." In *Literature and Psychoanalysis: The Question of Reading – Otherwise.* Ed. Shoshana Felman. Baltimore: The Johns Hopkins University Press, 1982, 338–95.

Jefferson, D. W. "The Moral Centre of *Little Dorrit.*" *Essays in Criticism* 26 (1976): 300–17.

Johnson, Samuel. "The Rambler, No. 4." In *Samuel Johnson: Rasselas, Poems, and Selected Prose.* Ed. Bertrand H. Bronson. 3rd ed. San Francisco: Rinehart Press, 1971.

Jones, John. *The Egotistical Sublime: A History of Wordsworth's Imagination.* London: Chatto & Windus, 1964.

Jordan, John E. *Why the "Lyrical Ballads"?: The Background, Writing, and Character of Wordsworth's 1798 "Lyrical Ballads."* Berkeley: University of California Press, 1976.

Kant, Immanuel. *The Critique of Judgement.* Trans. J. C. Meredith. Oxford: Oxford University Press, 1928; rpt. 1952.

Katz, Steven T. (ed.) *Mysticism and Philosophical Analysis.* New York: Oxford University Press, 1978.

Kawin, Bruce F. *Telling It Again and Again: Repetition in Literature and Film.* Ithaca: Cornell University Press, 1972.

  The Mind of the Novel: Reflexive Fiction and the Ineffable. Princeton: Princeton University Press, 1982.

Keats, John. *Poetical Works.* Ed. H. W. Garrod. London: Oxford University Press, 1956.

  The Letters of John Keats 1814–1821. Ed. H. E. Rollins. 2 vols. Cambridge, Mass.: Harvard University Press, 1958.

Kelly, Mary Ann. "Imagination, Fantasy, and Memory in *Little Dorrit.*" *Dickens Studies Newsletter* 13 (1982): 48–50.

Kenner, Hugh. *Dublin's Joyce.* Boston: Beacon Press, 1956.

Kermode, Frank. *The Sense of an Ending: Studies in the Theory of Fiction.* New York: Oxford University Press, 1967.

  "D. H. Lawrence and the Apocalyptic Types." In *Continuities.* New York: Random House, 1968, 122–51.

  D. H. Lawrence. New York: Viking Press, 1973.

  The Classic: Literary Images of Permanence and Change. Cambridge, Mass.: Harvard University Press, 1975; rpt. 1983.

  "Secrets and Narrative Sequence." *Critical Inquiry* 7 (1980): 83–102.

Kettle, Arnold. "Emily Brontë: *Wuthering Heights* (1847)." In *The Victorian Novel: Modern Essays in Criticism.* Ed. Ian Watt. London: Oxford University Press, 1971, 200–16.

Kiely, Robert. *The Romantic Novel in England*. Cambridge, Mass.: Harvard University Press, 1972.

Kinkead-Weeks, Mark. "The Marble and the Statue." In *Imagined Worlds: Essays on Some English Novels in Honour of John Butt*. Eds. Maynard Mack and Ian Gregor. London: Methuen, 1968, 371–418.

Samuel Richardson: Dramatic Novelist. Ithaca: Cornell University Press, 1973.

Kirkham, Margaret. *Jane Austen, Feminism and Fiction*. Sussex: The Harvester Press, 1983.

Klingopulos, D. G. "*Wuthering Heights*: The Novel as Dramatic Poem, II." *Scrutiny* 14 (1947): 269–86.

Knight, G. Wilson. *The Starlit Dome*. London: Oxford University Press, 1941; rpt. 1971.

"Lawrence, Joyce and Powys." *Essays in Criticism* 11 (1961): 406–7.

Knoepflmacher, U. C. *Religious Humanism and the Victorian Novel: George Eliot, Walter Pater, and Samuel Butler*. Princeton: Princeton University Press, 1965.

George Eliot's Early Novels: The Limits of Realism. Berkeley: University of California Press, 1968.

"Mutations of the Wordsworthian Child of Nature." In *Nature and the Victorian Imagination*. Ed. U. C. Knoepflmacher and G. B. Tennyson. Berkeley: University of California Press, 1977, 391–425.

Konigsberg, Ira. *Samuel Richardson and the Dramatic Novel*. Lexington: University of Kentucky Press, 1968.

Kroeber, Karl. *Romantic Narrative Art*. Madison: University of Wisconsin Press, 1960; rpt. 1966.

"Jane Austen, Romantic." *The Wordsworth Circle* 7 (1976): 291–6.

Lacan, Jacques. *The Language of the Self: The Function of Language in Psychoanalysis*. Trans. Anthony Wilden. Baltimore: The Johns Hopkins University Press, 1968. Rpt. New York: Dell, n.d.

Ecrits: A Selection. Trans. Alan Sheridan. New York: Norton, 1977.

Lane, Margaret. "The Drug-like Brontë Dream." *Brontë Society Transactions* 12 (1952): 79–87.

Langbaum, Robert. *The Poetry of Experience: The Dramatic Monologue in Modern Literary Tradition*. New York: Random House, 1957. Rpt. New York: Norton, 1963.

The Mysteries of Identity: A Theme in Modern Literature. New York: Oxford University Press, 1977.

"The Epiphanic Mode in Wordsworth and Modern Literature." *New Literary History* 14 (1983): 335–58.

Lawrence, D. H. *Women in Love*. New York: Viking Press, 1960.

Studies in Classic American Literature. New York: Viking Press, 1964.

Apocalypse. New York: Viking Press, 1966.

The Complete Poems of D. H. Lawrence. Ed. Vivian de Sola Pinto and F. Warren Roberts. New York: Viking Press, 1971.

Phoenix: The Posthumous Papers of D. H. Lawrence. Ed. Edward D. McDonald. New York: Viking, 1936; rpt. 1968.

Phoenix II: Uncollected, Unpublished, and Other Prose Works. Ed. Warren Roberts and Harry T. Moore. New York: Viking, 1968.

The Letters of D. H. Lawrence. Ed. James T. Boulton and Andrew Robertson. 3 vols. Cambridge: Cambridge University Press, 1979–84.

Leavis, F. R. *The Great Tradition.* New York: New York University Press, 1969.

Revaluation. London: Chatto & Windus, 1936.

D. H. Lawrence: Novelist. New York: Knopf, 1955. Rpt. New York: Simon & Schuster, 1969.

Leavis, Q. D. "A Fresh Approach to *Wuthering Heights.*" In *Lectures in America.* London: Chatto & Windus, 1969, 85–152.

Lévi-Strauss, Claude. *The Elementary Structures of Kinship.* Trans. James Harle Bell et al. Boston: Beacon Press, 1969.

Levine, George. "Determinism and Responsibility in the Works of George Eliot." *PMLA* 77 (1962): 268–79.

The Realistic Imagination: English Fiction from Frankenstein to Lady Chatterley. Chicago: University of Chicago Press, 1981; rpt. 1983.

Lewes, G. H. "Recent Novels: French and English." *Fraser's Magazine* 36 (1847): 687. Rpt. *Jane Austen: The Critical Heritage.* Ed. B. C. Southam. London: Routledge & Kegan Paul, 1968, 124–5.

"The Novels of Jane Austen." *Blackwood's Edinburgh Magazine* 76 (1859): 99–113. Rpt. *Jane Austen: The Critical Heritage.* Ed. B. C. Southam. London: Routledge & Kegan Paul, 1968, 148–66.

Lewis, Matthew G. *The Monk.* Ed. Louis F. Peck. New York: Grove Press, 1959.

Librach, Ronald S. "The Burdens of Self and Society: Release and Redemption in *Little Dorrit.*" *Studies in the Novel* 7 (1975): 538–51.

Liddell, Robert. "A Treatise on the Novel." In *Robert Liddell on the Novel.* Ed. Wayne C. Booth. Chicago: University of Chicago Press, 1969.

Lindenberger, Herbert. "Lawrence and the Romantic Tradition." In *A D. H. Lawrence Miscellany.* Ed. Harry T. Moore. Carbondale: Southern Illinois Press, 1959, 326–41.

Lindley, Arthur. "Richardson's Lovelace and the Self-dramatizing Hero of the Restoration." In *The English Hero, 1660–1800.* Ed. Robert Folkenflik. Newark: University of Delaware Press, 1982, 195–204.

Litz, A. Walton. "*Persuasion*: Forms of Estrangement." In *Jane Austen: Bicentenary Essays.* Ed. John Halperin. Cambridge: Cambridge University Press, 1975.

" 'A Developement of Self ': Character and Personality in Jane Austen's Fiction." In *Jane Austen's Achievement.* Ed. Juliet McMaster. New York: Barnes & Noble, 1976, 64–78.

Loxterman, Alan. "*Wuthering Heights* as Romantic Poem and Victorian Novel." In *A Festschrift for Professor Marguerite Roberts.* Ed. Frieda E. Penninger. Richmond, Va.: University of Richmond Press, 1976.

Lucas, John. *The Melancholy Man: A Study of Dickens's Novels.* London: Methuen, 1970.

MacAndrew, Elizabeth. *The Gothic Tradition in Fiction.* New York: Columbia University Press, 1979.

Macaulay, Thomas B. "The Diary and Letters of Mme D'Arblay." *Edinburgh Review* 76 (1843): 561–2. Rpt. *Jane Austen: The Critical Heritage*. Ed. B. C. Southam. London: Routledge & Kegan Paul, 1968, 122–3.

MacIntyre, Alasdair. *After Virtue: A Study in Moral Theory*. Notre Dame: University of Notre Dame Press, 1981.

Mackenzie, Henry. *The Man of Feeling*. Ed. Brian Vickers. London: Oxford University Press, 1967.

Maclean, Norman. "From Action to Image: Theories of the Lyric in the Eighteenth Century." In *Critics and Criticism: Ancient and Modern*. Ed. R. S. Crane. Chicago: University of Chicago Press, 1952, 408–60.

Mann, Karen E. "George Eliot and Wordsworth: The Power of Sound and the Power of Mind." *Studies in English Literature* 20 (1980): 675–94.

Martz, Louis L. *The Poetry of Meditation: A Study in English Religious Literature*. New Haven: Yale University Press, 1962.

Maturin, Charles Robert. *Melmoth the Wanderer*. Ed. William F. Axton. Lincoln: University of Nebraska Press, 1961.

McFarland, Thomas. *Romanticism and the Forms of Ruin: Wordsworth, Coleridge, and Modalities of Fragmentation*. Princeton: Princeton University Press, 1981.

McGann, Jerome J. *The Romantic Ideology: A Critical Investigation*. Chicago: University of Chicago Press, 1983.

McKillop, Alan D. *Samuel Richardson: Printer and Novelist*. Chapel Hill: University of North Carolina Press, 1936.

"Local Attachment and Cosmopolitanism: The Eighteenth-Century Pattern." In *From Sensibility to Romanticism: Essays Presented to Frederick A. Pottle*. Eds. Hilles and Bloom. New York: Oxford University Press, 1965; rpt. 1970, 191–218.

McMaster, Juliet. "Love and Pedagogy." In *Jane Austen Today*. Ed. Joel Weinsheimer. Athens, Ga.: University of Georgia Press, 1975, 64–91.

Medina, Angel. "Discussion: On Narrative and Narratives." *New Literary History* 11 (1980): 561–76.

Mellor, Anne K. *English Romantic Irony*. Cambridge, Mass.: Harvard University Press, 1980.

Miles, Rosalind. "A Baby God: The Creative Dynamism of Emily Brontë's Poetry." In *The Art of Emily Brontë*. Ed. Anne Smith. London: Vision, 1976, 68–93.

Miller, D. A. *Narrative and Its Discontents: Problems of Closure in the Traditional Novel*. Princeton: Princeton University Press, 1981.

Miller, J. Hillis. *Charles Dickens: The World of His Novels*. Cambridge, Mass.: Harvard University Press, 1958. Rpt. Bloomington: Indiana University Press, 1969.

The Disappearance of God: Five Nineteenth-Century Writers. Cambridge, Mass.: Harvard University Press, 1963.

"Ariadne's Thread: Repetition and the Narrative Line." *Critical Inquiry* 3 (1976): 57–77.

"Stevens' Rock and Criticism as Cure II." *Georgia Review* 30 (1976): 330–48.

"The Critic as Host." In *Deconstruction and Criticism*. New York: Seabury Press, 1979, 217–53.

Fiction and Repetition: Seven English Novels. Cambridge, Mass.: Harvard University Press, 1982.

Milton, John. *Paradise Lost.* Ed. Merritt Y. Hughes. New York: Odyssey Press, 1962.

Moler, Kenneth L. *Jane Austen's Art of Allusion.* Lincoln: University of Nebraska Press, 1968.

Monk, Samuel H. *The Sublime: A Study of Critical Theories in Eighteenth-Century England.* Ann Arbor: University of Michigan Press, 1960.

Moorman, Mary. *William Wordsworth: A Biography.* 2 vols. Oxford: Clarendon Press, 1957; rpt. 1968.

Morgan, Susan. *In the Meantime: Character and Perception in Jane Austen's Fiction.* Chicago: University of Chicago Press, 1980.

Morris, David B. "Gothic Sublimity." *New Literary History* 16 (1985): 299–319.

Muir, Edwin. *The Structure of the Novel.* New York: Harcourt, Brace & World, n.d.

Murfin, Ross C. *Swinburne, Hardy, Lawrence, and the Burden of Belief.* Chicago: University of Chicago Press, 1978.

The Poetry of D. H. Lawrence: Texts and Contexts. Lincoln: University of Nebraska Press, 1983.

Murrah, Charles. "The Background of *Mansfield Park.*" In *From Jane Austen to Joseph Conrad: Essays in Honor of James T. Hillhouse.* Eds. Robert C. Rathburn and Martin Steinmann, Jr. Minneapolis: University of Minnesota Press, 1958, 23–34.

Nelson, Lowry Jr. "Night Thoughts on the Gothic Novel." *Yale Review* 52 (1962): 236–57.

Newsom, Robert. *Dickens on the Romantic Side of Familiar Things: "Bleak House" and the Novel Tradition.* New York: Columbia University Press, 1977.

Newton, K. M. *George Eliot: Romantic Humanist, A Study of the Philosophical Structure of Her Novels.* London: Macmillan, 1981.

Nohrnberg, James. *The Analogy of "The Faerie Queen."* Princeton: Princeton University Press, 1976; rpt. with corrections, 1980.

Otto, Rudolf. *The Idea of the Holy: An Inquiry into the Non-rational Factor in the Idea of the Divine and Its Relation to the Rational.* Trans. John W. Harvey. Oxford: Oxford University Press, 1923.

Owen, W. J. B. (ed.) *Lyrical Ballads 1798.* London: Oxford University Press, 1969.

Park, William. "*Clarissa* as Tragedy." *Studies in English Literature* 16 (1976): 461–71.

Parker, Patricia A. *Inescapable Romance: Studies in the Poetics of a Mode.* Princeton: Princeton University Press, 1979.

"The (Self-)Identity of the Literary Text: Property, Propriety, Proper Place, and Proper Name in *Wuthering Heights.*" In *Identity of the Literary Text.* Eds. Mario J. Valdes and Owen Miller. Toronto: University of Toronto Press, 1985, 92–116.

Parrish, Stephen M. *The Art of Lyrical Ballads.* Cambridge, Mass.: Harvard University Press, 1973.

Patterson, Charles Jr. "Empathy and Daemonic in *Wuthering Heights.*" In *The English Novel in the Nineteenth Century: Essays on the Literary Mediation of*

Human Values. Ed. George V. Goodin. Urbana: University of Illinois Press, 1972.

Pease, Donald. "Blake, Crane, Whitman, and Modernism: A Poetics of Pure Possibility." *PMLA* 96 (1981): 64–85.

Perkins, David. *The Quest for Permanence: The Symbolism of Wordsworth, Shelley and Keats.* Cambridge, Mass.: Harvard University Press, 1965.

Pinney, Thomas. "George Eliot's Reading of Wordsworth." *Victorian Newsletter* 24 (1963): 20–22.

"The Authority of the Past in George Eliot's Novels." *Nineteenth-Century Fiction* 21 (1966): 131–47.

Plato. *The Dialogues of Plato.* Trans. B. Jowett. 3rd ed. 5 vols. New York: Oxford University Press, 1892.

Poovey, Mary. "Journeys from This World to the Next: The Providential Promise in *Clarissa* and *Tom Jones.*" *ELH* 43 (1976): 300–15.

The Proper Lady and the Woman Writer: Ideology as Style in the Works of Mary Wollstonecraft, Mary Shelley, and Jane Austen. Chicago: University of Chicago Press, 1984.

Porte, Joel. "In the Hands of an Angry God: Religious Terror in Gothic Fiction." In *The Gothic Imagination: Essays in Dark Romanticism.* Ed. G. R. Thompson. Pullman: Washington State University Press, 1974, 42–64.

Potter, Robert. *An Inquiry into Some Passages in Dr. Johnson's "Lives of the Poets"; Particularly His Observations on Lyric Poetry, and the Odes of Gray.* London: 1783.

Pottle, Frederick. *The Idiom of Poetry.* Ithaca: Cornell University Press, 1941.

Poulet, Georges. "Criticism and the Experience of Interiority." In *The Structuralist Controversy: The Languages of Criticism and the Sciences of Man.* Ed. Macksey and Donato. Baltimore: The Johns Hopkins University Press, 1972, 56–72.

Praz, Mario. *The Romantic Agony.* Trans. Angus Davidson. 2nd ed. London: Oxford University Press, 1933.

Price, Martin. *Forms of Life: Character and Moral Imagination in the Novel.* New Haven: Yale University Press, 1983.

Pritchett, V. S. *The Living Novel.* London: Chatto & Windus, 1949.

Propp, Vladimir. *Morphology of the Folktale.* Trans. Laurence Scott; rev. ed. Louis A. Wagner. Austin: University of Texas Press, 1968.

Pulos, C. E. *The Deep Truth: A Study of Shelley's Scepticism.* Lincoln: University of Nebraska Press, 1954.

Qualls, Barry. *The Secular Pilgrims of Victorian Fiction.* Cambridge: Cambridge University Press, 1982.

Radcliffe, Ann. *The Mysteries of Udolpho: A Romance, Interspersed with Some Pieces of Poetry.* Ed. Bonamy Dobree. London: Oxford University Press, 1970.

Rajan, Tilottama. *Dark Interpreter: The Discourse of Romanticism.* Ithaca: Cornell University Press, 1980.

"Deconstruction or Reconstruction: Reading Shelley's *Prometheus Unbound.*" *Studies in Romanticism* 23 (1984): 317–38.

Reed, Walter L. *Meditations on the Hero: A Study of the Romantic Hero in Nineteenth-Century Fiction.* New Haven: Yale University Press, 1974.

Reeve, Clara. "Preface to *The Old English Baron*, 1778." In *Novel and Romance 1700–1800: A Documentary Record*. Ed. Ioan Williams. London: Barnes & Noble, 1970, 298–300.

The Progress of Romance, through Times, Countries, and Manners; with Remarks on the Good and Bad Effects of It, on Them Respectively; In a Course of Evening Conversations. 2 vols. Colchester, 1785. Rpt. Dublin: Price, Exshaw et al., 1785.

Richardson, Samuel. *Clarissa or, The History of a Young Lady*. 8 vols. Oxford: Shakespeare Head Press, 1930.

Selected Letters of Samuel Richardson. Ed. John Carroll. Oxford: Clarendon Press, 1964.

Ricoeur, Paul. "Narrative Time." *Critical Inquiry* 7 (1980): 169–90.

Robbe-Grillet, Alain. *For a New Novel: Essays on Fiction*. Trans. Richard Howard. New York: Grove Press, 1965.

Rothstein, Eric. *Systems of Order and Inquiry in Later Eighteenth-Century Fiction*. Berkeley: University of California Press, 1975.

Restoration and Eighteenth-Century Poetry 1660–1780. Boston: Routledge & Kegan Paul, 1981.

Rousseau, Jean-Jacques. *The Reveries of a Solitary*. Trans. John Gould Fletcher. London: Routledge & Sons, 1927.

Ruoff, Gene W. "The Sense of a Beginning: *Mansfield Park*." *The Wordsworth Circle* 10 (1979): 174–86.

Ryle, Gilbert. "Jane Austen and the Moralists." In *Critical Essays on Jane Austen*. Ed. B. C. Southam. London: Routledge & Kegan Paul, 1968.

Ryskamp, Charles. "Wordsworth's *Lyrical Ballads* in Their Time." In *From Sensibility to Romanticism: Essays Presented to Frederick A. Pottle*. Eds. Hilles and Bloom. New York: Oxford University Press, 1965; rpt. 1970, 357–72.

Sanders, Andrew. *Charles Dickens Resurrectionist*. London: Macmillan, 1982.

Schlegel, Frederick von. *Lectures on the History of Literature, Ancient and Modern*. Trans. J. G. Lockhart. 2 vols. Philadelphia: Dobson, 1818.

Dialogue on Poetry and Literary Aphorisms. Trans. Ernst Behler and Roman Struc. University Park: Pennsylvania State University Press, 1968.

Schneider, Sister M. Lucy. "The Little White Attic and the East Room: Their Function in *Mansfield Park*." *Modern Philology* 63 (1966): 227–35.

Scholes, Robert. *Structuralism in Literature: An Introduction*. New Haven: Yale University Press, 1974.

Scott, Sir Walter. *The Miscellaneous Prose Works of Sir Walter Scott*. 6 vols. Edinburgh: Cadell, 1827.

The Poetical Works. Ed. J. Logie Robertson. Oxford: Oxford University Press, 1913.

"A Review of *Emma*." *Quarterly Review* 14 (1815): 188–201. Rpt. *Jane Austen: The Critical Heritage*. Ed. B. C. Southam. London: Routledge & Kegan Paul, 1968, 58–69.

Screech, Michael A. *Ecstasy and the Praise of Folly*. London: Duckworth, 1981.

Shakespeare, William. *The Complete Works of Shakespeare*. Ed. George Lyman Kittredge. Boston: Ginn, 1936.

Sheats, Paul D. *The Making of Wordsworth's Poetry, 1785–1798*. Cambridge, Mass.: Harvard University Press, 1973.

Shelley, Percy Bysshe. *Shelley's Poetry and Prose.* Ed. Donald H. Reiman and Sharon B. Powers. New York: Norton, 1977.

Showalter, Elaine. "Guilt, Authority, and the Shadows of *Little Dorrit.*" *Nineteenth-Century Fiction* 34 (1979): 20–40.

Simpson, Richard. [Unsigned review of the *Memoir of Jane Austen*]. *North British Review* 52 (1870): 129–52. Rpt. *Jane Austen: The Critical Heritage.* Ed. B. C. Southam. London: Routledge & Kegan Paul, 1968, 241–65.

Sitter, John. *Literary Loneliness in Mid-Eighteenth-Century England.* Ithaca: Cornell University Press, 1982.

Spacks, Patricia Meyer. *The Insistence of Horror: Aspects of the Supernatural in Eighteenth-Century Poetry.* Cambridge, Mass.: Harvard University Press, 1962.

Spilka, Mark. *The Love Ethic of D. H. Lawrence.* Bloomington: Indiana University Press, 1955; rpt. 1957.

"Lawrence Up-Tight." *Novel* 4 (1971): 252–67.

Squires, Michael. *The Pastoral Novel: Studies in George Eliot, Thomas Hardy, and D. H. Lawrence.* Charlottesville: University of Virginia Press, 1974.

Stace, W. T. *Mysticism and Philosophy.* London: Macmillan, 1961.

Stewart, Garrett. *Dickens and the Trials of Imagination.* Cambridge, Mass.: Harvard University Press, 1974.

Stockdale, Percival. *An Inquiry into the Nature, and Genuine Laws of Poetry; Including A Particular Defence of the Writings, and the Genius of Mr. Pope.* London: N. Conant, 1778.

Stone, Donald D. *The Romantic Impulse in Victorian Fiction.* Cambridge, Mass.: Harvard University Press, 1980.

Stone, Harry. *Dickens and the Invisible World: Fairy Tales, Fantasy, and Novel-Making.* Bloomington: Indiana University Press, 1979.

Stump, Reva. *Movement and Vision in George Eliot's Novels.* Seattle, Wash.: University of Washington Press, 1959.

Sulloway, Alison G. "Emma Woodhouse and *A Vindication of the Rights of Women.*" *The Wordsworth Circle* 7 (1976): 320–32.

Swinburne, Algernon Charles. "Emily Brontë." *Athenaeum* (June 16, 1983): 762–3.

Swingle, L. J. "The Perfect Happiness of the Union: Jane Austen's *Emma.*" *The Wordsworth Circle* 7 (1976): 312–19.

Tanner, Tony. "Introduction." In *Mansfield Park.* Ed. Tony Tanner. Harmondsworth: Penguin Books, 1966, 7–36.

Adultery in the Novel: Contract and Transgression. Baltimore: The Johns Hopkins University Press, 1979.

Tave, Stuart M. *Some Words of Jane Austen.* Chicago: University of Chicago Press, 1973.

"Jane Austen and One of Her Contemporaries." In *Jane Austen: Bicentenary Essays.* Ed. John Halperin. Cambridge: Cambridge University Press, 1975.

Thompson, G. R. "Introduction: Romanticism and the Gothic Tradition." In *The Gothic Imagination: Essays in Dark Romanticism.* Ed. Thompson. Pullman: Washington State University Press, 1974, 1–10.

Thurston, Norman. "Author, Narrator, and Hero in Shelley's *Alastor.*" *Studies in Romanticism* 14 (1975): 121.

Todd, Janet. *Women's Friendship in Literature*. New York: Columbia University Press, 1980.

Todorov, Tzvetan. *The Poetics of Prose*. Trans. Richard Howard. Ithaca: Cornell University Press, 1977.

Traugott, John. "*Clarissa*'s Richardson: An Essay to Find the Reader." In *English Literature in the Age of Disguise*. Ed. Maximillian E. Novak. Berkeley: University of California Press, 1977, 157–208.

Trickett, Rachel. "Jane Austen's Comedy and the Nineteenth Century." In *Critical Essays on Jane Austen*. Ed. B. C. Southam. London: Routledge & Kegan Paul, 1968, 162–81.

Trilling, Lionel. "*Little Dorrit*." In *The Opposing Self: Nine Essays in Criticism*. New York: Harcourt Brace Jovanovich, 1978, 44–57.

"*Mansfield Park*." In *The Opposing Self: Nine Essays in Criticism*. New York: Harcourt Brace Jovanovich, 1978, 181–202.

Turner, Victor. *The Ritual Process: Structure and Anti-Structure*. Aldine Publishing Co., 1969. Rpt. Ithaca: Cornell University Press, 1977.

Valéry, Paul. "Pure Poetry." In *The Art of Poetry*. Trans. Denise Folliot. New York: Bollingen, 1958. Rpt. New York: Vintage Books, 1961, 184–92.

Van Ghent, Dorothy. *The English Novel: Form and Function*. New York: Rinehart, 1953. Rpt. New York: Harper & Row, 1961.

Varma, Devendra P. *The Gothic Flame*. London: Arthur Baker, 1957.

Varnado, S. L. "The Idea of the Numinous in Gothic Literature." In *The Gothic Imagination: Essays in Dark Romanticism*. Ed. Thompson. Pullman: Washington State University Press, 1974, 11–21.

Von Rad, Gerhard. *The Message of the Prophets*. Trans. D. M. G. Stalker. London: SCM Press, 1968.

Walling, William A. "The Glorious Anxiety of Motion: Jane Austen's *Persuasion*." *The Wordsworth Circle* 7 (1976): 333–41.

Walpole, Horace. "The Prefaces to *The Castle of Otranto, A Story*, 1764 and 1765." In *Novel and Romance 1700–1800: A Documentary Record*. Ed. Ioan Williams. London: Barnes & Noble, 1970, 263–9.

Warner, William B. *Reading "Clarissa": The Struggles of Interpretation*. New Haven: Yale University Press, 1979.

Warren, Robert Penn. "Pure and Impure Poetry." In *Selected Essays*. New York: Vintage Books, 1951, 3–30.

Warton, Joseph. *Odes on Various Subjects*. London: R. Dodsley, 1746.

An Essay on the Genius and Writings of Pope. 4th ed., corrected. 2 vols. London: J. Dodsley, 1782.

Wasserman, Earl R. *Shelley: A Critical Reading*. Baltimore: The Johns Hopkins University Press, 1971.

Watt, Ian. *The Rise of the Novel: Studies in Defoe, Richardson and Fielding*. Berkeley: University of California Press, 1957.

Weinstein, Philip M. *The Semantics of Desire: Changing Models of Identity from Dickens to Joyce*. Princeton: Princeton University Press, 1984.

Weiskel, Thomas. *The Romantic Sublime: Studies in the Structure and Psychology of Transcendence*. Baltimore: The Johns Hopkins University Press, 1981.

Wellek, René and Austin Warren. *Theory of Literature*. 3rd ed. New York: Harcourt, Brace & World, 1956.

Welsh, Alexander. *The City of Dickens*. Oxford: Clarendon Press, 1971.

Wendt, Alan. "Clarissa's Coffin." *Philological Quarterly* 39 (1960): 481–95.

Whalley, George. "Jane Austen: Poet." In *Jane Austen's Achievement*. Ed. Juliet McMaster. New York: Barnes & Noble, 1976, 106–33.

Whately, Richard. [Unsigned review of *Northanger Abbey* and *Persuasion*]. *Quarterly Review* 24 (1821): 352–76. Rpt. *Jane Austen: The Critical Heritage*. Ed. B. C. Southam. London: Routledge & Kegan Paul, 1968, 87–105.

White, Hayden. "The Value of Narrativity in the Representation of Reality." *Critical Inquiry* 7 (1980): 5–28.

Whitehead, Alfred North. *Science and the Modern World*. New York: Macmillan, 1926. Rpt. New York: Free Press, 1967.

Widdowson, Peter. "Emily Brontë: Romantic Novelist." *Moderna Språk* 66 (1972): 1–19.

Wiesenfarth, Joseph. *The Errand of Form: An Assay of Jane Austen's Art*. New York: Fordham University Press, 1967.

George Eliot's Mythmaking. Heidelberg: Carl Winter, 1977.

Wilden, Anthony. "Lacan and the Discourse of the Other." In Lacan, *The Language of the Self: The Function of Language in Psychoanalysis*. Baltimore: The Johns Hopkins University Press, 1968. Rpt. New York: Dell, n.d., 159–311.

Williams, Anne. "Natural Supernaturalism in *Wuthering Heights*." *Studies in Philology* 82 (1985): 104–27.

Williams, Ioan. *Novel and Romance 1700–1800: A Documentary Record*. London: Barnes & Noble, 1970.

Williams, Raymond. *The Country and the City*. New York: Oxford University Press, 1973; rpt. 1975.

Willy, Margaret. "Emily Brontë: Poet and Mystic." *English* 6 (1946): 117–22.

Wilson, Milton. *Shelley's Later Poetry: A Study of His Prophetic Imagination*. New York: Columbia University Press, 1959.

Winner, Anthony. "Richardson's Lovelace: Character and Prediction." *Texas Studies in Language and Literature* 14 (1972): 53–75.

Witemeyer, Hugh. *George Eliot and the Visual Arts*. New Haven: Yale University Press, 1979.

Wolff, Cynthia Griffin. *Samuel Richardson and the Eighteenth-Century Puritan Character*. Hamden, Conn.: Archon Books, 1972.

Woodman, Ross. *The Apocalyptic Vision in the Poetry of Shelley*. Toronto: University of Toronto Press, 1964.

Woolf, Virginia. *The Common Reader*. New York: Harcourt Brace Jovanovich, 1925.

To the Lighthouse. New York: Harcourt, Brace & World, 1927.

The Second Common Reader. New York: Harcourt Brace Jovanovich, 1932.

Granite and Rainbow: Essays. New York: Harcourt Brace Jovanovich, 1958; rpt. 1975.

Wordsworth, Jonathan. *The Music of Humanity: A Critical Study of Wordsworth's "Ruined Cottage."* New York: Harper & Row, 1969.

"Wordsworth's 'Borderers.'" In *English Romantic Poets: Modern Essays in Criticism.* Ed. M. H. Abrams. 2nd ed. New York: Oxford University Press, 1975, 170–87.

Wordsworth, William. *Lyrical Ballads.* Eds. R. L. Brett and A. R. Jones. London: Methuen, 1963; rev. ed. 1968.

"The Ruined Cottage" and "The Pedlar." Ed. James Butler. Ithaca: Cornell University Press, 1979.

The Poetical Works of William Wordsworth. Ed. Ernest de Selincourt. 2nd ed. rev. Helen Darbishire. 5 vols. Oxford: Clarendon Press, 1951–4.

The Prelude, or Growth of a Poet's Mind. Ed. Ernest de Selincourt. 2nd ed. rev. Helen Darbisher. Oxford: Clarendon Press, 1959.

The Prose Works of William Wordsworth. Eds. W. J. B. Owen and Jane W. Smyser. 3 vols. Oxford: Clarendon Press, 1974.

The Letters of William and Dorothy Wordsworth: The Early Years 1787–1805. Ed. E. de Selincourt. 2nd ed. rev. Chester L. Shaver. Oxford: Clarendon Press, 1967.

The Letters of William and Dorothy Wordsworth: The Middle Years. Ed. Ernest de Selincourt. 2nd ed. rev. Moorman and Hill. 2 vols. Oxford: Clarendon Press, 1970.

Yeazell, Ruth Bernard. "The Boundaries of Mansfield Park." *Representations* 7 (1984): 133–52.

INDEX